PRECONDITIONS OF REVOLUTION

THE JOHNS HOPKINS SYMPOSIA IN HISTORY

The Johns Hopkins Symposia in History are occasional volumes sponsored by the Department of History at The Johns Hopkins University and The Johns Hopkins Press. Each considers an important topic of current historical interest and comprises original essays by ranking scholars in the United States and other countries. The present volume is the first. Its preparation has been assisted by the James S. Schouler Lecture Fund.

PRECONDITIONS
OF REVOLUTION IN
EARLY MODERN EUROPE

Edited with an Introduction by
Robert Forster
and
Jack P. Greene

THE JOHNS HOPKINS PRESS

Baltimore and London

Preface

This book grew out of a colloquium on the comparative history of modern revolutions given by the editors during the academic year 1968–69 in the Department of History at The Johns Hopkins University. During the spring semester of that year each of the essays of which this volume is composed was presented in abbreviated form as a lecture and followed by a seminar.

Professors Herbert H. Rowen of Rutgers University; Perez Zagorin of the University of Rochester; Ruth Pike of Hunter College; Orest Ranum, then of Columbia University and now of The Johns Hopkins University; and Michael Cherniavsky, then of the University of Rochester and now of the State University of New York at Albany, each participated in one of the seminars as critic and discussion leader. The editors and the authors are grateful to them for their questions and suggestions, all of which presumably contributed to the final drafts of the essays.

Paris and Baltimore   R.F. and J.P.G.

Contents

Introduction   1
ROBERT FORSTER AND JACK P. GREENE

1   The Netherlands Revolution   19
J. W. SMIT

2   The English Revolution   55
LAWRENCE STONE

3   Revolts in the Spanish Monarchy   109
J. H. ELLIOTT

4   The Fronde   131
ROLAND MOUSNIER

5   Pugachev's Rebellion   161
MARC RAEFF

NOTES ON CONTRIBUTORS   203

INDEX   205

PRECONDITIONS OF REVOLUTION

ROBERT FORSTER AND JACK P. GREENE

Introduction

In planning this book, we had two objectives. First, and most important, we intended to explore through the five authoritative and self-contained essays here included the full range of conditions that generated political and social upheaval in Europe during the two centuries immediately preceding the great revolutions at the end of the eighteenth century. Second, we wanted to consider whether there were sufficient similarities among the origins of these obviously unique and largely discrete events to warrant any general hypotheses about the preconditions of political and social disturbance in early modern Europe.

With these objectives in mind, we consciously adopted a very wide working conception of revolution. Borrowing and broadening the definition of Eugene Kamenka, we considered as a revolution *any sharp, sudden change or attempted change in the location of political power which involved either the use or the threat of violence and, if successful, expressed itself in the manifest and perhaps radical transformation of the process of government, the accepted foundations of sovereignty or legitimacy, and the conception of the political and/or social order.*[1]

Such a comprehensive definition gave us wide latitude in the choice of subjects and enabled us to include as revolutions not only the English Revolution, the one obviously great national revolution of the period, but also such apparently different phenomena as the separatist movements that occurred in the Netherlands, Catalonia, and Portugal; an abortive attempt by a segment of the ruling elite and its adherents to overturn the existing regime, the *Fronde*; and a large-scale regional uprising,

[1] Eugene Kamenka, "The Concept of a Political Revolution," in *Revolution*, ed. Carl J. Friedrich (New York, 1966), p. 124.

1

Pugachev's Rebellion. The definition also permitted us to exclude two other categories of events: (1) public and private palace revolutions or *coups d'état* which, though they produced a change in regime, wrought little alteration in the structure of either government or society; and (2) the many localized *jacqueries* which sought redress of immediate grievances but no change in the nature of existing social and political arrangements. By employing the term *preconditions,* we sought, following the example of Harry Eckstein, Lawrence Stone, and others, to focus on "long-run, underlying causes . . . which create a potentially explosive situation" as distinguished from *precipitants,* those "immediate, incidental factors . . . which trigger the outbreak and which may be nonrecurrent, personal, and fortuitious," and thus probably are somewhat less susceptible to analysis on a comparative basis.[2]

Perhaps because the authors were not asked to be explicitly comparative and because their respective subjects, with the notable exception of that of J. H. Elliott, did not require them to be, the first and most pronounced impression conveyed by these essays is that of extraordinary diversity of the preconditions for political unrest in the period under consideration and the seemingly totally separate and distinctive character of each of the eight events considered. Not surprisingly, however, a close inspection reveals sufficient similarities to make it possible both to construct a preliminary system for classifying these disturbances, by fitting them into five generic categories, and to register some general observations about the nature and range of the underlying causes and character of revolutions and revolts in early modern Europe.

Despite many obvious dissimilarities, the Netherlands Revolution, described by J. W. Smit, and the English Revolution, analyzed by Lawrence Stone, seem to fit together into one category which we may call *great national revolutions.* It is significant, perhaps, that both authors, in contrast to the other three contributors, chose to label the events they describe as revolutions and that both took considerable pains to relate their ma-

[2] Lawrence Stone, "Theories of Revolution," *World Politics* 18, no. 2 (January, 1966):1964.

terials not merely to the extensive earlier literature on each
subject but also to the growing corpus of theoretical writing on
revolution. It is also revealing that the search for preconditions
carried both of them into the entire *monde,* the whole society,
in which the revolution occurred.

For what these two essays disclose is a depth and extent of
social and political strain and a degree of social and political
dysfunction far more extensive than that discovered by any of
the other writers, with the possible exception of Roland Mousnier on the *Fronde.* Smit and Stone emphasize the profound
structural weaknesses of the existing political and social system; the severe status inconsistencies and inter- and intra-group
and regional tensions created by fundamental changes in the
economy and corresponding alterations in the distribution of
income and rates of economic growth and social mobility; the
fragmentation of elites through the alienation of important segments of the ruling class—disgruntled burghers and unpre-
ferred nobility in the Netherlands, and the "country" in England; the widespread hostility to the state church which enabled
religious extremists to play a far greater role than their numbers
would have warranted; and a marked tendency among the discontented to moralize about public men and institutions as
manifest in a growing belief in the "corruption" of the regime
and a corresponding loss of confidence in it. They also stress a
rising resentment of the government's extensive fiscal demands
to meet military expenses; the emergence of a strong and potentially competing focus of authority capable of supplying both
organization and leadership for revolutionary forces—the provincial estates in the Netherlands and the House of Commons
in England; frustrated expectations among both the elite and
lower social groups caused by the sudden worsening of economic
conditions; and, finally, the intransigence—Stone adds "folly"—
of the regime.

Coupled with new, badly conceived, and clumsily executed
policies, these many social and political "fissures" encouraged
the many existing discontented elements—subsections of larger
social groups—to coalesce in a common opposition, in response
to a series of myopic and irritating measures on the part of the
government, gradually gained cohesion against an identifiable
and, they believed, dangerous and morally corrupt "enemy" or

group of enemies: in the Netherlands, the emperor, his viceroy, his mercenary army, and the Catholic Church; and in England, the court, the episcopate, the crown's evil advisers, and, finally, the King himself.

But these many similar components, which of course existed in a very different combination in the two events, should not obscure the differences between the Netherlands and English revolutions. True, by discounting the importance of national-ist tendencies within the Netherlands, Smit minimizes, at least as a precondition, the one major difference traditionally empha-sized by historians from J. L. Motley to Pieter Geyl: nascent Dutch nationalism and its linguistic, religious, and cultural roots. He thereby makes the Netherlands Revolution somewhat less of a separatist movement and more of a constitutional one similar to the English Revolution than most writers have pre-viously supposed. But there were real differences: the extraor-dinarily complex and varied character of social divisions from one town or province to another which militated against class solidarity on a national scale; the great economic diversity and political particularism among provinces; the absence of effective political integration on the national level; and the apparently corresponding lack, at least at the beginning of the revolt, of a common political ideology that could bring many constituent elements among the revolutionaries together. Each of these differences inevitably gave the Netherlands Revolution some-thing of the character of a series of separate local revolts. Only the deep antagonism to the Catholic Church and the widespread desire for religious change could serve, initially, as a unifying force.

By contrast, the English Revolution occurred within a nation-ally integrated political system, and, far more than the provincial estates in the Netherlands, the English Parliament served as an excellent vehicle—the word is scarcely adequate to convey the intensive legalism and reverential constitutionalism represented by Parliament—for organized national resistance. Moreover, dis-contented elements operated out of a coherent body of widely generalized beliefs, a revolutionary ideology that had gradually emerged over the previous half-century from a fusion of various strands of Puritanism, the tradition of the common law, the social and political values of the "country" group, and the skepticism associated with the new learning. This ideology, which was accompanied by a degree of alienation among intellectuals far greater than seems to have occurred in the Netherlands, gave direction, purpose, and unity to the opposition in its struggle against the regime.

Yet, these differences in national political integration and ideological development can be overemphasized. For Smit makes clear that, as the Netherlands Revolution unfolded, the revolutionary elements succeeded in uniting the economically advanced and socially heterogeneous provinces of Holland and Zeeland behind a program of "liberties," toleration, and patriotism which would receive institutional embodiment in a single Estates-General. This program had much less appeal in the more rural provinces, but it led to the creation of a new type of Estates-General in 1576. Fostered by events of the following century, these "liberties" were central ingredients in the emergence of a new national consciousness.

Ultimately, of course, the consequences, as well as the preconditions, make it possible to classify the Netherlands and English revolutions as great national revolutions. As Smit and Stone point out, each resulted in the substitution of a new political order for the old, and, perhaps even more important, in the breakthrough of a new conception of the social and political order. The fact that this conception—the ideal of the Netherlands as a capitalist and bourgeois republic "with a strongly marked, very mercantile national identity"—*followed* in the wake of the actual political revolution, means, of course, that the Netherlands Revolution was a less complete national revolution than the English. The fact that the conception did eventually emerge from the new political order which developed out of the revolution, however, suggests perhaps that it was no less revolutionary in its long-range potential.

The five revolts discussed by J. H. Elliott and Roland Mousnier can be grouped into three separate categories. The Sicilian and Neapolitan uprisings in 1647–48 were *urban jacqueries*, popular outbursts born of social distress and directed not at the government but at the local ruling social group. With no comprehensive program for reform and no elite support, these

movements lacked the commitment to a set of unifying generalized beliefs or the leadership and organization necessary to
sustain a successful revolt against powerful alliances between
local elites and the central government in Madrid.

The Catalan and Portuguese revolts and the *Fronde,* despite
certain important differences among them, can be considered
together, although the Portuguese revolt falls into a different
category from the other two. Unlike the revolutions in the
Netherlands and England, they cannot be traced *primarily* either
to long-term social and economic changes or to a gradual decline in the power of the central government. Rather, the *main*
source of discontent in all three cases seems to have been the
centralizing tendencies of the early seventeenth-century warfare
state, which was attempting by every available means to marshal
national resources and increase state revenue. Energetic first
ministers dedicated to "reason of state" and the new absolutism
—Olivares in Spain and Richelieu in France—sought through
the Castilianization of Portugal and Catalonia and the extension into the French provinces of a burgeoning royal bureaucracy to consolidate and increase the power of the central government. In the process, they tried to counteract ancient centrifugal tendencies by excluding local notables from any share
in the patronage to the new royal offices and, in many instances,
ignoring or openly violating special provincial, local, or group
liberties, exemptions, and privileges that had traditionally protected their possessors from the exertion of certain kinds of
power by the central government.

By undermining the authority, income, prestige, and status
of old regional and provincial elites, by challenging local interests and traditional loyalties and conceptions of the state, and
by calling into question the authority of ancient institutions and
customs, these attempts to concentrate power in a bureaucratic
center that was not yet recognized as the focus of national loyalties had two important results. The first was the creation of
profound status inconsistencies that led to the progressive alienation of important segments among the elite: in Portugal and
Catalonia, a large proportion of the local notables, and in
France, the princes of the blood, *les grands,* the magistrates of
the parlements, local officials, leaders of the municipalities,
members of the provincial estates, and the rural military nobility (the *gentilshommes*).

The second result was the creation and/or intensification among the discontented of a generalized belief antagonistic to the existing regime. In Portugal and Catalonia, these beliefs revolved around an apparently expanding conception of the *patrie*, an ideal of a national community which rested upon a combination of "the constitutionalism of the privileged classes and the general antipathy to the outsider felt by the population at large."[3] Deriving, in Portugal, from "the recent fact of national sovereignty and independence" and a "deep pride in . . . [its] epic achievements" overseas and, in Catalonia, from "memories of a magnificent . . . past" and "the survival from that past of a constitutional system built on the firm foundations of law and representation," this "idealization of their own communities as historical, national, and legal entities" served both as a normative standard against which the actions of the central regime in Madrid could be measured and as a focus of opposition. In France, the customary constitution—that bundle of unwritten customs, traditional liberties, and royal edicts registered by the parlements—functioned in much the same way: it provided a defense for group and regional interests and privileges against the aggressive and "unconstitutional" claims and actions of the crown and served as a rallying point for opposition.

Like the Netherlands and English revolutions, of course, these three revolts exhibited many significant divergencies. The Portuguese and Catalan revolts occurred on the periphery of the Spanish Monarchy, while the *Fronde* erupted at the very center of the French political nation, in Paris as well as in the provinces. The chain of personal, quasi-feudal loyalties (*fidélités*) that cut through the entire social hierarchy and bound men from different social classes inextricably together seems to have been far more influential in the *Fronde* than it was in either the Catalan or Portuguese revolts. All three revolts occurred after a long period during which the central regime had placed increasingly burdensome fiscal demands upon the populace, although the Portuguese and Catalan tax burdens seem to have been significantly lighter than the French. Indeed, Portuguese and Catalan notables appear to have been moved less by discontent with the existing tax burden than by fear that the heavy demands already placed upon Castile by the Madrid government

[3] J. H. Elliott, "Revolution and Continuity in Early Modern Europe," *Past and Present* no. 42 (February, 1969):51.

would soon be extended to them, while the Portuguese seem to have been motivated at least in part by expectations that greater commercial opportunities would follow independence from Castile. Of the three, only the Portuguese was ultimately successful, and not simply its success but the ease with which that success was attained and the absence of any popular participation constitute significant differences between it and either the Catalan revolt or the *Fronde*. These differences prevent us from concluding that the other two revolts, had they succeeded, would have been as unrevolutionary in their consequences as the Portuguese. Bringing about no alterations in either basic social and political processes or in prevailing conceptions of the social and political order, it cannot be said to have been much more than a simple *secessionist coup d'état*.

To be sure, one of the primary distinctions between the Catalan revolt and the *Fronde* on the one hand, and the Netherlands and English revolutions on the other, was that the former, like the Portuguese revolt, failed to generate a new and comprehensive conception of the social and political order. But this failure does not necessarily mean that the two revolts had as little revolutionary potential as the Portuguese. The absence of the kinds of strong religious undercurrents that existed in the Netherlands and English revolutions and, despite the presence of powerful internal social tensions, especially in Catalonia, the continuing strength and vitality of traditional patterns of social organization may indeed have rendered the situation in both Catalonia and France less conducive to the emergence of a revolutionary mentality or a revolutionary ideology.

But Mousnier clearly shows that political thought veered off in a genuinely revolutionary direction during the *Fronde*. What began as an appeal for "a return to a golden age in the past"[4] wound up, as seems to have happened so often in these early modern uprisings, in demands by the Parlement of Paris that went far beyond the tenets of the customary constitution and would have required fundamental alterations in traditional political and constitutional relationships. To the very large extent to which these constitutional theories of the parlements were neither widely understood nor deeply felt among the revolting

[4] *Ibid.*, p. 43.

nobles and their followers, there was obviously little chance of their ever being implemented. But had the alienation of French notables been more extensive and the power and influence of the crown weaker, these "revolutionary" theories might well have provided the foundations for a basic reconception of the political order. If this assessment is correct, then it can be suggested that the main reason why the *Fronde* failed to develop into a revolution of a magnitude and character similar to the English was that the government of Louis XIV, in contrast to the clumsy and feeble instrument of Charles I, had sufficient astuteness to exploit divisions within the ranks of dissident groups and enough power and support ultimately to put down the revolt. The revolutionary potential of the Catalan rising is less clear. But the depth of the revolt and the breadth of participation in it suggests that, as in the case of the earlier and at least externally similar Netherlands Revolution, a prolonged military struggle with Madrid might have led to its escalation from a separatist and nationalist revolt into a revolution capable of altering political and social institutions. Whatever their potential, however, the failure of the Catalan revolt and the *Fronde*, as well as the absence of extensive social dysfunction and any religious content, prevented them from becoming great national revolutions like those of the Netherlands and England and requires us to classify them merely as *national revolts with the potential to become revolutions*.

Although it also failed to develop into a revolution, Pugachev's rebellion, as treated by Marc Raeff, belongs to still a different category. To be sure, like the earlier revolts in the Spanish Monarchy and France, it was, at least in its first two stages, largely the result of deep and growing antagonisms created by the aggressive centralizing activities of the national government in St. Petersburg. The Petrine state—perhaps more gradually than Spain and France a century before—persistently increased the tax burden and multiplied all kinds of "regulations" which disrupted the habits and customs of numerous groups in the region of the rebellion in unforeseen and irritating ways. The czarist state also encouraged activities which upset traditional patterns of life among various seminomadic tribes such as the

Bashkirs and sought to whittle away local autonomy, particularly in matters of military recruitment and discipline among the several Cossack communities. Along with the government's efforts at cultural "Russification" (especially, in the area of religion, the attempts to convert pagan nomads to Christianity and to tamper with Church-state relations in ways potentially offensive to the numerous Old Believers in the region), these many centralizing activities by the government in St. Petersburg created severe status inconsistencies among the Cossacks and contributed to a growing desire to return to the "old law" and the "old order." This desire served as a unifying force among the various discontented elements in the region.

But there was another powerful factor behind this desire which, if not entirely peculiar to Pugachev's rebellion, was missing from all of the other revolts considered in this volume. For at the same time that the czarist government was extending "direct state control over regions and social groups that heretofore had lived in a traditional and autonomous framework," it was also "removing itself from exercising direct control over the common people by allowing the 'interposition' of the serf- and landowning nobles." Forced into such measures by the weakness and smallness of the czarist bureaucracy in the region, the central government thus inadvertently created an extremely volatile situation. By handing over virtually all direct administration to the resident nobility and placing the control of serfs exclusively in their hands, the central government made possible a harsh "noble reaction" that saw the substitution of free labor services (corvées) for money payments among the serfs on private estates and, by 1770, the disappearance of the serf's right to petition the czar. By dashing partially fulfilled expectations for greater freedom among the serfs which derived from the earlier reforms of Peter the Great, this noble reaction fed the desire to return to the old order and, according to Raeff, was probably the central ingredient in stirring the broad discontent that made the third stage of the rebellion—the mass peasant uprising—possible.

Another distinctive feature of Pugachev's rebellion was the exceptionally mutable social situation from which it emerged. None of the other events here considered, not even the English and Netherlands revolutions, seem to have occurred in a society that was quite so much in flux. The product, among other factors, of a heavy immigration of free peasants and escapees from the central provinces, the uprooting of nomads as grazing lands were converted to arable, the ascription of unwilling serfs to work in the mines and factories of the Urals, and the general social unsettledness so often found in frontier areas, the rapid and sweeping social changes that occurred throughout the region of the revolt during the eighteenth century, Raeff suggests, predisposed a wide variety of elements to follow Pugachev.

Like the Catalan revolt and the *Fronde*, Pugachev's rebellion failed to develop into a great national revolution. Nor did it have the potential to become even a separatist movement. As in the case of the Netherlands Revolution and the later revolts in the Spanish Monarchy, it was a regional affair that happened on the periphery of the empire. But, unlike those events, it took place in a region that was almost wholly rural, socially diffuse, and largely lacking in any sense of regional identity or, to use Elliott's phrase, "local *patrie*." Exhibiting few of the characteristics of a traditional elite such as the magistrates and nobles of the Netherlands or the notables of Catalonia, its Cossack leaders were at best only a rudimentary elite without the habitual loyalties and ancient ties that bound their counterparts in the other revolutionary societies more closely to their peasant followers. Because of their mutual dislike of the state-preferred nobility, however, Pugachev and his Cossack and Old Believer followers were able to appeal to the peasants on the basis of a program that promised a return to an idealized past of paternalistic czarism and revived local autonomy which would provide protection against both bureaucrats and local nobles. Resting as it did on the quasi-mystical appeal of Pugachev as the redeemer, the "true czar," this program was not, however, capable either of sustaining the revolt once Pugachev's defeats had rendered his pretentions to be the real czar unbelievable or of uniting the many heterogeneous groups among the discontented for a prolonged period.

Along with other external factors, such as the absence of either elite or peasant support elsewhere in Russia and the military superiority of the state, the many internal weaknesses of the revolt meant that it was unable to survive even a series of limited defeats, much less to develop into a revolution. Nevertheless, Pugachev's program, like the constitutional appeals of the *Frondeurs* and the patriotic pronouncements of the Catalan notables, did contain the rudiments of a new and potentially revolutionary challenge to the political and social order. While it was true that toward the end of the revolt Pugachev and his Cossack followers displayed little interest in the fate of the peasants and neither controlled nor understood the peasant uprising they had sparked, Pugachev's notion that "the basis of the political organization of society was service to state . . . by commoner and noble alike" and his promise to remove the nobles as intermediaries between peasant and czar were, in eighteenth-century Russia, genuinely radical. Had the movement been successful, these ideas might have provided the basis for a redefinition of existing social and political arrangements. In a class by itself, Pugachev's rebellion was thus a *large-scale regional rebellion with limited potential to become a revolution.* Although it remained largely a Cossack affair, it elicited widespread support from peasants, and, although its social and political aims were couched in terms of an appeal to the past and were never fully elaborated, it assumed an increasingly revolutionary posture before it was finally put down.

The eight uprisings here considered must then be grouped into at least five categories, only the first three of which clearly fall under the flexible definition of revolution with which we began: (1) *great national revolutions* (the Netherlands and English revolutions); (2) *national revolts with the potential to become revolutions* (the Catalan revolt and the *Fronde*); (3) a *large-scale regional rebellion with limited potential to become a revolution* (Pugachev's rebellion); (4) a *secessionist coup d'état* (the Portuguese revolt); and (5) *urban jacqueries* (the Sicilian and Neapolitan uprisings).

But we do not wish to emphasize only the many differences among these events. As both the discussion above and the essays themselves suggest, it is possible also to venture a number of brief and tentative general observations about both the preconditions for political upheaval in early modern Europe and the character of the five early modern revolutions or potentially revolutionary uprisings that fall into the first three categories.

First, what Elliott has elsewhere referred to as "fierce social antagonisms"[5] were present in all five events. But these antagonisms were not among economic classes, not even among broad social orders. Instead of the conventional polarities of noble-bourgeois, rich-poor, or urban-rural, there were *everywhere* complex tensions among the multiple tiers and corps in the social hierarchy and/or competing status groups within the elite. As Stone has remarked about the English situation, elites were "fissured and fragmented by differences about constitutional arrangements, religious aspirations, and cultural patterns, by conflicts of interest and conflicts of loyalty, as well as by the unsettling effects of rapid economic development and social change." The most politically dangerous social antagonisms in early modern Europe thus seem to have derived not from class hostility but from status inconsistencies arising not only out of changing economic conditions and frustrated material expectations but also, and even more important, from government actions which directly threatened the *situations acquises* and the local power of traditional elite groups ranging from municipal councilmen to high nobles. As all of these essays reveal, an understanding of these kinds of complicated social tensions requires the subtle analysis of an infinite variety of social relationships and of the psychological effects of changes in income, status, political power, education, and other elements that gave men "standing" in the early modern period.

Second, the operation—as well as the nature—of these social antagonisms casts strong doubt upon their causal primacy in these early modern uprisings. To one degree or another, serious social divisions and adverse economic conditions were present in all of them. But such factors were a sufficient—as opposed to a necessary—cause for revolt only in the abortive and limited *jacqueries* in Sicily and Naples. Elsewhere, they contributed to shaping in important ways the responses of participants to events and thus to influencing the course of the disturbances. But there seems to be general agreement among the essayists that existing social and material discontents (especially those based on economic distress), as intensive and extensive as they were in several cases, would not by themselves have caused any

[5] *Ibid.*, p. 42.

of the five uprisings. Moreover, the fate of the Sicilian and Neapolitan revolts suggests that severe economic hardship among the lower orders of society and deep hostilities between social classes were insufficient either to sustain a revolt for a long period or to produce a successful revolution. On the other hand, of course, the experience of both the Netherlands and English revolutions seems to indicate that powerful socioeconomic sources of discontent may have been necessary to transform a revolt or a rebellion into a revolution.

Third, in view of these observations about the role of socioeconomic factors, it is clear that, however powerful their social and economic content, all five events were primarily the result, to use Stone's words, of "a crisis within the regime rather than a crisis within the society." To some extent these crises were the products, as Hugh Trevor-Roper has remarked, of "serious structural weaknesses" in the existing political systems,[6] in the inability of these systems to deal effectively with major problems presented by prolonged involvement in foreign wars, mounting debts, religious divisions, separatist aspirations, and social dislocations deriving from structural changes in the economy. Even more important, however, were the regimes' relentless fiscal pressures upon the taxpayers and their vigorous—and often clumsy—efforts at bureaucratic centralization. By establishing new offices whose jurisdictions overlapped those of old ones, replacing old officials with new ones, fomenting quarrels over patronage, threatening the status—and material position— and challenging the customary privileges of established corporations or social groups, and ignoring the aspirations of emergent groups, these efforts to achieve more effective central control weakened older political bonds and alienated significant elements within the ruling class.

Fourth, the defection of at least a part of the established elite was characteristic of all of these events, although the Catalan notables and the Cossacks who supported Pugachev were of course only regional elites. Only the Sicilian and Neapolitan revolts, which sputtered out almost as suddenly as they had begun, did not have elite leadership. In all of the other events, resentment against the activities of the regime or the prevailing

---

[6] As quoted in *ibid.*, p. 37.

style of government among a significant segment of the elite was so great as to strain their loyalty to the government or to erode traditional upper-class fears of social upheaval to the point that they were willing to take up arms against the regime. As Elliott has observed in reference to the Sicilian and Neapolitan revolts, purely popular uprisings may have been doomed to failure from their inception, and the cooperation and leadership of some section of the elite appears to have been essential for any possibility of success. As the experience of Pugachev's rebellion suggests, however, a movement which drew its leaders entirely from a regional—as opposed to a national— elite also had little chance of a favorable outcome unless, perhaps, its leaders, as in the cases of Catalonia and Portugal, were willing to limit their aspirations simply to separation from the central government. Clearly, the neutrality, if not the support, of influential elite elements at the center of the political nation would seem to have been a necessary precondition for a successful revolt or revolution.

Fifth, all five of the main events here discussed rested upon a coherent, well-defined, and solid ideological base, a cluster of generalized beliefs which was deeply antagonistic to the existing regime or to its policies, dominant figures, or prevailing style of government. These beliefs hardly constituted an ideology in one, modern sense of the term: in no case did they form an all-encompassing, logical, and unified world view of the historical process. Not blueprints for comprehensive and fundamental social and political reform, they carried no demands for social equality, universal political privileges, or economic improvement for the masses. Like most human beings, the men who held and acted on these beliefs were drastically limited in their behavior and their objectives by traditional patterns of thought, patterns so repressive in character as to make it extremely difficult for the men who held them to break through ancient and deeply engrained conceptions of society and the polity or accepted modes of political action. The result, as Elliott has pointed out, was that, at least initially, they were everywhere "dominated . . . by the idea, not of progress, but of a return to a golden age in the past," by a passion, not for innovation, but for renovation.[7] Thus their appeals and their justifi-

[7] *Ibid.*, pp. 43–44.

cations for taking up arms against the regime were almost invariably framed in terms of a defense of certain normative standards, of the need to guard the local *patrie* against the usurpations of outsiders or to protect the ancient constitution from illegal encroachments by the misguided or malevolent actions of the existing regime. But the backward thrust of these ideas did not prevent them from functioning effectively as an ideology for revolt or revolution or from serving as an alternative focus of loyalty which permitted the discontented among the elite to rise above petty antagonisms within the state, to endow their behavior with a sense of exalted purpose, and even to gain support from the lower orders of society. Present in all of these events, such a unifying belief was obviously an essential precondition for either revolution or a potentially revolutionary uprising in early modern European society.

Sixth, the atavistic character of these early modern revolutionary ideologies, the absence of any notion of progress, did not mean that they were incapable of generating new conceptions of the political and social order. In the crucible of political and social debate, revolt, and military conflict, thought moved to at least some degree in unforeseen, unintended, and even new and radical directions. Only in the English Revolution did there emerge any serious demands for fundamental changes in existing patterns of social relationship, and only in Pugachev's rebellion did there develop even the suggestion of a desire for alterations in the distribution of property or the existing system of property control. But, in every case, what started as a movement to restore and preserve a heritage by forcing changes in the regime or government eventuated in demands for basic alterations in the political system or constitutional structure. The fact that the most comprehensive and sweeping programs for reform were spawned by the Netherlands and English revolutions, the only events in which religion seems to have played a crucial role, suggests that religious division and a strong moral content may have been powerful catalytic agents in pushing the thought of discontented groups beyond traditional bounds and that a major intellectual breakthrough was possible only in large upheavals that stimulated prolonged and intense debates about the fundamental postulates of political and social organization.

Seventh, if an alternative ideology antagonistic to the regime was necessary for the outbreak of a potentially revolutionary disturbance in early modern Europe, so also was the existence of some institutional vehicle. However unlike the parties and conspiratorial groups that are presumed to provide the leadership and the institutional base for contemporary revolutionary activities, the Netherlands provincial estates and Estates-General, the English House of Commons, the Catalan *diputats,* the French parlements (especially the Parlement of Paris), and the Russian Cossack societies actually functioned as revolutionary organizations through which dissident elements could pursue their political and military objectives. Without such organizations, sustained or successful revolt would have been impossible.

Eighth, as several of the contributors to this volume have pointed out or implied, some possibility for success was also an important precondition for revolt in early modern Europe. It appears that before even seriously disaffected elements within traditional elites could be brought to open rebellion the regime had to be, or at least seem to be, sufficiently weak as to make it doubtful that it could offer sustained resistance.

Ninth, and finally, the great national revolutions seem to have been distinguished from the revolts primarily by the extent— the multiple character—of social and, more important, political dysfunction in the polities within which they occurred, the inability of the existing regime to put them down, and their capacity to generate a major reorientation in accepted ideas about the social and political order.

Social tensions born of conflicts over status and authority more than of material stress, weaknesses in political structure, state ambitions, discontent with existing regimes and government policies, elite participation, an alternative ideology capable of uniting dissident elements, an institutional vehicle for opposition activity, and some prospects for success—these appear to have been the major ingredients of the revolutions and revolts treated in this volume and important preconditions of political upheaval in early modern Europe. Yet the mix was very different in every case, and, whatever the similarities among these events, the divergencies and the extraordinary and peculiar complexity of each must be kept constantly in mind.

Revolutions are almost as difficult to reconstruct as they are to predict. By offering such clear and perceptive reconstructions of these early modern political disturbances, as well as by providing the foundations for the general observations above, the authors of the essays that follow have made a notable contribution to our understanding of the origins and character of revolutions in modern history.

J. W. SMIT

1 | The Netherlands Revolution

When a contemporary historian is confronted by a problem like the one implied in the title of this book, he knows that he must be prepared for a lot of logical and terminological trouble. In the last century, John Lothrop Motley solved the problem of the "preconditions" of his *Rise of the Dutch Republic* with that once-famous series of sketches of the protagonists of the drama. His vivid picture of Emperor Charles V's eating habits was especially memorable.[1] The image of the ogre devouring disgusting quantities of food transformed itself in the minds of his benevolently liberal audience into an allegory of despotic misgovernment; a perfect capsule statement of the preconditions of the Netherlands Revolution, it seemed to explain satisfactorily why the Netherlands stood up in the name of liberty after the old emperor had been succeeded by a son whose consuming appetites, Motley implied, could ultimately be satisfied only by the unrestrained letting of human blood. All Motley's picture does to us now, though, is make us hungry. But it is no use yearning for the lost innocence of narrative history. The present-day audience wants to know: What is a revolution? What are preconditions?

Looking to the historians of the Netherlands Revolution for an answer does not help much. Some argue that there was no revolution at all, just a revolt, although the distinction between these two terms is scarcely ever made clear. Others try to place the event at the beginning of the long series of revolutions which propelled European and American society toward political and social progress. But the most striking features of all of these

[1] John Lothrop Motley, *The Rise of the Dutch Republic* (New York: Harper & Brothers, 1875), 1:123.

19

interpretations are their arbitrariness and their failure to develop, much less to use, systematic categories.

Pirenne, whose narrative account of the Netherlands Revolution is still by far the most convincing, is a case in point. In
brilliant style he persuades us that a rapidly growing capitalist
economy, the formation of bourgeois and workers classes, and
the demands of a growing national state and national consciousness produced the tensions which led naturally to the uprising
against an alien, Spanish Habsburg government.[2] It is precisely
this brilliant style which makes us forget that the booming
capitalist economy did not characterize all of the Netherlands,
that the categories of feudality, bourgeoisie, and proletariat do
not easily fit the social realities of most of the sixteenth century,
even in the Netherlands, and that national consciousness was
largely in a state of unconsciousness. Similar observations apply
to Pieter Geyl, who bases his *Revolt of the Netherlands* on that
same assumption of a strong national movement (although defined more narrowly in cultural and linguistic terms) and con-
tinues to argue, in contrast to Pirenne, that what happened in
the Netherlands was a conservative *Stände* revolt rather than
anything progressive.[3] Still other historians have described the
Netherlands Revolution as the result of an irresistible religious
impulse or, to use terminology that is more strictly Marx's than
Pirenne's, an early bourgeois revolution against feudal society.[4]

[2] H. Pirenne, *Histoire de Belgique*, vol. 3; *idem*, "Une crise industrielle
au XVIᵉ siècle," *Bulletin de l'Academie Royale de Belgique, Classe des
Lettres*, 1905. See E. Coornaert, *La draperie-savetterie d'Hondschoote*
(Paris: Les Presses Universitaires de France, 1930).
[3] P. Geyl, *The Revolt of the Netherlands* (London: Williams & Norgate,
1932); see also his essays in *De Groot-Nederlansche Gedachte*, 2 vols.
(Haarlem: Tjeenk Willink, 1925); *Kernprobleem en van onze Geschiedenis*
(Utrecht: A. Oosthoek, 1937); and *Debates with Historians* (Groningen:
J. B. Wolters, 1955).
[4] For a summary of these controversies see J. W. Smit, "The Present
Position of Studies Regarding the Revolt of the Netherlands," in *Britain
and the Netherlands*, ed. J. S. Bromley and E. H. Kossmann, vol. 1 (London: Chatto & Windus, 1960). For the Marxist point of view add T. Wittman, "Quelques problèmes relatifs à la dictature révolutionnaire des
grandes villes en Flandre, 1577–1579," *Studia Historica* (Budapest), 40
(1960); *idem, Les Guex dans les Bonnes Villes de Flandre, 1577–1584*
(Budapest: Akadémiai Kiadó, 1960).
Attempts to interpret the sixteenth-century revolutions as the beginning
of the capitalist era are, however, at variance with the views of more
modern Marxist historians; see E. J. Hobsbawm, "The Crisis of the Seventeenth Century," in *Crisis in Europe*, ed. Trevor Aston (New York: Basic
Books, 1965), and P. Vilar, "Problems in the Formation of Capitalism,"
Past and Present, 1956.

A historiographical survey would not, however, be of much help in understanding the revolution. It would only make clear that all of the explanations so far advanced are mainly rhetorical simplifications—at once plausible and often contradictory—of a tremendously complicated process, hypotheses rather than solutions. What is needed is some conceptual apparatus that will make it possible to differentiate among various preconditions and their relative importance, and to discover which, if any, have been really revolutionary in their operation and implications.

The first thing we must do, then, is to face what we have been side-stepping so far: the definition of the terms "revolution" and "preconditions." Given such definitional problems, the modern historian sagely looks to the social sciences for help. From a quick glance at the rapidly increasing literature in this field, he learns with some dismay and certain glee that among social scientists the discussion of the theory of revolutionary phenomena is no less a Babel of tongues. That need not discourage us, however. Because we are looking at theories mainly in order to formulate problems, we might as well proceed nominalistically and arbitrarily and test whatever theory seems most promising.

The selection of theories for discussion is facilitated by the fact that they generally fall into two classes: political and societal. Political theories of revolution tend to focus on breakdowns in the political system, the failure of the legitimate government to maintain its monopoly of power, and the incidence of violence. Especially interesting for our purpose is the concept of *internal war* developed by several political scientists to replace the term "revolution." In this concept, *internal war* is defined as "any resort to violence within a political order to change its constitution, rulers, or policies," revolutions being "large-scale and prolonged instances of internal war, notable chiefly for the fact that they combine, in strikingly similar sequences, many different types of violence."[5] Violence, not necessarily an expression of essential changes in the political or social structure, is thus the critical element in this nation of revolution. By con-

[5] H. Eckstein, ed., *Internal War* (New York: Free Press of Glencoe, 1964); *idem,* "On the Etiology of Internal War," *History and Theory,* 1965.

trast, in the second, societal type, revolution implies a basic social transformation involving dislocations within class and status systems and basic shifts in the traditional social foundations of political power.[6]

The two approaches are quite different, but both are heuristically useful. The internal-war theory concentrates rather bluntly on the use of violence, and in its obvious link with the conflict model of society it conceives of social order as a precarious balance of power, always challenged but sufficiently resilient, stable, and in control of the situation so as to claim that the use of violence is clearly "a deviation from previously shared norms." It follows quite naturally that in this context Clausewitz's famous definition of war as the continuation of diplomacy by violent means may be applied to internal politics as well: revolution is the continuation of the regular sociopolitical bargaining process by the use of force. In the case of the Netherlands Revolution, this approach may help us to focus on the nature of the power relations, to identify the contending power groups, and to take into account the government's facilities for repressing an internal war, a factor which is often neglected because of our abiding belief in the inexorable character of revolutionary events.

There are obvious disadvantages to this approach. Lawrence Stone has pointed out that the concept of violence as a deviation from previously shared norms prohibits its application to those societies, such as Western Europe in the Middle Ages, and, we might add, in the sixteenth century, in which the use of political violence was common.[7] I will return to this point later, although it should be suggested here that, in spite of the weakness of the central government and the nobility's and free burghers' insistence on the right to bear arms in both the Middle Ages and the sixteenth century, the role of the sovereign as the sole source of legitimate violence and the distributor of justice remained at least nominally unchallenged; the private use of force was still theoretically abnormal. The objection has also been raised that the concept of political violence employed by the internal-war

---

[6] On the concept of societal change see Edward A. Tiryakin, "A Model of Societal Change and its Lead Indicators," in *The Study of Total Societies*, ed. S. Z. Klausner (Garden City, N.Y.: Anchor Books, 1967).
[7] Lawrence Stone, "Theories of Revolution," *World Politics*, 1965.

approach tends to treat all forms of antigovernment violence—from palace revolutions to the collapse of total social systems—as essentially similar phenomena and does not distinguish the different levels of the social meaning of violence. But this objection need not bother us as long as we remember that the internal-war theory generally restricts its attention to the political structure, thus implying the same restrictions for the validity of its conclusions.

Precisely because this theory cannot account for total societal breakdown, the historian also has to be prepared to analyze his material in terms of theories of societal change. The first such theory to come to mind, of course, is that of Karl Marx and his followers. Several features of this theory are of potential interest here: the explanation of the transition from feudal to early capitalist production relations, the concept of class as an economic entity which at the same time by necessity aims at the monopoly of power, the idea of revolution as the expression of class struggle, and the argument that changes in the spiritual and intellectual superstructure depend on earlier alterations in the economic substructure.

Despite its many attractions, Marxist theory has serious disadvantages for the study of early modern revolutions. To begin with, its vital concept of class is rather ambiguous: on the one hand, the class struggle is supposed to be characteristic of all history; on the other, class consciousness is required to transform a potential class into a real one—a requirement which condemns almost all classes in the sixteenth century to existence in the limbo of "false consciousness." [8] Furthermore, the classes in between the various types of nobility, the bourgeoisie, and the proletariat (whose existence Marx admitted even for the nineteenth century, although he thought they would ultimately disappear) were much too numerous in the sixteenth century to permit Marx's class schema to be easily applicable. Moreover, the exclusive economic characteristics of sixteenth-century Marxist classes were so mixed up with those of typical status groups that they can be used only with great caution. Finally,

---

[8] Karl Marx, *Das Elend der Philosophie* (Stuttgart: J. H. W. Dietz, 1885), p. 187; *idem, Das Kapital* (Berlin: Verlagsgesellschaft des Allgemeinen Deutschen Gewerkschaftsbundes, 1932), 1: 13; K. Marx and F. Engels, *Manifest der Kommunistische Partei* (Berlin: Dietz, 1957), p. 87.

however useful Marxist theory may be in calling attention to the importance of crucial aspects of economic and societal change, it is considerably less successful in defining the role of values and beliefs, with the result that the seemingly palpable modes of relation between economic substructure and intellectual and spiritual conditions remain elusive and hypothetical.

It is fair to say, I think, that the Marxist model has been more successful in explaining long-range processes than in analyzing the specific dynamics of early modern societies. Nevertheless, its limitations should not discourage us from using either it or other models of the total society, such as, for example, Talcott Parsons' four-part structural approach.[9] Historians tend to shrink from such grandiose schemata and thus surrender the possibility of systematically fitting, at least hypothetically, any of the results of their detailed research into a larger context, albeit they frequently attempt to do so through idiosyncratic common-sense generalizations. Consider how much could be learned from testing Merton's typology of the modes of individual adaptation to change and his analysis of anomie and deviant behavior.[10] A well-designed study of data on crime rates; changing types of crime; the economic and social meaning of vagrancy and migration; attitudes towards sexuality, the family, education, and generation gaps; and other lead indicators of social behavior should yield insights into the depth to which societal change had penetrated before the outbreak of the Netherlands Revolution. When one approaches this problem from such an angle, however, one finds only gaps in our knowledge; at best, most of these topics have been dealt with only in a very impressionistic manner.

Our lengthy elucubrations so far have led us to advocate the use of both the political and societal models of revolution. In the case of the Netherlands Revolution, this approach should conclude the useless debate over such labels as *revolt* versus *revolution, conservative* versus *progressive*.[11] We may decide to label as a *political revolution* (according to the internal-war

---

[9] Talcott Parsons, *The Social System* (Glencoe, Ill.: Free Press, 1951); see also Klausner, *The Study of Total Societies*, chaps. 1 and 4.

[10] Robert K. Merton, *Social Theory and Social Structure* (New York: Free Press of Glencoe, 1968), pp. 185–87.

[11] Such an approach should also help us to discard terminological confusion elsewhere, as in Griewank's thesis on revolution, which denies true revolutionary character to the sixteenth- and seventeenth-century rebellions because they were devoid of a progressive revolutionary conscience and

theory) any violent attempt to alter the government, expanding this term, if one wishes, to *sociopolitical revolution* when clashing social interests are paramount among the contending power groups. Because all social clashes are not necessarily indicative of essential changes in the social structure, however, the next step would be to assess whether the sociopolitical revolution of the Netherlands was also a *societal* revolution.

When we accept these flexible and tentative criteria for revolution, it still remains to consider what we shall call the "preconditions." Within the restrictions of their conceptual framework, the political and societal approaches allow us to distinguish to some degree between long-term preconditions and the incidental precipitants of the revolutionary process. In the internal-war thesis the preconditions consist of alterations in the regular rules of political bargaining and possibly of shifts in the power constellation. In the societal models, we can differentiate between, for example, long-range changes in the modes of production and incidental economic crises caused by external wars or climatological circumstances. Equally clear is the difference between dislocations of class and status groups caused by the incidental decline of a single industry or those related to a general irreversible socioeconomic development.

Although the distinction between precipitants and preconditions thus seems relatively clear, it presents many difficulties. Eckstein presents the terms in a seductive comparison of the revolutionary process with a cigarette lighter: preconditions, i.e., the general structure of the lighter, "make it possible to produce a flame" by the action of the participants, i.e., the turning of the flint wheel. It remains to be seen whether it is not sometimes possible that revolutionary movements are tipped off by the intensification of one of the structural strains in the general structure itself, which would be comparable to a process of

---

ideology. Although I am unwilling to admit that an awareness of societal change was totally absent in the case of the Netherlands Revolution, it is true that almost all propaganda on the side of the rebels was couched in conservative terminology, which justified the rebellion as the restoration of a time-honored situation. The Marxist model, however, as well as more recent sociological theories of change such as Merton's (*Social Theory and Social Action*, chap. 3), maintains quite effectively that societal revolutionary movements may have a latent character, i.e., need not be recognized as, or intended as such to represent, societal change. See K. Griewank, *Der neuzeitliche Revolutionsbegriff*, (Weimar: H. Bohlaus Nachfolger, 1955).

spontaneous combustion. An additional danger of this concentration on preconditions is that it may yield nothing more than a simple list of long-range developments that suggest a potential, but not necessarily an inevitable, revolutionary outburst. To try to avoid this danger it is necessary to devote some attention as well to the outcome of the revolutionary events. One may then assess the comparative strength of the several so-called preconditions from the perspective supplied by the later developments.[12]

It will be clear that I have much less confidence in the handling of the term "preconditions" than is perhaps desirable in a symposium devoted entirely to their study. But the preceding pages have at least the merit of clarifying the order of the rest of the discussion. We will first sketch the political system (or systems) of the Netherlands and single out the preconditions of internal war. We will then try to identify the most important strains in the social, economic, and ideological spheres. Finally, we will follow these factors through some of the crucial stages of the revolution, namely (1) from the ascension of Philip II through the first stage of the outbreak of violence (1555–67); (2) the resumption of the revolution in Holland and Zeeland (1572–73); (3) the resumption of the revolution in the rest of the Netherlands (1576–85); (4) the situation around 1600, after the actual revolutionary phase had ended and new regimes had been established as well in the free northern provinces, the Republic of the United Netherlands, as in the southern Netherlands, reconquered by the Spanish.

Our first task in this section is to describe the political system in which the Netherlands Revolution broke out, or, in the terms of internal-war theory, the institutionalized bargaining system in which regular peaceful negotiations gave way, at a specific

---

[12] In thus trying to read the history of a revolution backward, one finds some theoretical comfort in Neil Smelser's *Theory of Collective Behavior* (London: Routledge & Kegan Paul, 1962). Smelser not only gives a typology of revolutionary collective behavior, but he also tries to analyze collective movements in a hierarchical arrangement in which the most elaborate form, the value-oriented movement, subsumes lower forms such as, for example, hysterical or hostile outbursts. When collective behavior attains the stage of a value-oriented movement it indicates that the strains in the social system have become so powerful that only a value-oriented change is capable of satisfying the needs of the participants.

moment, to internal war. Although I intend to focus on those pressure groups within that system which had the facilities for power enforcement, we must also keep in mind that no political system can survive on power alone; a functioning political community is bound to be a moral community, having authority structures and legitimacy norms which usually militate against excessive violence.[13]

Accordingly, the first observation that we have to make about the political system of the Netherlands on the eve of the revolution is that such a moral community hardly existed. During the fifteenth and sixteenth centuries the Burgundian princes and their Habsburg successors had collected, but not united, a number of economically and politically very dissimilar Netherlands provinces. Before the revolution, the Estates-General, which has often been mistaken for a national representative body, did not serve this function at all, except on a few occasions when the individual provinces collectively used the institution to block Hapsburg efforts at unification. Only one session, that of 1558, offered any indication of an awareness among the provinces that they could more easily resist the prince if they would act in concert.[14] This session represented the only anticipation of the revolutionary situation in the late seventies and eighties, when William of Orange was to try to promote the idea of the Estates-General as the representational legislative body for all the Netherlands provinces. Thus, this type of Estates-General, which to the extent that William of Orange was successful survived the establishment of the Dutch Republic, was a result, not a precondition, of the revolution.

Before the revolution the Estates-General was by tradition a mere convention of provincial embassies who ordinarily met only to hear the general tax proposals of their common prince and then, significantly, proceeded to bargain about their provincial quota in separate sessions with the sovereign's representatives. Also important in preventing the Estates-General from serving as a focal point for the development of a national moral community was the fact that several provinces had been conquered by Charles V only recently: Friesland, Utrecht, and

[13] Talcott Parsons, "Some Reflections on the Place of Force in Social Process," in *Internal War*, ed. Eckstein, pp. 33–38.
[14] K. Verhofstad, *De regering van Philip II in de Nederlanden* (Nijmegen: J. J. Berkhout, 1939).

Groningen in the twenties and thirties, and Gelderland as late as 1543. The provinces of *nouvelle Conquête*, as the late acquisitions were still called in the 1560s, were generally regarded as foreign countries by the older, so-called patrimonial provinces, and they in turn fiercely defended their right *not* to be called to the Estates-General. But even the patrimonial provinces did not consider the Estates-General a national representative body. On the one occasion before the sixteenth-century revolution when they took independent action as a body—in 1477, during the crisis after the death of Charles the Bold—their objective was not, as Pirenne would have it, to constitute themselves as a nation-wide parliament. Rather, the purpose of the Grand Privilege, which they extorted from Charles's helpless successor, was to safeguard and expand their provincial privileges.[15]

Thus, the only bodies that could appeal to a primitive awareness of unity and national feeling and that possibly could be called moral communities with definite norms of legitimacy were the individual provinces. But, even in their case, qualifications have to be made. They may be described more accurately as confederations or leagues of towns and noble and ecclesiastic landholders than as integrated political systems. The real loci of power were the noble dynasties and the towns. The towns most deserve the name of political communities; they were semi-autonomous corporations with highly developed political lives of their own, for a highly integrative socialization process had found expression in a peculiarly republican political consciousness. Flanders is a case in point. As Professor Dhondt has shown, the traditional model of the harmonious corporative state is scarcely applicable there.[16] During the later Middle Ages a confederation of towns controlled the provincial estates; through its militia each town maintained a virtual power monopoly over its section of the countryside, and together the towns tried to impose their will on the prince. In spite of their diminished power, the towns continued this policy in the sixteenth century. To a lesser degree the same thing happened in Holland and Brabant.

---

[15] F. W. N. Hugenholtz, "The 1477 Crisis in the Burgundian Duke's Dominions," in *Britain and the Netherlands,* ed. Bromley and Kossmann, vol. 2.

[16] J. Dhondt, "Ordres ou Puissances," *Annales E. S. C.,* 1950; for Brabant see E. Coornaert, "L'état et les villes à la fin du Moyen Age," *Revue Historique* 207 (April-June, 1952):201–4.

The confederation or league was the accepted form of political organization, and even the rural, nobility-controlled provinces were actually based on a confederative power balance of the noble dynasties, with their clientele of lesser noblemen, the large abbeys, and some towns.

The consequences of this political fragmentation for the analysis of the Netherlands Revolution are obvious. Because every province, even every town, to a large extent constituted an autonomous system, each with its peculiar socioeconomic and political structures, revolution or internal war can be studied and explained only in local terms. The study of the revolution of the second half of the sixteenth century should then concentrate on the question of why in most of the towns and provinces the internal struggle for political domination was directed against the same target: the prince.

An examination of the internal and external political conduct of the towns reveals not only striking similarities, which can easily be reduced to the usual generalizations about urban politics, but also individual peculiarities resulting from the specific economic interests, social structure, position in the provincial power structure, tradition, and so on, of each town. These differences are no less important for the explanation of the revolution than the similarities.

In the internal politics of the towns we find factions everywhere struggling for political power. These struggles fall into two broad patterns. In some, generally mercantile towns, the guilds had been too weak to claim a share in the government, and party struggle was among factions within the patriciate, which occasionally allied itself with the guilds or the wealthy bourgeoisie. Amsterdam and the towns of the province of Holland generally followed this pattern.[17] In towns with large-scale industry—Ghent is the extreme example—the guilds had forced their way into the government. They always got their share of political power in a corporative form, becoming a constitutive member of the town council and obtaining the right to elect

---

[17] For Amsterdam see J. E. Elias, *Geschiedenis van het Amsterdamse Regenstenpatriciaat* (The Hague: M. Nijhoff, 1923). In the industrial city of Leiden the guilds were politically weak; see N. W. Posthumus, *Geschiedenis van de Leidsche Lakenindustrie* (The Hague: M. Nijhoff, 1908), 1:365–70.

their own member of the governing magistracy.[18] Within this second framework the broader social interests of the town found much more direct expression in politics. Most of the Brabant and Flemish town governments were in fact reflections on a smaller scale of the larger structure of the estates, and town government was often an exemplary bargaining institution of social groups. In towns with such political arrangements, potential violence and the control of repressive facilities were pivotal factors in the governmental process. The militia, dominated numerically by the artisanal lower middle class, was as much an instrument of a particular class as of the town government. But recurrent economic recessions, even when they were of an incidental nature, used to hit the artisans almost as hard at it did the unruly unskilled workers. Generally, the artisans and skilled workers were quite anxious to underline the difference in their status from that of the "proletarians" and to crush their uprisings. But several times during the sixteenth century they refused to do so, and then town government was in danger. The urban uprisings of 1566, 1572, and 1576–78 all were ushered in by the defection of the militia,[19] which was composed of artisans and skilled workers.

Apart from lower-class pressure and the dangerous temporary coalitions among artisans, industrial workers, and unskilled laborers, town governments were also frequently upset by shifts within the governing families or attacks on the oligarchy from the wealthy social layer just below them, often new wealth, which rankled under its exclusion from politics. In both cases the militia could be a decisive factor. The clearest example of this occurred in Amsterdam when a coalition of patricians and merchants who were out of power tried to dislodge the governing clique in 1564. The magistrates succeeded in implicating

---

[18] For Ghent see V. Fris, *Histoire de Gand* (Brussels: G. van Oest & cie, 1913), and H. van Werveke, *Gand* (Brussels: La Renaissance du livre, 1946); for Brussels see A. Henne and A. Wauters, *Histoire de Bruxelles*, (Brussels: Librairie encyclopédique de Perichon, 1845).

[19] For this phenomenon in general, see H. A. Enno van Gelder, *Revolutionnaire Reformatie* (Amsterdam: Van Kampen & zoon, 1943), and for some Holland towns see J. C. Boogman, "De overgang van enige Hollandse steden in 1572," *Tijdschrift voor Geschiedenis*, 1942. Before the revolution the revolt of Ghent in 1536–40 belonged to some extent in this category; see A. Henne, *Histoire du règne de Charles Quint en Belgique*, vol. 6 (Brussels: E. Flatau, 1859), chap. 25. The role of the urban militias deserves a more thorough investigation.

the leaders in the rebellious acts of 1566, most of whom went into exile. In 1578, following William of Orange's victory, these refugees came back and with the help of the militia threw out the old oligarchy.[20]

So far the emphasis in this description of political dynamics has been on the inveterate autonomy of the towns and the primacy of local interests in the interaction between town politics and general policy. It is necessary to take a further step, however, and to note how in the provincial structure the towns found their place in a common front against the nobility. Control of the countryside and food production, as well as the effective prohibition of rural industry, was a vital interest to most towns. In order to obtain that control, the towns attempted to push the nobility out of their sphere of jurisdiction and to encroach upon their autonomy.[21] This is a familiar story throughout the fifteenth and sixteenth centuries, and it accounts for many events in the revolution. But it must also be emphasized that, in spite of this hostility, the nobility often learned to collaborate with the towns in strengthening the provincial estates against the prince and his hated henchmen in the provincial courts.

The nobility had the option to seek the prince's help against their common bourgeois enemy or to ally with the bourgeoisie against the prince, who was no less prone to want to curtail the power of the nobles. During the reign of Charles V the nobility seemed to have opted for the prince. The higher nobility rose rapidly in the emperor's service, while the lower nobility was content either with lesser administrative functions or with service in the army. At both levels the grandees used their patronage to build up a vast clientele. A few of the most brilliant noblemen had command over a *bande d'ordonnance*, the positions for which they could fill at will.[22] Rivalry among the famous houses prevented direct danger for the prince. Throughout the revolution, jealousies between clans, such as that between Orange-Nassau and Croij, were a powerful factor in shaping parties. The nobility was also engaged in a constant battle against the

[20] Elias, *Geschiedenis*, pp. 7–10.
[21] For Holland this has been studied in detail by E. Chr. Brünner, *De order op de buitennering van 1531* (Utrecht: Oosthoek, 1918), pp. 155 ff.
[22] For the nobility see H. A. Enno van Gelder, "De Nederlandsche Adel in de Opstand tegen Spanje," *Tijdschrift voor Geschiedenis*, 1928.

intrusions of the government—personified by generally bourgeois
legalists—into the affairs of the central and provincial adminis-
trations. Their resentment, however, was rather slow to materialize. Although the nobility often opposed these intrusions prior
to the 1560s, it did not unite aganst the government before the
abdication of Charles V.

Power relationships began to change greatly under the emperor's government, a process that had, in fact, begun under his
predecessor. The princely mercenry army now dwarfed the militias of the towns. But none of the money that was needed to
maintain this army could be raised without the consent of the
provincial estates and the towns and nobility they represented,
and no prince would lightheartedly entertain the idea of using
force against them. Thus a precarious balance was achieved in
which the power groups recognized that peaceful negotiation
was preferable to internal war. In his position as arbitrator,
Charles V, backed by the implicit threat of his army, made
intelligent use of the inclination toward peace. Wherever he
could, he used the social and political conflicts within the towns
to support the magistrates and make them into dependent tools
of his policy. Likewise, he profited from the tensions within the
provincial estates, from the interurban competition, and from
dynastic jealousies between noble houses. Tensions that had
often built up into internal wars in the preceding century now
were utilized to divide and govern. Local urban revolts provided
opportunities to dismantle town walls or to impose the building
of citadels garrisoned by Charles's troops. The higher nobility
was pacified by the new and brilliant role it was given to play in
the Netherlands government and in the Hapsburg imperial army
and government.

But such cooperation with the prince did not result in much
progress in Charles's attempts at unification. In 1534, for example, the provinces flatly rejected his project for a defensive
alliance among them. Furthermore, although Charles had ex-
pressly forbidden the formation of leagues as a form of lese
majesty, he was nevertheless confronted time and again with
confederations of towns and even of the Brabant abbots, who
founded the first order of the estates of that province. Several
towns rebelled in the 1520s and 1530s. Most serious was the
Rebellion of Ghent (1536–40). That proud city defied the em-

peror, refused to pay taxes granted by the Estates of Flanders, and almost succeeded in bringing about a general revolt in Flanders, as it had so often done before. Thus the confederation of towns, noble clientele groups, and provinces at the beginning and subsequent stages of the revolution were to a great extent simply repetitions of traditional modes of political action.

In this context the development of the provincial estates is a fascinating phenomenon. Nowhere does the impotence of central government present itself so convincingly as in the government's dealings with the provincial authorities. Upon the relatively undisturbed provincial systems, Charles V had begun to build a superstructure of central government. In 1531 he created three collateral councils for all the possessions of the Hapsburg Netherlands and transformed the provincial courts into local branches of the Brussels government. Charles had reason to expect that at least the nobility and the delegates from the town magistrates, who depended so much upon his protection, would support his policy. The opposite, however, was true. The ever-increasing financial needs of Hapsburg international policy required that the provincial estates be asked almost every year to consent to new taxes, and the estates invariably seized this opportunity to present grievances and to demand clarifications or extensions of privileges. The content of the demands varied according to the socioeconomic and political structures of the provinces, but in general the estates insisted on the defense of their right of absolute veto on new taxes and their right to convene without being summoned. In many provinces the estates also waged a constant war of nerves against the provincial courts, which were filled with the *créatures* of the central government.[23]

The town magistrates developed classic syndromes of role conflict. They were constantly reminded of their dependence

[23] There are almost no modern histories of the major provincial estates. For Artois see C. Hirschauer, *Les États d'Artois* (Paris: Champion, 1923). For the tax problems see J. Craybeckx, "Aperçu sur l'histoire des impôts en Flandre et au Brabant au cours du XVIe siècle," *Revue du Nord*, 1954; M. Arnould, "L'impôt sur le capital en Belgique au XVIe siècle, "*Le Hainaut économique*, 1946; J. Dhondt, "Bijdrage tot de kennis van het financiewezen der Staten van Vlaanderen," *Nederlandsche Historiebladen*, 1940; H. Terdenge, "Zur Geschichte der holländischen Steuern im 15. und 16. Jahrhundert," *Vierteljahrschrift für Sozial- und Wirtschaftsgeschichte*, 1925.

upon the king and of their helplessness toward their own constituents. In the provincial estates they had first to defend the interests of their own towns, which were often the interests of a particular group that could cause a commotion at home. Next, they generally had to collaborate in the formulation of an urban point of view and then come to an understanding with the nobility and clergy in order to present a common front against the prince. Moreover, although they knew that their own class interests were often best served by yielding to the prince, they also knew that the insatiable thirst for money on the part of the central government would not spare the interests of the groups with which they were most closely allied, the merchants and entrepreneurs. While they consented to the conversion of the old *taille*-type taxes into excises on consumer commodities, which fell heavily upon the lower classes,[24] they fought with all their might against proposals for tax reform that would hit entrepreneurial gains and capital, even, as in 1542, when the government threatened to introduce them *potestate absoluta*.[25] In all provincial estates there thus developed a consistent pattern of obstruction, sabotage, and struggle against the agents of the central government.

Paradoxically, the government, lacking a bureaucratic and tax-collecting apparatus of its own, was forced to leave many administrative tasks to the estates. Most of the provinces developed a bureaucracy of some complexity with a chancellery, a receiver-general of the taxes, a treasury, secretaries (usually trained jurists), and in many cases a permanent committee of deputies for current affairs. Thus the estates became full-fledged political bodies, obeying the law of all institutions: whichever does not expand its power, loses it. Their dealings with the central government often left the impression of a tiresome, ritualistic repetition of dilatory moves and invocations of precedent and thus gave rise to those mistaken interpretations which label *Stände* revolutions as merely conservative phenomena. On the contrary, it is most fascinating to observe how underneath that ritualistic behavior new ideas and new perceptions helped strengthen the representative bodies and created a corps con-

---

[24] For Artois see Hirschauer, *Les États*, pp. 136–37; Dhondt, "Ordres ou Puissances," pp. 301–2.

[25] *Archief Sociaal-economische Geschiedenis*, 1922, p. 134.

sensus of political ideas in spite of internal economic and social antagonisms. This consensus was not necessarily directed against the government. There was much traditional provincialism and xenophobia in it. But the government was bound to feel the power of the provinces as soon as the latter simultaneously began to blame their local troubles on the prince. In the wake of Philip II's bankruptcy the session of the Estates-General in 1558 had shown a momentary but nevertheless surprising unity of action against the prince.[26] The estates even created the office of receiver-general to administer the little money they were willing to grant. Action through the Estates-General was not yet very effective; its sessions still did not include the northeastern provinces. Nevertheless, its appeal was sufficiently widespread to make the demand for a free deliberating Estates-General the rallying cry of the opposition in the early 1560s. Indeed, this demand was finally met in 1576, during the revolution, by the creation of a brand-new type of estates-general which assumed the duties of a representational legislative, and sometimes even executive, body.

This rapid sketch of the political system of the Netherlands has revealed a loose structure in which social distrust, the pride of autonomy, and local xenophobic economic anxieties abounded and the willingness to cooperate easily yielded to threats of quasi-legitimate action on all levels. The resulting particularism was all the more serious because of the endemic and often organized illegitimate violence of banditry and personal feuds, which could imperceptibly coalesce with political resistance movements. The king kept the peace by playing dangerous groups and individuals off against one another, but he himself could easily become the object of various types of discontent.

The instability of the political structure was, therefore, one of the prime preconditions of the Netherlands Revolution. The instability was a traditional feature of the system, however, and its presence does not seem to be an indication of a structural breakdown under the stress of innovative political or social forces. But there were some new ingredients, the most impor-

---

[26] P. A. Meilink, "De Staten-Generaal van 1557–1558," *Bijdragen en Mededelingen van het Historisch Genootschap te Utrecht* (Utrecht: A. Oosthoek, 1924).

tant being the simultaneous strengthening of the central, royal power and that of the representative bodies, mainly the provincial estates. This double—and contradictory—process was an increasingly disturbing element and also has to be counted among the preconditions of the revolution. Whether this development was in any way a response to changes occurring in the social structure is a difficult question to answer. But it is possible that new organizational problems rising out of rapid demographic expansion had much to do with the demand for regional political integration which found expression in the attempts to strengthen the provincial estates. The obvious efforts of the prince to use this demand to further his own dynastic interests enjoyed only limited success, however, because the forces of both cautious integration and particularism ultimately turned against him.

One more element in the political situation must be stressed: the lack of an ideology capable of unifying all potentially revolutionary but mutually hostile social and local interest groups. Without such an ideology, local revolts were bound to remain isolated and limited affairs. The existence of innovative ideologies is one of the crucial criteria for sociopolitical or societal revolutions. Historians generally have tended to deny the revolutionary character of the political program of the Netherlands Revolution. But the conservative terminology in which most of the rebel demands were presented may easily deceive us. After all, the rebels were asking for the establishment of *new* political forms, notwithstanding the efforts of their theorists to prove that those forms had existed for more than a thousand years. Of course, other possible sources of ideological cohesion were nationalism or protestant religion; the fact that they were of some importance in this respect emphasizes the insufficiency of a purely constitutional or social program to serve as a "generalized belief," as a revolutionary ideology. As we will see, however, neither was strong or widespread enough to sustain and justify the revolution—a clear indication of the pluralistic character of the events. We shall come back to this problem later. First we must ask the next question: Were the changes we described mere shifts of power within a basically static society or were they the results of more fundamental changes in economy and society?

The obvious way to investigate this crucial problem is to describe the general socioeconomic development of the Netherlands and to measure its effect on the political behavior of the three main constituents of the political system: the nobility, town populations, and the prince. That, however, is not easily done. In spite of the impressive studies made by economic and social historians over the last twenty years, the conclusions are still ambiguous and inconclusive.

According to the theoretical literature, a revolution may be the result of a reaction of socioeconomic groups to changes in either an expanding or a declining economy. In an expanding economy a newly risen class may attempt to appropriate the political power denied it by an antiquated political structure,[27] and the result is always fundamental, irreversible change. In a declining economy violent action may be taken to redistribute power to the suffering classes. Finally, there is the interesting combination of the two hypotheses: in an expanding economy a temporary recession or slowdown may frustrate the expectations of rising classes.

Each of these interpretations has been implicitly tried out by the major historians of the Netherlands Revolution. Pirenne argues the case for the bourgeois-capitalist thesis, seeing the revolution as the result and expression of a growing desire for unfettered economic freedom, the expansion of a new entrepreneurial class in Antwerp and in the southern textile industry, the emergence of new forms of exploitation, and the breaking up of traditional social relations. He sees in these developments a classic case of the bourgeois revolution, complete with the accumulation and concentration of capital and the proletarization of the artisanal middle class, the *Verelendung*.

Marxist historians have been particularly ambivalent in their sympathies as well as in their analysis, wavering between support for any revolution in which the progressive forces of bourgeois and proletarians took part, and the knowledge that classes in the sixteenth century were still extremely inchoate and that the time for a proletarian revolution had not yet come. This

[27] See the discussion of the pertinent literature in Lawrence Stone, "Theories of Revolution," pp. 170–72.

38 J. W. SMIT

ambivalence is well illustrated in Kuttner's study of the events of 1566–67. He overemphasizes the significance of proletarian action, which, he points out, was caused by poverty and aggravated by sudden price rises and bourgeois exploitation; characteristically he blames the nobility and the bourgeoisie for not having trusted the forces of the proletarian revolution. Even more contradictory is the treatment of the urban revolts in Flanders and Brabant by Wittman. He stresses the role of the reactionary corporative guild bourgeoisie as a revolutionary force but at the same time finds, quite surprisingly, all the signs of a revolution of the antifeudal urban and agrarian masses.[28]

Non-Marxist authors such as Charles Verlinden also devote much attention to the bleak situation of the wage-earning masters, journeymen, and unskilled workers. Wages had lagged behind prices from the early 1520s through the rest of Charles V's reign, improving only slightly during the early years of Philip II's government. "In those conditions commotions could not fail to occur," Verlinden concludes, and this conclusion seems especially reasonable in view of the decline of the buying power of a journeyman's wages to the absolute subsistence level. Even in good harvest years, short-term price *Hausses* drove wages below the critical line, causing starvation and massive death. Moreover, Verlinden finds evidence of widespread poverty and unemployment, the *réserve armée* of Marxist theory.[29]

Recently, Van der Wee has come up with a totally different economic interpretation of the revolution which is close to the "frustrated expectations" model. In his view the Netherlands economy around the middle of the century was rapidly expanding; the population was increasing, and wages were keeping up with prices. There was a growing artisanal middle class and a declining number of industrial workers, all enjoying full employment, and poverty was on the decline. The sudden economic recession of the 1560s hit the middle classes in the midst of this

[28] Erich Kuttner, *Het Hongerjaar 1566* (Amsterdam: Boek-en Courantmij, 1949); Wittman, "Quelques problèmes."
[29] Ch. Verlinden, "Crises économiques et sociales en Belgique à l'époque de Charles Quint," in *Charles Quint et son temps* (Paris: Centre National de la Recherche Scientifique, 1959); for the workers budget see E. Scholliers, "De levensstandaard der arbeiders op het einde der 16e eeuw te Antwerpen," *Tijdschrift voor Geschiedenis*, 1959. See also Ch. Verlinden, ed., *Dokumenten voor de geschiedenis van prijzen en lonen* (Gent: vol. 1, 1959; vol. 2, 1965).

unprecedented prosperity and thus propelled them into a radical posture in which they subsequently provided massive support first for the Reformation and then for the revolution.[30]

None of these interpretations can be rejected out of hand or completely. It is possible to be quite conclusive about specific long-range developments like demographic expansion and inflation, but the impact of such developments—the ways in which they were felt in the various economic and social structures— differs considerably from one region to another; the resulting variations are of enormous importance in the case of the very rapid and unbalanced development of the sixteenth-century Netherlands, for only a few regions took part in the process of modernization. It is impossible to generalize, in the manner of Pirenne and Van der Wee, about the entire Netherlands economy on the basis of important but very advanced and atypical industrial and commercial innovations in Antwerp and in the textile industry of the south. Van der Wee obviously is right when he emphasizes the importance of the growth of a new middle class in Antwerp and its territories, but the evidence given by Verlinden and Scholliers for the subsistence-level wages of workers and the lagging of wages behind prices is also totally convincing for the categories of people with which they are concerned.

On the whole, in fact, Van der Wee probably describes the situation in the Antwerp region as much rosier than it actually was. He himself admits that the number of unskilled workers in Antwerp was growing and that the case for full employment is shaky even for Antwerp. Even if his thesis is correct for Antwerp and several other places, however, the picture looks much gloomier from the perspective of a large number of slowly dying cities. In Flanders, Brabant, and Holland there was without a doubt an obvious concentration of capital and population and a high level of employment; in Antwerp and its quarter, Amsterdam and its dependencies in North Holland, Hondschoote and

---

[30] H. van der Wee, *The Growth of the Antwerp Market* (The Hague: M. Nijhoff, 1963), 2:133–40; *idem*, "Das Phänomen des Wachtums und der Stagnation im Lichte der Antwerpener und Südniederländischen Wirtschaft des 16. Jahrhunderts," *Vierteljahrschrift für Sozial- und Wirtschaftsgeschichte*, 1967; *idem*, "De economie als factor bij het begin van de opstand in de Zuidelijke Nederlanden," *Bijdragen en Mededelingen Historisch Genootschap Utrecht*, no. 83 (1969).

its environs, and a few other regions, the tendency was toward large industrial organizational forms. But at the same time towns like Gouda and Leiden in South Holland, Louvain and the Walloon quarter in Brabant, and Gent in Flanders went through difficult times.[31] The picture is even more somber when other provinces are taken into account. The progress of the booming centers was obviously based partly on the misery of others. Altogether, I think too much emphasis is placed on the prosperous middle classes in Van der Wee's explanation of the revolution. A similar distortion may be found in his interpretation of the reformed religious movement as basically a middle-class phenomenon. This interpretation may be true in some cases, but in others the Pirenne thesis, which argued that the Reformation followed in the wake of social disorganization and despair in the industrial areas, is a much more satisfactory explanation.

The important point is that all of these speculations about the class structure of the socioeconomic system of the Netherlands have a limited applicability because economic classes were still so intertwined with traditional status groups and because a general Netherlands economy or market simply did not exist. A weaver in Gent differed in status and economic function from his counterpart in Hondschoote or Utrecht or Leiden. The same was true for all other trades. Classes—i.e., economic groups with class consciousness and solidarity and the will to obtain power in the national political structure—in the form of a bourgeoisie, *artisanat,* proletariat, or peasantry did not exist at the national level. They *did* exist at the local level, but their political significance was restricted to the specific localities in which they operated. To be sure, there were some instances of cooperation among men of the same class across local boundaries, but they were few and, to the extent that they were conscious, generally followed the more traditional pattern of animosity of towns toward nobility and the countryside, or vice versa.

[31] For Holland see Posthumus, *Geschiedenis;* Brünner, *De order;* W. van Ravesteyn, *Onderzoekingen over de economische en sociale ontwikkeling van Amsterdam gedurende de 16e en het eerste kwart der 17e eeuw* (Amsterdam: S. L. van Looy, 1906). For Brabant see R. van Uytven, "De sociale crisis der XVIe eeuw to Leuven," *Belgisch Tijdschrift voor Philologie en Geschiedenis,* 1958.

The fact stands, however, that in the revolution the frustrated prosperous bourgeois of the booming towns joined the desperate declassed craftsmen and thriving or declining nobles, and local riots coalesced into a general revolution. Can changes in the social and economic structure account for these phenomena? Did traditional patterns of life everywhere break up? Any number of factors—the sudden advent of a new generation or an increase in vertical and horizontal social mobility, migration, unemployment, vagabondage, and criminality—either singly or in combination could have created the atmosphere of restlessness and unpredictability in which huge collective outbursts often take place. But most of these factors have never been systematically studied, and, until they are, the problem of causality will never be satisfactorily explained.[32] Nevertheless, it is necessary to try to make some tentative assessment of the major effects of socioeconomic conditions on the political system and the revolution.

The nobility, to begin with the group which was perhaps closest to being a nation-wide, as well as the oldest, class, did not everywhere suffer to the same degree from economic phenomena like inflation. In some rural areas, mostly in the south and east, part of the peasants' dues were still paid in kind. Similarly, their economic and political power remained strong. Especially in the rural areas, the nobility continued in control, although even in Hainaut—the bastion of noble power—there was a slight increase in bourgeois landholding. The towns in the Walloon provinces were generally too weak to threaten the position of the nobility seriously; if the noblemen could hold onto their political power, they could also preserve their income from the performance of judicial and administrative functions. How much the nobles feared the loss of these functions is revealed by their bitter clashes with the towns and especially with the gentlemen of the *longue robe*. The count of Hoogstraten expressed the general sentiments of his class when he threatened to cut the robes of the hated jurists so short that they would not cover their owners' backsides.

But it is difficult to determine whether such hostility was

---

[32] I am thinking here of a series of the type being worked out by students of Professor Chaunu, for instance, J. Cl. Gegot, "Étude par sondage de la criminalité dans le baillage de Falaise," *Annales de Normandie*, 1966.

inspired primarily by concern to preserve their economic standing or by the desire to maintain their social status. The higher nobility still received considerable income, but its relative economic position, like that (to a lesser extent) of the lower nobility, seems to have been declining because of conspicuous spending. Obviously, economic pressures were only one of the nobility's many grievances, but they constituted a major incentive for revolution in a class which felt beleaguered on all sides. Precisely because of the omnipresence of pressures of so many different kinds, economic motives were as likely to push the nobility toward revolution as toward loyalism. As a class the nobility had traditionally tried to safeguard its interests by choosing sides in clan feuds and in larger internal wars. Many of the poorest noblemen chose the side of rebellion, while others remained loyal, allowing themselves to be bought by the king; many simply followed their patron or automatically chose the side opposite a traditional enemy. In most case histories it remains difficult to assess which motive was strongest, but the financial one was everywhere prominent.

In the case of the populations of the towns, the effects of economic and social factors on behavior are much more clearly visible. Again, similar causes did not always produce the same results. Town magistrates could choose to oppose the central government and ride out the storm with their citizens, as they did in Antwerp; or they could, because of special circumstances, decide to side with the government, as they did in Amsterdam. The handworkers could join the unskilled workers in their hostile outbursts or self-consciously refuse to cooperate with men of lesser status. The frightful recession of the 1560s, however, brought the lower classes and the middle bourgeoisie much closer together as both became increasingly resentful of the government. The frequent acts of violence and the pillaging of the countryside by organized bands of industrial workers were clearly expressions of hostility toward the government.[33] Even though they had a great deal to lose, the middle and upper bourgeoisie had their own convincing reasons for turning cautiously against the government. Van der Wee has pointed to the democratization of long-distance trade during the wave of expan-

---

[33] Kuttner, *Het Hongerjaar 1566*, pp. 72–79.

sion from 1540 to 1565, and there is also sufficient evidence to show that many of the wealthier artisans as well as merchants had invested in *rentes*. This group of large and small proprietors had many reasons for discontent over the money-raising and fiscal policies of the government. It had become an important source of governmental loans. Charles V had increased his short-term and consolidated debt on the Antwerp market from some fifty to sixty thousand pounds Flemish in 1515 to eight million pounds by the early 1550s. Much of this money had been provided by small investors, and the crash caused by Philip II's bankruptcy in 1559 must have dragged with it many members of the lower bourgeoisie.[34] Sharply increasing taxes did the rest. The town magistrates were deeply involved in both taxation and *rentes:* they had to negotiate the taxes and often guaranteed or sold the *rentes*. Their ambivalence toward the government has been mentioned earlier. It is likely that the government's *va banque* policy and the situation in urban finances led many urban patricians as well as small investors down the road to firm opposition and finally to revolution.

In summary, we cannot fail to be impressed by the importance of the socioeconomic situation as a precondition of the Netherlands Revolution. Whether it also indicated the existence of any profound structural change, however, is less clear. There are signs of a partial breakthrough of new economic structures and of a growing bourgeois consciousness among the merchants, but the lack of a systematic study of either subject makes precise conclusions difficult. Indeed, one of our most basic needs is an analysis of bourgeois mentality. At the very least, however, we can say that our knowledge of the socioeconomic situation suggests that the dynamic element in the opposition was represented by progressive forces as well as by the victims of the new developments.

If the role of political and socioeconomic factors in the origins of the Netherlands Revolution is complex and obscure, the significance of ideological and religious preconditions is infinitely more so.

[34] F. Braudel, "Les emprunts de Charles Quint sur la place d'Anvers," in *Charles Quint et son temps*.

Initially, the attempts to justify the resistance were of the old-fashioned feudal type, but the statement of the Estates of Holland in 1572 that it had the right to convene without the prince's approval represented something different. The proliferation of illegal acts after 1576 made it difficult to adhere to a conservative constitutional position, and in that period there was a significant increase in natural-law arguments as well as in willful distortions of constitutional precedents. The establishment of causal links between theory and action is difficult, however, because the new formulations of the rights of citizens and princes were mostly later rationalizations of revolutionary action and hence presumably not indications of earlier discontent or ideological goals.

Also, in the later 1570s there were many attempts to appeal to a greater-Netherlands national feeling, a fact which has been duly recorded by Pirenne and Geyl. William of Orange employed such an appeal to overcome the divisive effects of the Calvinist monopolization of the revolution; quite clearly, however, national consciousness was not strong enough to serve as a general unifying belief. Like the constitutional arguments, it was a result rather than a precondition of the revolution. It could, however, be used by the many non-Protestants among the rebels to justify their resistance, and national or patriotic arguments were infused in the literature of the time, thus constituting an additional, minor element in the movement.[35]

The importance of religion can be established more easily, though the problem remains a tantalizing one. What in the reformation process represented a more or less autonomous spiritual emancipation and what was directly reducible to social and economic developments is a problem which will keep historians busy for a long time. All I intend to do here is to point out the many contradictory strains in the current against orthodoxy. The Reformation as a movement of spiritual emancipation can be seen in the critical attitude among the elite, but it can also be studied, in another segment of the population, in the character of popular devotion.

Toussaert has investigated very thoroughly the fifteenth- and sixteenth-century fascination with the ritualistic and supernatu-

[35] See G. Malengreau, L'Esprit particulariste et la Révolution des Pays-Bas au XVIᵉ siècle (Louvain, 1936).

ral elements of religion, with processions, miracles, devotions, indulgences, and patron saints.[36] This undercurrent was potentially heterodox, but, in an almost diametrically opposite sense from the enlightened, rational discourses of the humanists, it aimed at purification of the Church and the return to the simplicity of early Christianity. The popular religion was often scarcely Christian. Nevertheless, coastal Flanders, the region which Toussaert studied, became one of the earliest centers of widespread Protestantization. Obviously, mysterious psychological transitions from the ritualistic and magic brand of Catholicism to the most austere type of Calvinism were possible. The unreformed, but hardly Catholic, people of Toussaert's book often show a sharply felt need for purity in religious life rather obscurely mixed with an equally strong practice of impurity, both being expressions of rage and hostility toward the traditional religious establishment. But examples of this unmitigated anger and aggressiveness are also found in the Protestant propaganda and in the interrogations and confessions of their martyrs: incapable of controlling their contempt, they often answer their inquisitors in strings of profanity. This anticlerical aggressiveness had been fed by very palpable inconsistencies between the ideals and practices of the servants of the Church; it was further strengthened in the towns by a long tradition of fighting ecclesiastic jurisdiction and by the economic competition between guilds and monasteries which had so often erupted in violence.

More important for our purpose, however, is the extent to which the Reformation served as an alternative to the established sociopolitical order. The monopoly of the Church was being challenged, and, judging from what happened in the Netherlands cities during the revolution, a majority of the people were happy to see the monopoly broken, even though they did not become convinced Protestants themselves. The support for toleration was widespread, and the application of Charles V's ordinances against heretics was lax. In this ambiguous and and anxious situation, which may be sufficiently explained by the socioeconomic and political strains previously described, many people must have lived in a constant state of tension

[36] J. Toussaert, Le sentiment religieux en Flandre à la fin du Moyen Age (Paris: Plon, 1963).

between the poles of libertinism and asceticism—a tension which was so well combined in the extreme Münsterites and for which the total abandoning of self in a new religion could be either a permanent or a temporary solution. In this general sense the urge for religious change was probably a powerful precondition of the revolution. It helped people define the evil, identify the scapegoat, and justify their hostility. It did not necessarily succeed in committing them to a revolutionary posture, but it did help to undermine their allegiance to time-honored institutions. Because of the widespread hostility toward the Church, the die-hard Protestants could, in spite of their minority, make the religious issue a tool of divisiveness. In the 1570s the undogmatic leaders of the revolution, such as William of Orange, either became nominal Calvinists or supported their party. In this later, more clearly bourgeois phase, Catholicism became synonymous with Spain and the aristocracy, Calvinism with patriotism and the bourgeoisie, the twin elements in the new order of things.

In the preceding section I analyzed a number of possible preconditions of the Netherlands Revolution. As I suggested at the outset, however, this method yields a confused picture of violent movements fragmented along local and social lines. Now I shall consider the question of whether this confusion was the ultimate stage of a revolution that was little more than an ephemeral and incidental coalescence of local events or represented one of the convulsions of an innovating social process. The question can best be approached through an examination of some of the crucial phases of the revolution.

To bring some order to the confusion of the *histoire événementielle,* it is desirable to keep Smelser's theory of collective behavior in mind. Smelser defines collective behavior as mobilization on the basis of a belief which redefines social action and thereby answers the need to restructure an ambiguous, anxiety-producing situation. The vital determinants in his analytical schema are the spread of such a generalized belief and the mobilization, on the basis of that belief, of the participants. Smelser applies this schema to the analysis of a number of forms of revolutionary behavior, from simple forms like hysteria and collective outbursts to complicated value-oriented movements. For the topic at hand the crucial questions raised by Smelser are: first, whether the events of the revolution were of a simple and limited or more complex and inclusive value-oriented type; and second, whichever was the case, whether the revolution produced generalized beliefs capable of successfully mobilizing the participants on a nation-wide scale.

Let us turn now to the first of our periods, the prelude of the revolution, 1555–66. From our previous discussion we know that the Netherlands was an incompletely integrated state in which class and regional warfare existed just beneath the surface of everyday life. Nevertheless, there was no violence on a national scale prior to 1566; the governing elite was relatively loyal, and violence was limited to local revolts usually involving specific social groups.

Striking changes occurred during the period 1555–66. A worsening economic situation created antagonism between the responsible magistrates and the ever more demanding prince. Whether these economic events were preconditions or actual precipitants is difficult to tell; economic competition with England, bad harvests, and the financial demands of princely warfare—undoubtedly the main factor—were of a contingent nature. But they could affect the population severely because the Netherlands was so heavily involved in secular economic expansion. However that may have been, the alienation of the magistracy was one of the factors which disturbed the balance of the political system. In spite of the provincialism which persisted in the Estates-General, the free discussion of the session of 1558 brought a turn in the history of that body. Thereafter, the belief that its intervention would bring redress of grievances became increasingly generalized among dissident elements in the Netherlands.

In the same period, another part of the governing elite—the nobility—became estranged from royal government. After Philip II's departure for Spain, the grandees tried to force through the reform of the Council of State into an exclusively aristocratic executive body. They failed, but in their attack on the king's position they secured the removal of the Spanish troops, an event of incalculable significance because it left the government with no power except the nobility's *bandes d'ordonnance* and the urban militias. Faced with the choice between revolt and obedience, many of the grandees withdrew sulking, but their place was taken by a substantial part of the lesser nobility under the tacit leadership of a hard core of antigovernment grandees (William of Orange among others).

These events, beginning in the early 1560s, coincided with serious economic trouble and growing distrust of the government's financial policy. On a lower social level the discontent showed itself in demonstrations against the establishment in general, especially against its weakest spot, the Church. Religiously indifferent mobs attacked prisons, the hated symbols of oppression, and freed Protestants.[37] Toleration became the general slogan and, in conjunction with the demand for a free Estates-General, became the core of the opposition's political program. For some time these slogans worked as perfect generalized beliefs of a national, or interprovincial, scope; they were simple principles and above all were socially neutral. Because the government strongly resisted both demands, they continued to be the rallying cries of the opposition, and came increasingly to exercise wide emotional appeal. From the perspective of the discontented, where one stood on these issues readily identified him as friend or foe, patriot or villain.

But the events of 1566 were to demonstrate the weakness of both issues as unifying concepts. Tension had been growing. In April, 1566, the lower nobility had drawn nation-wide attention to its demands for change; in the early months of the year skyrocketing prices prepared the ground for a wild, iconoclastic movement in the summer. The nobility refused to suppress it, as did most of the town militias. It was the classical case of a power vacuum. The elite had wanted only limited action, but in the southern towns the movement developed all the characteristics of a revolt of artisans and proletarians, which was equally threatening to the higher bourgeoisie and the nobility. The orgy of fraternity soon gave way to more sober reactions. The lower nobility, alarmed at this turn of events, withdrew its demands and disbanded, the rebel towns were forced to surrender, and the scene was set for repression, which came in the form of the duke of Alva's reign of terror.[38]

[37] A. J. C. de Vrankrijker, "De Opstand in het industriegebied," *Bijdragen Vaderlandsche Geschiedenis*, 1937.
[38] For 1566 see R. van Roosbroeck, *Het Wonderjaar te Antwerpen* (Antwerp: De Sikkel, 1930); and Kuttner, *Het Hongerjaar 1566*.

The failure of the 1566 revolution brings out some specific characteristics of the Netherlands Revolution as a whole. On the popular level the primitive, hostile outburst that accompanied it had at most developed into the traditional local social revolution, without much of a program and with a total lack of interest beyond local borders. The emerging national ideology failed to unite dissident groups not only because of regional differences but even more because no program could have bridged the enormous gaps among the discontented classes. Initially, in fact, the hatred among class and status groups increased as a consequence of the revolution. Only the terror of Alva maintained the antagonism of the bourgeoisie and nobility toward the government. Of the duke's measures, it was typically his new sales tax which was chiefly responsible for keeping some revolutionary fervor alive within the Netherlands after his suppression.[39]

For those noble leaders of the revolution who had been forced into exile, the stakes for keeping the fires of revolution burning were far higher. Among them, William of Orange brooded about the failure of the revolution of 1566 and came to an understanding of its weaknesses. Thereafter, he worked tenaciously to unite the opposition in a program of privileges, toleration, and patriotism. But this desperate effort to impose ideological unity on a movement that had to gather its force from so many conflicting camps was predoomed to failure. Given the diverse goals of the various components of the opposition and the many deep social antagonisms among them, Orange's program was simply too ephemeral, too narrow, and too dependent upon an as yet inchoate sense of national consciousness to succeed in channeling all local hostile potential exclusively against the government. Class consciousness, on the other hand, did not evolve into clearer and more modern forms, an indication that in this respect the society had not yet been sufficiently shaken by the socioeconomic changes that had already taken place as to call forth new and perhaps more descriptive perceptions of the newly emergent social order.[40]

But Orange's program was capable of uniting Holland and Zee-

---

[39] See J. Craybeckx, "De 10ᵉ penning een mythe?" *Tijdschrift voor Geschiedenis*, 1964.

[40] The best works for this period are L. Delfos, *Die Anfänge der Utrechter Union* (Berlin: E. Ebering, 1941); and Malengreau, *L'Esprit particulariste* (1924 ed.).

land behind him, as was indicated after his successful invasion of those provinces in 1572. Following the invasion, the power vacuum of 1566 was repeated. Alva had to concentrate his army in the south, and in Holland and Zeeland the urban militias refused to defend the towns against Orange's irregular troops. The fact that, socially, Holland and Zeeland were much more homogeneous provinces than Flanders and Brabant was of the utmost importance to the success of this venture. The nobility did not count for much and now lost even more of its influence in the Holland and Zeeland estates. The towns had always been rather safely in the hands of the merchant patriciates and lacked the unruly revolutionary tradition of their Flemish and Brabant sisters. William of Orange came to power as the hero of the lower middle classes, who hoped to settle their account with the patriciate. Ultimately, however, the democratic tendencies of the lower middle classes were neither sufficiently strong nor sufficiently articulate to threaten the oligarchy. Like Charles V before him, Orange finally decided to protect the magistrates, his only concession to the radicals being the abolition of Catholicism. So in Holland and Zeeland the revolution finally assumed a definitive character: it represented the victory of the bourgeois estates over the nobility and the central government. But it was a character which was suited to the structure of these particular provinces only.

How different the situation was elsewhere was revealed in the period 1576–79. In 1576, dissatisfied with the Spanish regime, the southern provinces, led by the nobility and magistracy, rejoined the revolt, as did the eastern provinces. The southern nobility finally carried out the narrowly defined aristocratic *coup d'état* which William of Orange had envisioned in the early sixties. The nobility allied with Orange but did not want to accept him as leader. At the same time, the old guild democratic hatred of the patriciate and nobility broke loose again in general urban revolts in Flanders and Brabant. The astonishing fact now was that William of Orange, who had instituted an oligarchy in Holland, was hailed as the hero of guild democracy in the south. Just as paradoxically, Calvinism, which was the anchor of the new establishment in the north, became the weapon against the moderates and the wealthy bourgeoisie in the south. The story that followed is too complicated to give in capsule form here.

It is interesting to note, however, that in this totally anarchic situation internal war broke out in essentially the same forms and with many of the same ideological patterns as had appeared in the fourteenth and fifteenth centuries: town *ligues* against nobility, noble dynasties against one another. William of Orange tried desperately to keep the revolutionary front united, and more and more his appeal was formulated in terms of national consciousness and unity. But his efforts were of no avail; social antagonism in the south was too strong to permit the kind of intergroup cooperation which had permitted Holland and Zeeland to achieve stable self-government. In this situation military power would decide. The Spanish reconquered the south, while the northern provinces were forcefully drawn into the power system of Holland, which had been strengthened by a massive immigration of capital and skilled labor from the south. The geographical division became a social, economic, and religious division as well. The northern provinces became predominantly bourgeois and mercantile, and, although many of the immigrants from the south were Catholic, the Calvinists achieved dominance. The southern provinces, on the other hand, were primarily oriented toward agriculture and remained under the social and political dominance of the nobility; the restoration of the Catholics to power assured that they would be largely Catholic.

The above factual sketch should enable us to answer the two main questions we posed at the beginning of this paper: first, whether it is possible to establish priorities among the several preconditions of the Netherlands Revolution; and second, whether there actually was an element of societal change in what seems, even from my survey, to have been a classical case of the merely political internal war.

To begin with the political preconditions, it will have become clear that the insufficient subjection of regional and socio-economic interests to the state contributed heavily to the outbreak of the revolution. On the one hand, there was a tendency, even an internal necessity, toward some form of unification. The Hapsburg princes did not merely try to impose unification on their own volition; they also responded to the need of an expanding economy for more integration and a better system of communications. On the other hand, the princes were a force against unification because suspicions were raised by their economic and foreign policies. In this ambivalent situation a national consciousness and a feeling of national identity could not become the basis for a nation-wide movement on either side. The outcome of the revolution—i.e., the confederative constitution of the Dutch Republic—seems to suggest that the provinces were simply incapable of overcoming their traditional regionalism and that provincial autonomy was the most important element in the political creed of the rebels. But we should beware of the usual depreciating comments on the so-called particularism of the Dutch Republic. Braudel has rightly observed that around 1600 the middle-sized state was the most viable.[41] Indeed, although the constitution of the republic is often derided as unworkable, it functioned much better and permitted the achievement of a higher degree of economic integration than any of the monarchies of Europe. The bourgeoisie of Holland had carried through exactly the degree of reform it needed to promote economic expansion and yet feel free from overcentralization.

The interpretation of the economic and social facts reveals similar contradictions. The unmistakable economic expansion and innovation seem to have been of too limited and local a nature to have caused the irresistible and widespread breakthrough of a new social order. Similarly, ideological and religious factors are too ambiguous or too little investigated to permit us to conclude that significant anomie or an unequivocal strain of intellectual or spiritual disorientation accompanied these societal changes. Nevertheless, the socioeconomic preconditions seem to have been rather influential from the perspective of the outcome of the revolution. After all, in spite of the qualifications we must make, the new republic became the first real capitalist and bourgeois nation with a strongly marked, very mercantile national identity.

The key to an understanding of our problem resides, I think, in the fact that the revolution succeeded in only part of the Netherlands. I would like to defend the thesis that the Nether-

[41] F. Braudel, *La Mediterranée et le monde mediterranéen*, vol. 2 (Paris: A. Colin, 1966).

lands Revolution was indeed, among many other things, an innovative, progressive, societal revolution. But the mercantile bourgeois class, which fought its own revolution, was too weak to establish its government in all of the Netherlands; it had too little sense of class consciousness and too little solidarity from one region to another to organize on a nation-wide scale; but it was also too strong to be defeated by a government aiming at its destruction. It could found a state in its own image only in Holland, where the market economy, already in an advanced stage of development, was swollen by southern capital, people, and skills, and where it had no major opposition from rival social groups. The emergence of the Dutch Republic was not the result of an irresistible process of world history, leading to the triumph of capitalism. Too many incidental facts, such as the avarice and stupidity of the Spanish government, geographical position, and military developments played a large part in its untimely birth. But in its curious mixture of unconscious progressiveness and misunderstood traditionalism, the republic [42] embodied a premonition of the future as well as the persistence of the past: as such it was a perfect image of the sixteenth century.

A NOTE ON FURTHER READING

The chief standard histories of the Netherlands Revolution are still H. Pirenne, *Histoire de Belgique*, vols. 3 and 4 (Brussels: Lamertin, 1907 and 1911), and P. Geyl, *The Revolt of the Netherlands* (London: Williams & Norgate, 1932); they are useful, but each in its own way is biased. Pirenne's book is also important because of its clear-cut theses on the revolution's economic, institutional, and religious factors, which have constituted the point of departure of many later works. Also to be mentioned is F. Rachfahl's *Wilhelm von Oranien und der niederländischen Aufstand*, 4 vols. (Halle: M. Niemeyer, 1906–24), for its strong emphasis on the role of the estates. Still indispensable is A. Henne's *Histoire du règne de Charles Quint en Belgique*, 8 vols. (Brussels: E. Flatau, 1858–60), for the wealth of archival material it uses. The most recent survey is *Algemene Geschiedenis der Nederlanden*, ed. by J. A. van Houtte *et al.*, vols. 4 and 5 (Utrecht: W. de Haan, 1951–52).

The complicated discussions about the revolution, mostly of a

---

[42] See Hobsbawm's analysis of the relative backwardness of the Dutch economy of the seventeenth century, "The Crisis of the Seventeenth Century," p. 45.

strong religious and political nature, have been summarized in my
article "The Present Position of Studies Regarding the Revolt of the
Netherlands"; to the "progressive" interpretations mentioned in the
article should be added H. A. Enno van Gelder, *De Nederlandse
Staten en het Engels Parlement* (Amsterdam: Noord-Hollandse Uitg.
Mij-Amsterdam, 1960), and to the Marxist interpretations we should
add the work of T. Wittmann mentioned in note 4. In English we
have the rather unsuccessful attempt by G. Griffiths to fit the Netherlands case into the framework of Crane Brinton's *Anatomy of Revolution;* see Griffiths' "The Revolutionary Character of the Revolt in the
Netherlands," *Comparative Studies in Society and History* 2 (1959–
60). I. Schöffer offered some necessary corrections of Griffiths' chronology in *ibid.* 3 (1961–62), but in both articles the regional differen-
tiations of the revolution are neglected. Institutional historiography
provides a very fragmented picture. Most of the studies have been
written from an anachronistic nineteenth- and twentieth-century
conception of the state. Excellent work has been done, though, in
the many issues of *Ancien Pays et États—Standen en Landen.* Good
case studies of provincialism also appear in A. Zijp, *De Strijd tussen
de Staten van Gelderland en het Hot, 1543–1566* (Arnhem: S. Gouda
Quint, 1913), and J. Woltjer, *Friesland in de Hervormingstijd*
(Leiden: Universitaire pers, 1962); for the regular monographs of
institutional history I refer the reader to the bibliographies in the
Algemene Geschiedenis der Nederlanden, vols. 4 and 5.

For economic history the first volume of H. van der Wee, *The
Growth of the Antwerp Market* (The Hague: M. Nijhoff, 1963), has
an extensive bibliography which completes the bibliography of the
Algemene Geschiedenis for the southern Netherlands. Because the
emphasis in my paper has been on regionalism I should indicate the
opposite interpretation of J. A. van Houtte, "Het Nederlandse Markt-
gebied in de 15ᵉ Eeuw," *Bijdragen en Mededelingen Historisch
Genootschap Utrecht* 70 (1956). Analyses of the social situation are
rare: I should mention E. Scholliers, *Loonarbeid en honger* (Antwerp: De Sikkel, 1960), a model of its kind, but, unfortunately,
published only in Dutch.

Religion in its social significance is also an underdeveloped area;
there is not much apart from straight Church history and generalizations like Kuttner's (see note 4). At present, however, much is being
done; see J. Decavele, "De reformatorische beweging te Axel en Hulst
(1556–1566), *Bijdragen Geschiedenis der Nederlanden* 23 (1968–69),
and M. Delmotte, "Het Calvinisme in de verschillende bevolkingsla-
gen te Gent (1566–1567)," *Tijdschrift voor Geschiedenis* 76 (1963).
An article of my own on religion and social stratification in Utrecht
is forthcoming.

LAWRENCE STONE

2 | The English Revolution

PRESUPPOSITIONS

Before advancing an explanation for a historical event, it is first necessary to establish what kind of event it is which needs explaining. What happened in England in the middle of the seventeenth century? Was it a "Great Rebellion," as Clarendon believed, the last and most violent of the many rebellions against particularly unprepossessing or unpopular kings, which had been staged by dissident members of the landed classess century after century throughout the Middle Ages?[1] Was it merely an internal war caused by a temporary political breakdown due to particular political circumstances?[2] Was it the Puritan Revolution of S. R. Gardiner, to whom the driving force behind the whole episode was a conflict of religious institutions and ideologies?[3] Was it the first great clash of liberty against royal tyranny, as seen by Macaulay, the first blow for the Enlightenment and Whiggery, a blow which put England on the slow road to parliamentary monarchy and civil liberties?[4] Was it the first Bourgeois Revolution, in which the progressive and dynamic elements in society struggled to emerge from their

The footnotes to this article are intended to draw attention to the great body of research which has been published during the last twenty years and upon which so much of the argument is based. Facts which have long been familiar and are in all the textbooks are not footnoted.

[1] E. Hyde, Earl of Clarendon, *The History of the Rebellion and Civil Wars in England,* ed. W. D. Murray (Oxford, 1888).
[2] C. V. Wedgwood, *The King's Peace, 1637–41* (London, 1955).
[3] S. R. Gardiner, *History of the Great Civil War, 1642–9,* 3 vols. (London, 1886–91).
[4] T. B. Macaulay, *The History of England from the Accession of James II* (London, 1849); G. M. Trevelyan, *England Under the Stuarts* (London, 1925).

feudal swaddling clothes? This is how Engels saw it, and how many historians of the 1930s, including R. H. Tawney and C. Hill, tended to regard it.[5] Was it the first Revolution of Modernization, which is the Marxist interpretation in a new guise, now perceived as a struggle of progressive and dynamic forces to remold the institutions of government to meet the needs of a more efficient, more rationalistic, and more economically advanced society?[6] Or was it a Revolution of Despair, engineered by the decaying and backward-looking elements in society, the mere gentry of H. R. Trevor-Roper, who, consumed with hatred, jealousy, and ideological intolerance bred of sectarian religious radicalism, attempted to turn back the clock and to re-create the decentralized, rural, agrarian, inward-looking, socially stable, and economically stagnant society of their hopeless, anachronistic dreams.[7]

There is a grain of truth in each of these theories. Each author displays one facet of a many sided whole, but tends to ignore the sides which do not fit his stereotype, choosing instead to focus too exclusively on that particular stage of a many staged process which best illustrates his particular hypothesis.

In order to clear the way for the long-term analysis which will follow, it is first necessary to set out certain basic presuppositions on the acceptance of which the whole structure depends. The first and most fundamental is that there is a profound truth in James Harrington's assertion that "the dissolution of this Government caused the War, not the War the dis-

[5] F. Engels, *Socialism: Utopian and Scientific* (London, 1892), pp. xix–xxiv; C. Hill, *The English Revolution, 1640* (London, 1940), pp. 9–82; R. H. Tawney, "The Rise of the Gentry, 1558–1640," *Economic History Review* 11 (1941); idem, "Harrington's Interpretation of His Age," *Proceedings of the British Academy* 27 (1941); M. Dobb, *Studies in the Development of Capitalism* (London, 1946), pp. 109–51, 161–76, 186–220, 224–39.

For a neo-Marxist interpretation, see Barrington Moore, Jr., *Social Origins of Dictatorship and Democracy* (Boston, 1966), pt. 1, chap. 1. For a modified Marxist interpretation giving a greater role to religion and ideas, see C. Hill, "La Révolution anglaise du XVIIe siècle," *Revue Historique* 221 (1959), and his *Century of Revolution, 1603–1714* (London, 1961).

For a savage onslaught on these theories, see J. H. Hexter, "The Myth of the Middle Class in Tudor England," in his *Reappraisals in History* (London, 1961).

[6] C. E. Black, *The Dynamics of Modernization* (New York, 1966), pp. 72–74, 90, 106–8.

[7] H. R. Trevor-Roper, "The Gentry, 1540–1640," *Economic History Review*, suppl. 1, 1953.

solution of this Government."[8] This means that to concentrate upon Clarendon's "Great Rebellion" or Miss Wedgwood's "Civil War" is to miss the essential problem. The outbreak of war itself is relatively easy to explain; what is hard is to puzzle out why most of the established institutions of state and Church—crown, court, central administration, and episcopacy—collapsed so ignominiously two years before.

The second assumption is that this is more than a mere rebellion against a particular king. Sigmund Neumann has defined a revolution as involving "a sweeping, fundamental change in political organization, social structure, economic property control, and the predominant myth of a social order, thus indicating a major break in the continuity of development."[9] If we accept this definition, it is evident that the English Revolution fulfills some, but not all, of these requirements. There was undoubtedly a fundamental change in political organization, and in the predominant myth of a social order, and the Levellers certainly demanded a fundamental change in social structure, although, admittedly, they were soon crushed. On the other hand, much (but not all) of the old political organization was restored in 1660, and, although economic property control was seized (temporarily) from the hands of the crown and the episcopacy, both Independents and Presbyterians were satisfied with the existing distribution of private property within the society. Such attempts to change the distribution as were made, notably by the confiscation and sale of the estates of important Royalists, are now known to have been largely unsuccessful. In terms of the distribution of wealth between social groups, and even between individual families, England at the end of the revolution in 1660 was barely distinguishable from England at the beginning in 1640.[10] Within these limits, however, the English Revolution is nonetheless unique for its radicalism among the many rebellions of early modern Europe and therefore cannot easily be

[8] J. Harrington, *Oceana* (London, 1737), p. 70.
[9] S. Neumann, "The International Civil War," *World Politics* 1 (1949): 333–34, n. 1.
[10] J. Thirsk, "The Sale of Royalist Land during the Interregnum," *Economic History Review*, 2d ser., vol. 5 (1952); *idem*, "The Restoration Land Settlement," *Journal of Modern History* 26 (1954); H. J. Habakkuk, "Landowners and the Civil War," *Economic History Review*, 2d ser., vol. 18 (1965); *idem*, "The Parliamentary Army and the Crown Lands," *Welsh Historical Review* 3 (1967).

compared with the anti-colonial revolts of the Netherlands, Catalonia, or Portugal, with the aristocratic and official revolt of the *Fronde*, or with any of those desperate, blind, and bloody movements of popular fury by peasantry or urban poor which tore at seventeenth-century Europe from Calais to the Urals.

The revolutionary nature of the English Revolution can be demonstrated partly by its deeds and partly by its words. Its achievements included not merely the killing of a king (the English had a long tradition of murdering unwanted kings, from William Rufus to Edward II to Richard III), but the abolition of monarchy; not merely the execution of the persons and confiscation of the property of a few noblemen, but the abolition of the House of Lords; not merely a protest against Hobbes's "unpleasing priests," clergy and bishops, but the sweeping away of the Established Church and seizure of episcopal properties; not merely an attack on unpopular officials, but the abolition of a range of critically important administrative and legal institutions of government. The revolutionary nature of the English Revolution is perhaps even more convincingly demonstrated by its words than by its deeds. The mere fact that it was such an extraordinarily wordy revolution—22,000 pamphlets and newspapers were published between 1640 and 1661[11]—would by itself strongly suggest that this is something very different from the familiar protest against an unpopular government. Here is a clash of ideas and of ideologies, and the emergence of radical concepts affecting every aspect of human behavior and every institution in society from the family to the Church to the state.

Some have argued that because much of the rhetoric, particularly in the early stages, was couched in terms of a return to some imagined Golden Age in the past, because the word "revolution" itself meant not a change to something totally new, but a circular or elliptical rotation to a position which had been occupied at some earlier moment in time, the movement was therefore basically conservative, and consequently not a revolution at all as the word is defined today. Now it is perfectly true that reformers and reactionaries in 1640 were each looking backward to a (different) mythical past. The Puritans, of whatever shade of opinion, were seeking a return to what they

[11] *Catalogue of the Thomason Tracts in the British Museum, 1640–1661* (London, 1908), p. xxi.

imagined to have been the state of the primitive Christian church of the Early Fathers, before it had been distorted and corrupted by later, sinful, accretions. The lawyers were seeking to go back to what they believed to be the medieval situation— and were they not assured by Chief Justice Sir Edward Coke in immensely learned folio volumes that it was no more than the historical truth?—when kings, bureaucracies, and church courts were all guided and controlled by the opinions of common lawyers and the conventions of common law.[12] The antiquarians provided the more advanced lawyers and parliamentarians with the theory of the Norman Yoke, the notion that before 1066 the Anglo-Saxons had lived as free and equal citizens, enjoying self-government through representative institutions, but that these liberties had been destroyed by an alien tyranny of kings and aristocrats imposed by the Norman Conquest.[13] Somewhat imprudently exploited by the landed opposition to the crown in the 1630s and the early 1640s, the theory of the Norman Yoke was taken up by the Levellers in the late 1640s as a weapon against landlords as a whole. The parliamentary gentry dreamed of a Golden Age of social stability, political harmony, and a Protestant domestic and foreign policy, which they believed to have existed in the good old days of Queen Elizabeth and to which they hoped to return.

Charles I and his authoritarian supporters similarly looked back to the reigns of rich and powerful kings like Henry II, Edward I, or Henry VIII. Laud cast envious eyes back to the vastly wealthy, politically powerful, and socially well-connected church of the late Middle Ages, while Charles himself and some of his advisers had visions of going back to an antediluvian past when social hierarchy was respected, deference reigned supreme, social mobility was at a minimum, and every man knew his place. The fact that these notions were cast in an antiquarian mold does nothing to alter one way or another the degree of radicalism or conservatism which they represent. This must be

---

[12] C. Ogilvie, *The King's Government and the Common Law, 1471–1641* (Oxford, 1958); M. Judson, *The Crisis of the Constitution* (New Brunswick, 1949), chap. 2; C. Hill, *Intellectual Origins of the English Revolution* (Oxford, 1965), chap. 5; W. S. Holdsworth, *A History of English Law*, vol. 5 (London, 1937), pp. 425–93.

[13] C. Hill, "The Norman Yoke," in his *Puritanism and Revolution* (London, 1958), pt. 1, chap. 3.

judged against the contemporary situation, and it makes no difference whatever whether the idealized Golden Age is in the past or in the future. All that matters is the degree to which the vision differs from the reality of the present.

It is perfectly true that the country gentry and nobility assembled in Westminster in 1640 were reformers, not revolutionaries. They had no intention whatever of tampering with the social structure, and, although they wished to make far-reaching changes in the essential organs of Church and state, they stopped far short of any radical overthrow of established institutions. In 1640 no one dreamed of abolishing monarchy or the House of Lords, and only a minority hoped to abolish episcopacy or tithes. Notions of participatory democracy were beginning to circulate among the more radical Puritan congregations, but none of the elite saw this as anything more than a small cloud on the distant horizon.

On the other hand, even if the Parliamentary opposition leaders were political and religious reformers rather than revolutionaries, and were undeniably social conservatives, even if most of their arguments were legalistic and backward-looking, it should not be forgotten that as early as 1640 many of them were using, and complacently listening to, language which was genuinely and frankly radical and forward-looking in tone and content. In November, 1641, Sir John Dryden of Canons Ashby, M.P., a highly respectable, wealthy, and well-established Northamptonshire gentleman, wrote from London to his uncle in the country to describe the activities of the Long Parliament: "I ask that I shall have your prayers. . . . I can only bring straw and stubble to that great work. God be praised, here want not skilful agents for that great work; it hitherto goeth on fast. . . . The walls go up fast, though they cannot be suddenly finished. The ruins be such, both in Church and Commonwealth, that some years will hardly repair all the breaches." If Sir John spoke the language of radical change, some of the things he listened to were even more inflammatory. In 1641 Thomas Case delivered a sermon before the assembled members of the House of Commons, in which he urged them on to ever greater efforts. "Reformation must be universal. . . . Reform all places, all persons and callings. Reform the benches of judgment, the inferior magistrates. . . . Reform the universities, reform the cities, reform the counties, reform inferior schools of learning. Reform the Sabbath, reform the ordinances, the worship of God. . . . You have more work to do than I can speak. . . . Every plant which my heavenly Father hath not planted shall be rooted up."[14] This is not the language of aristocratic rebellion or civil war, with limited, largely personal, objectives; it is the language of revolution in the modern sense, and the language of "Cultural Revolution" at that. And yet it was preached in 1641, before the war began, to an approving audience of sober-sided members of Parliament.

From all this one may reasonably conclude that, by the time the government collapsed in 1640, there existed among very large numbers of normally conservative noblemen and gentlemen a strong desire for widespread change: a change in the political myth away from the Divine Right of Kings; a change in the constitution away from an all-powerful executive and toward a "balanced constitution" in which authority would be distributed more evenly between the King and his servants and the representative assembly of the political nation; a change in administrative institutions, with the destruction of most of the so called Prerogative Courts; a change in the powers, wealth, and organization of the Established Church; and, finally, a modest but strictly limited change in the concept of social hierarchy, by which gentlemen would be treated more or less as equals, regardless of discrepancies in titular rank.

The third assumption upon which this essay is founded is that the class-war theory of the Marxists has only limited applicability to the seventeenth century. The great contribution of Marxism to the interpretation of the period has been to stress the extent and significance of early capitalist growth in trade, industry, and agriculture in the century before the revolution. Marxist or Marxist-influenced historians have taken the lead in investigating these developments, and it is important to recognize how much their work has influenced all subsequent interpretations. Their weakness, however, has been their persistent efforts to link these developments to the revolution by means of a theory of class warfare which may work reasonably well for England in the early nineteenth century, but which seriously

---

[14] Historical Manuscripts Commission, *Second Report* (London, 1874), p. 63; M. Walzer, *The Revolution of the Saints* (Cambridge, Mass., 1965), pp. 10–11.

distorts the historical reality of earlier periods. A more fruitful way of linking social and economic change to revolution is through the theory of status inconsistency, which holds that a society with a relatively large proportion of persons undergoing high mobility is likely to be in an unstable condition. The reason for this instability is that mobility affects some of the many components of status (wealth, education, power, position, etc.), but not others, and this produces individuals whose status is poorly crystallized. Such persons are likely to turn to new ideas and to demand a change (to the left or to the right) in religious, political, and social arrangements, and their aspirations will therefore conflict with the established conventions of the political order.[15]

The revolution was certainly not a war of the poor against the rich, for one of its most striking features was the almost total passivity of the rural masses, the copyholders, and agricultural laborers. In contrast to the peasant uprisings during the French or Russian revolutions or in France or Russia in the seventeenth century, the rural poor in England were almost entirely passive during the 1640s and 1650s. A few enclosures were torn down in the early 1640s, the Diggers made a few pathetic and easily crushed attempts to take over the common lands here and there in the late 1640s, but that was all. The only serious interventions by the rural poor in the whole course of the revolution were the assemblies of "club-men" who gathered in several counties during the latter stages of the war.[16] These were no more than desperate attempts by the rural poor to protect their fields, crops, cattle, and women from the depredations of both armies, and themselves from the clutches of the recruiting officers on both sides.

In the towns the urban wage-earners were equally passive, even in London. Yet there can be no doubt that one stage up the social ladder, among the small freeholders and yeomen in the countryside, and among the apprentices, artisans, and small shopkeepers in the towns, there was a definite tendency to side with Parliament. But the rich merchant oligarchies in the cities either were cautiously and selfishly neutral or they sided with the King as the protector and patron of their political and eco-

---

[15] G. E. Lenski, "Status Crystallization: (A Non-Vertical Dimension of Social Status," *American Sociological Review* 19 (1954).
[16] Gardiner, *History of the Great Civil War*, 2:230–32, 277–79.

nomic privileges. The only exceptions to this rule arose when religious convictions triumphed over the calculations of interest. The bourgeoisie, therefore, was either neutral or divided. Moreover, the fissure did not run along lines of class, or employer against employee, but rather along lines of relative wealth and access to political and economic privilege. The gentry were equally neutral or divided, again with a tendency, but no more than a tendency, for the richer gentry to side with the King. Yet there were plenty of rich gentry who were active Parliamentarians, especially in the early stages, and an analysis of the political affiliations of the richer gentry M.P.s in the Long Parliament reveals an almost even split on either side.[17] Nor can the poorer parish gentry be legitimately identified with either side. With the radicalization of the parliamentary party in the middle and late 1640s under the pressure of a long-drawn and inconclusive war, a minority of lesser gentry thrust themselves to the fore, both in the local county committees and in national politics. Many, perhaps a majority, of the "Political Independents" were of lesser gentry origin. But this does not mean that the "mere gentry" can be described as parliamentarian. In the north and west these little men, these archetypal mere gentry, formed the backbone of the Royalist army and party in the 1640s, and were to be the most fanatical of Church-and-King men in the post-revolution era. Equally damaging to the simplistic and superficial hypothesis of the mere gentry as predominantly parliamentarian is the discovery that the mere gentry of Kent formed the core of the Royalist opposition as well as the core of the Parliamentary County Committee.[18] In short, the fact that many members of the radical group which seized control of the Parliamentary forces in the late 1640s were lesser gentry does not at all mean that the lesser gentry as a whole were mostly Parliamentarian. There is a logical fallacy in this chain of reasoning which is too obvious to be worth dwelling upon any further.[19]

[17] Based on a study of the biographies in M. F. Keeler, The Long Parliament, 1640–41 (Philadelphia, 1954).

[18] A. Everitt, The Community of Kent and the Great Rebellion, 1640–60 (Leicester, 1966), pp. 143, 242.

[19] For this and other objections, see C. Hill, "Recent Interpretations of the Civil War," in his Puritanism and Revolution; P. Zagorin, "The Social Interpretation of the English Revolution," Journal of Economic History 19 (1959); and Hexter, Reappraisals in History, pp. 129–31.

A more promising argument about the division of the gentry in the revolution is that the money minded, enterprising, entrepreneurial (i.e. bourgeois) gentry tended to side with Parliament, and the paternalistic, conservative, *rentier* (i.e., feudal) gentry tended to side with the King.[20] This is an attractive notion, but there is at present not a shred of evidence to support it, except the fact that the south and east were mostly in the hands of the Parliamentarians and the north and west in the hands of the Royalists. But to shift from this geographical division to the identification of individual characteristics in the two areas is to fall into the well-known ecological fallacy.[21] It is possible to think of a number of reasons—closer propinquity to London, stronger puritan leanings, greater exposure to initial seizure by Parliamentary forces from London when war began, etc.—why the geographical split should have occurred the way it did, without concluding that it necessarily represents a bourgeois-feudal dichotomy.

To sum up, the only sociological conclusions which seem plausible for the early stages of the war are that there was a clearly marked tendency for the yeomen in the countryside and middling groups in the towns and industrial areas to side with Parliament, and a much less marked tendency for the aristocracy and the merchant oligarchies to side with the King. None of the polarities of feudal-bourgeois, employer-employee, rich-poor, country gentry–parish gentry seem to have much relevance to what actually happened in the early 1640s. What we have to explain is a complex struggle of orders and status groups, largely confined to members of various elites which were fissured and fragmented by differences about constitutional arrangements, religious aspirations, and cultural patterns, by conflicts of interest and conflicts of loyalty, as well as by the unsettling effects of rapid economic development and social change. Before civil war could break out, the major institutions of the central government had to lose their credibility and to collapse. Although the crisis becomes intelligible only in the light of social and economic change, what has to be explained in the first place is not a crisis within the society but rather a

[20] Engels, *Socialism;* Tawney, "The Rise of the Gentry," pp. 183–89, 203.
[21] W. S. Robinson, "Ecological Correlations and the Behavior of Individuals," *American Sociological Review* 15 (1950).

crisis within the regime, the alienation of very large segments of the elites from the established political and religious institutions. The first stage of the crisis was a conflict between conflicting elites rather than a challenge to the existing social order. This was a political revolution with potential, but abortive, social consequences, just as the French Revolution was a political revolution with partially realized social consequences. As the Levellers bluntly put it to the House of Commons in 1647, "the grounds of the late war between the King and you was a contention whether he or you should exercise the supreme power over us."[22]

Any analysis of so complex a thing as a revolutionary challenge to an established regime, even one mounted largely from within the ruling elites, must necessarily range backward over a long period of time and be multi-causal in its approach. It must lay as much stress on constitutional defects and ideological passions as it does on social movements or economic changes, if it is to have any hope of grasping all the threads that lead to the crisis. Such an approach raises serious problems of organization, and for analytical purposes it seems best to unravel the tangled skein of the developing crisis stage by stage, examining first the long-term preconditions, next the medium-term precipitants, and lastly the short-run triggers.[23] Such an organization of the material does not imply that the seamless web of history tears neatly apart into hard and fast categories of this kind, for it clearly does nothing of the sort. All that is claimed is that this seems the most appropriate way of arranging the mass of material into an easily intelligible and logically consequential order.

The second difficulty with a multi-causal approach is how to arrange the factors in a rank order of relative importance. If no such ordering is attempted, the reader is left with an unweighted shopping list, but he must recognize that in the last resort the imposition of a rank ordering depends not on objec-

---

[22] D. M. Wolfe, *Leveller Manifestoes of the Puritan Revolution* (London, 1944), p. 237.

[23] The theoretical framework of this paper is basically that of Chalmers Johnson, *Revolution and the Social System* (Stanford, Calif., 1964), pt. 1, and *Revolutionary Change* (Boston, 1966), chaps. 4 and 5. For a critique of this and other models, see L. Stone, "Theories of Revolution," *World Politics* 18 (1966).

tive and testable criteria but on the judgment, sensibility, or bias
of the historian.

THE PRECONDITIONS, 1529–1629

The Instability of the Tudor Polity

If one looks, with all the wisdom of hindsight, at the structure
of the Tudor polity in its heyday during the first twenty-five
years of the reign of Elizabeth, that age of relative tranquillity
before the storm clouds began to gather in the late 1580s, one
can see that it was essentially unstable. This is not the place to
reopen the question of what the Early Tudors were striving to
achieve. Was it no more than an efficient bureaucracy at the
center and a political balance summed up by the concept of
sovereignty residing in a "king in Parliament"? Or was the
Spanish ambassador nearer the mark when in 1498 he reported
home that Henry VII "would like to govern England in the
French fashion, but he cannot"?[24] There are good reasons for
believing that Henry VII, and more particularly Henry VIII, cast
envious eyes across the Channel, and were only too anxious to
acquire those powers upon which were founded the strong
Renaissance monarchies of Europe. It was Henry VIII who
bluntly told the Irish, "of our absolute power we be above the
law," and Edward Lord Herbert in the seventeenth century
seems to have had a shrewder idea of the Early Tudors' real
attitude toward the law than some twentieth-century historians,
who are more easily impressed by conformity to the letter than
by allegiance to the spirit. Lord Herbert remarked of Henry VII
that "he used to take their [the common lawyers'] advice
obliquely, and no otherwise than to discover how safe his own
designs were, and so with less danger to vary from them. Which
deviations yet he would so regulate, as that his actions at home
had still, if not their ground, yet at least their pretext from the
Common Law."[25] After many years in which it has not been
respectable to use the phrase in academic circles, the concept of
"Tudor despotism," as an aspiration if not a reality, is at last

[24] Calendar of State Papers Spanish, 1:178.
[25] Edward Lord Herbert, The Life and Reign of King Henry VIII (London, 1683), p. 4.

becoming something that can be talked about again.[26] It is arguable that between 1470 and 1558, and particularly between 1529 and 1547, there was in England a desire in official quarters to acquire some of the tools for strong monarchical government; that Henry VIII was not a constitutional monarch, but a powerful autocrat working perforce through legal and constitutional channels to acquire new sources of untrammeled authority. This movement was ultimately frustrated, partly because of the survival of medieval institutions and traditions, notably in the common law and in Parliament, partly because the King did not devote himself single-mindedly to the task, and partly because of the diversion of governmental energies and the dissipation of governmental resources in a major foreign war between 1543 and 1551—a war which, even as wars go, appears exceptionally futile in its ends and exceptionally wasteful in its means.[27] After 1558 Elizabeth and her advisers abandoned all ambitions of developing a continental-style monarchy, and settled down to manage what they found at their disposal. Unfortunately for them, the system they inherited was a peculiarly brittle one.

To argue along these lines does not at all imply that any society which is not founded on a substantial degree of consensus is liable to disintegration. The structural-functionalists among sociologists and political scientists have tended to underestimate both the degree of conflict and tension and the number of largely obsolete or dysfunctional institutions which exist in any society, and which can be tolerated and absorbed without too much discomfort. On the other hand, the Tudor state lacked the brute force to beat down opposition, and only temporarily enjoyed the united support that would make such force unnecessary. When the elites began to quarrel, either the structure would have to change or the whole edifice would begin to totter and shudder under the strain.

[26] The liberal-constitutional view of Henry VIII and Cromwell was established in the early 1950s by Professor G. R. Elton and became the standard interpretation with the publication of his *England under the Tudors* (London, 1955). The first major attack on it came with J. H. Hurstfield, "Was There a Tudor Despotism After All?" *Transactions of the Royal Historical Society*, 5th ser., vol. 17 (1967), and has been followed up by J. J. Scarisbrick, *Henry VIII* (London, 1968).

[27] A. F. Pollard, *Henry VIII* (London, 1905), pp. 397–415, and R. B. Wernham, *Before the Armada: The Growth of English Foreign Policy* (London, 1966), chaps. 12, 13, and 14, have tried to fit the war into a grand strategy. The fallacies of their arguments have been pointed out by Scarisbrick, *Henry VIII*, p. 424.

The Elizabethan state was remarkably deficient in some of the essential components of power. Let us begin with money, the sinews of all government. This was a problem which the Early Tudors seemed to be on the verge of solving. In 1522, for the first time in nearly one hundred years, and the last time for more than one hundred years, a new and relatively honest assessment was carried out to form the basis for a parliamentary tax on property.[28] Moreover, the customs revenue soared as trade increased, and a revived fiscal feudalism squeezed wealth out of the landed classes.[29] Most important of all, however, was the fact that between 1536 and 1552 the crown laid hands on the vast property of monasteries and chantries, usually reckoned (without much hard statistical evidence) to amount to at least a quarter of the country. Had this property been retained and exploited, both for the wealth it could produce and for the political and religious patronage it carried with it, it could have provided the state with overwhelming resources, which would have made it virtually independent of parliamentary taxation. But before it had even been assimilated and absorbed, the bulk of the property was sold off to pay for war, so that by 1562 the crown was left with an independent income which, with a tight rein on expenditure, was sufficient, but no more than sufficient, for peacetime purposes.[30]

Having deprived itself of the financial and political benefits of confiscated Church property, the crown failed to develop those alternative sources of revenue which were so important to other European powers. Monopoly of an essential mineral was one. Alum was the prime support of the papacy, gold and silver of Spain, salt of France, and copper of Sweden. The adverse decision by the common-law judges in the case of the earl of Northumberland in 1568 deprived the English crown of its chance to make a profit from the almost limitless reserves of England's coal and non-precious metals. It tried to exploit first

---

[28] H. Miller, "Subsidy Assessments of the Peerage in the Sixteenth Century," *Bulletin of the Institute of Historical Research* 28 (1955); F. C. Dietz, *English Government Finance, 1485–1558*, University of Illinois Studies in the Social Sciences, no. 9 (Urbana, 1920), p. 94.

[29] J. Hurstfield, "The Profits of Fiscal Feudalism, 1541–1602," *Economic History Review*, 2d ser., vol. 8 (1955).

[30] Dietz, *English Government Finance*, chaps. 10, 11, 12, and 14.

copper and then salt and alum, but failed to make a profit from any of them. [31]

The second great resource of continental states was the sale of offices in administration and the law. But the English bureaucracy remained pitifully small, Elizabeth's efforts to increase the number of legal offices were defeated by the judges in the *Cavendish* case in 1587, and such offices as existed were bought and sold by the officials and courtiers themselves with no benefit accruing to the crown.[32] James I entered the field late, in 1616, but the profits he reaped failed to compensate for the unpopularity he earned. Equally serious was the fact that the administrative weakness of the monarchy, and its reliance on the gentry and the merchants for support, rendered it unable—or unwilling—to adjust old taxes to new conditions. The Elizabethan government put political good will before fiscal efficiency, and as a result the Book of Rates, which declared the value of goods for customs, was altered only once in eighty years, despite the steady rise in prices, receipts from wardship fell, and assessments for parliamentary subsidies were left unchanged, unable either to cope with inflation or to incorporate new wealth. By 1603 the propertied classes had become accustomed to avoiding taxation, and efforts by the Stuarts to tighten things up by means of impositions, fines for wardship, forced loans, or ship money inevitably ran into serious legal and political obstacles.[33] The English crown was financially boxed in at all points.

If it lacked money, the English monarchy also lacked troops. In the 1530s some elements in government had toyed with the idea of a large standing army financed by Church wealth, and in the 1540s a considerable army of Italian and German mercenaries had been stationed on English soil.[34] But they were paid

[31] M. B. Donald, *Elizabethan Copper* (London, 1955), chaps. 6 and 11; E. Hughes, "The English Monopoly of Salt in the Years 1563–71," *English Historical Review* 40 (1925); R. B. Turton, *The Alum Farm* (Whitby, England, 1938).

[32] G. Aylmer, *The King's Servants* (London, 1961), chaps. 3 and 4; K. W. Swart, *Sale of Offices in the Seventeenth Century* (The Hague, 1949), chap. 3.

[33] F. C. Dietz, *English Public Finance, 1558–1641* (New York, 1932), pp. 235, 265–66, 303–4, 362–79, 391; L. Stone, *The Crisis of the Aristocracy, 1558–1641* (Oxford, 1965), pp. 496–98.

[34] L. Stone, "The Political Programme of Thomas Cromwell," *Bulletin of the Institute for Historical Research* 24 (1951):4–18; W. K. Jordan, *Edward VI: The Young King* (London, 1968), p. 466, n. 2.

off in 1551 as an economy measure, and thereafter the crown had to rely on a poorly armed and poorly trained militia, on a tiny personal bodyguard, and, in emergencies, on a rallying of the traditional forces of the magnates and their retainers, tenants, and servants.[35] The Tudor and Stuart kings were in no position to mount a large-scale offensive against their own subjects without powerful voluntary support from a considerable number of those subjects.

To strengthen its judicial authority, the crown set up a series of new courts to exercise powers of justice and administration over certain geographical areas (the north, the west, Wales), certain categories of people (Wards, Exchequer), and certain categories of offenses (Star Chamber, Requests, Admiralty). These courts were more subjected to royal controls than the common-law courts, their procedures were swifter and cheaper, and their officials were more concerned with the firm administration of justice than with the preservation of obsolete legal archaisms. But the common law's powers survived, ready for use in the coming political struggles.[36]

In the first half of the sixteenth century the government succeeded in creating a unified central administration with the Lord Treasurer at its head, and the Privy Council as the main executive body. But even here anomalies persisted (e.g., the Court of Wards), and old-fashioned officials fought long-drawn-out and often successful interdepartmental battles to the detriment of efficiency.[37] Far more serious, however, was the failure of the government even to attempt to establish more than a skeleton bureaucracy of its own in the towns and the countryside. The reason for this failure is obscure, largely because historians have not asked themselves why it was that the so-called administrative revolution of the early sixteenth century was confined to Westminster. What seems to have happened is that the early

---

[35] Stone, *Crisis of the Aristocracy*, pp. 201–17; C. G. Cruikshank, *Elizabeth's Army* (Oxford, 1966), chaps. 1 and 2; L. Boynton, *The Elizabethan Militia, 1558–1638* (London, 1967), chaps. 1–4.

[36] The most recent and balanced survey of this problem is E. W. Ives, "The Common Lawyers in Pre-Reformation England," *Transactions of the Royal Historical Society*, 5th ser., vol. 18 (1968), pp. 162–73.

[37] W. C. Richardson, *Tudor Chamber Administration, 1485–1547* (Baton Rouge, 1952), pp. 433–42; G. R. Elton, *The Tudor Revolution in Government* (Cambridge, 1953), pp. 223–24; *idem*, "The Elizabethan Exchequer: War in the Receipt," in *Elizabethan Government and Society*, ed. S. T. Bindoff, J. Hurstfield, and C. H. Williams (London, 1961).

Tudors deliberately built up the authority of the gentry as a means of destroying the local power bases of their over-mighty subjects, the great territorial magnates of the late Middle Ages. No sooner had the old nobility been brought to heel, however, than the crown was overwhelmed by the crisis of the Reformation, for which it desperately needed parliamentary support, while its finances were rapidly undermined by foreign war and inflation. The classes represented in the House of Commons were willing enough to give the King their support in his religious and political policies, but only so long as they were left to rule the countryside and the towns. The crown was thus in no position to proceed to the next stage in the creation of a strong monarchy, the replacement of the local gentry by paid officials of its own. As a result there was a tacit agreement to divide responsibility, and the main burden of local administration was perforce left in the hands of unpaid gentry and urban worthies, whose loyalty and efficiency was dependent upon a careful regard being had for their interests, privileges, and prejudices.[38] So far from being progressively weakened, local county particularism grew step by step with the growth of the central government. A national power base at Westminster and a series of local power bases in the countryside, developed in parallel as the legislative activities of the former thrust an increasingly heavy burden of social and economic administration on the latter. In the sixteenth and early seventeenth centuries the phrase "my country" meant "my county," and rising sentiment for national unification around "the King in Parliament" was paralleled and offset by rising local loyalty to the quarter sessions meeting in county towns.[39]

To counteract these centrifugal tendencies, Henry VIII, after he had broken with Rome for reasons of dynastic security, did his utmost to create a self-consciously national church which would unify the country around the King. Despite ferocious treason and heresy laws, he failed in the attempt, largely because he lacked the troops and the administrators to enforce his will. Once he had started on the Reformation, Henry found himself riding the back of a tiger: he could neither control its move-

---

[38] For two good local studies, see W. B. Willcox, *Gloucestershire: A Study in Local Government, 1590–1640* (New Haven, 1940); T. G. Barnes, *Somerset, 1625–40* (London, 1961).

[39] P. Zagorin, *The Court and the Country* (London, 1969), pp. 33–34.

ments nor jump off as it plunged ahead. The subsequent extreme religious oscillations of the reigns of Edward VI and Mary, each imposed on a reluctant and bewildered population by a tiny minority of zealots, only deepened the confusion and threatened religious anarchy. The official Elizabethan policy was to bolster up the unconvincing political compromise of the Anglican church with a lukewarm and a cynical Erastianism. It was a brilliant success in cooling religious passions and avoiding an outbreak of doctrinal warfare linked to rival aristocratic factions. But it was not designed—indeed, by its very nature it could not be made—to satisfy the needs of a population that was starved of spiritual nourishment. The hungry flock was obliged to look elsewhere. The lack of assertive self-confidence of the Established Church, coupled with the half-heartedness of its persecution of dissidents, permitted the development of substantial and influential groups of enthusiastic nonconformists to the left and to the right, Puritans and Catholics. Moreover, because the crown had given away to the laity the patronage of many livings along with the estates of the monasteries, it could not even be sure of controlling its own clergy.

This weakness on the religious front was compounded by equally serious weaknesses in social structure. The over-mighty subjects of the late Middle Ages had been largely, if not entirely, eliminated by 1540, thanks to a royal policy of attainders and confiscations which was powerfully assisted by natural demographic attrition. But in order to secure local and national support for the Reformation settlement and the dynastic succession, Henry felt obliged to replace these magnates with a new official and military aristocracy established as great territorial landlords on the ruins of the monasteries and the old nobility. No sooner had this been done than the financial pressures generated by the wars of the 1540s forced the crown to sell large parts of the newly acquired Church property to a greedy class of gentry, a gentry whose aspirations and interests would eventually have to be accommodated somehow or other within the political system.[40]

To conclude this catalog of weaknesses, potential or actual,

[40] W. T. McCaffrey, "England: The Crown and the New Aristocracy, 1540–1600," *Past and Present* 30 (1965); Stone, *Crisis of the Aristocracy*, p. 97; S. B. Liljegren, *The Fall of the Monasteries and the Social Changes in England Leading up to the Great Revolution* (Lund, 1924).

the government had inadequate control over the written and spoken word. Censorship of the press was firmly established by law, but its effectiveness was weakened by aristocratic protection of Puritan pamphleteers, the smuggling of books from abroad, and the operation of clandestine printing presses in England.[41] The most important propaganda instrument of the day was the pulpit, but loss of the patronage of many livings to the laity, which was itself divided, meant that there was never a time when some preachers were not urging upon their congregations ideas that were displeasing and even dangerous to the government. Moreover, the grammar schools and universities could be filled with teachers whose sympathies with the Established Church might be less than absolute.[42] In an age of ideological conflict this lack of firm control of the communication media was a very serious handicap to a government.

All these weaknesses might not have mattered so much, had there not survived from the medieval past a powerful national representative body, which after a bitter struggle in the early sixteenth century (the full story of which has not yet been told) had succeeded in preserving for itself the powers to consent to taxation and to vote on legislation. Over against this was set the ill-defined powers of the so-called prerogative, and the increasingly charismatic nature of Renaissance kingship. The Holbein portrait of Henry VIII, arms akimbo and legs astride like a colossus, expresses perfectly the image of the new monarchy.[43] Elizabeth inherited something of her father's irritable and authoritarian temperament, as well as his capacity for charm when he cared to exercise it, so it is hardly surprising first that she had serious trouble with her parliaments from the moment she ascended the throne, and second that she usually managed to get her own way.[44]

[41] F. S. Siebert, *Freedom of the Press in England, 1476–1776* (Urbana, 1965), pts. 1 and 2; A. G. Dickens, *The English Reformation* (London, 1964), pp. 26–37, 68–82, 190–92, 264–79; P. Collinson, *The Elizabethan Puritan Movement* (London, 1967), pp. 48–55, 141–47, 432–47; idem, "John Field and Elizabethan Separatism," in *English Government and Society*, ed. Bindoff, Hurstfield, and Williams.

[42] C. Hill, *The Economic Problems of the Church* (Oxford, 1956), chap. 4; E. Rosenberg, *Leicester: Patron of Letters* (New York, 1955), chap. 4.

[43] Scarisbrick, *Henry VIII*, pl. 3.

[44] J. E. Neale, *Elizabeth I and Her Parliaments, 1559–81* (London, 1953). For an international comparison, see J. P. Cooper, "Differences between English and Continental Governments in the 17th Century," in *Britain and the Netherlands*, vol. 1, ed. J. S. Bromley and E. H. Kossman (London, 1960).

In short, whether one looks at its political support, financial resources, military and administrative power, social cohesion, legal subordination, religious unity, or control of propaganda, the Elizabethan polity appears to have been shot through with contradictions and weaknesses. It is to the development of those contradictions and weaknesses over the seventy years from 1559 to 1629 that attention now must be directed.

The Development of Dysfunctions

Because one of the most important political developments was the growing inability of the state to adjust to new social forces, it seems logical to begin with the economic changes which generated those forces. In the first place there was a significant increase both in population and in total economic resources. Agricultural output increased at a rate sufficient to feed a population that by 1620 was nearly double what it had been in 1500.[45] Overseas trade did not expand very much between 1551 and 1604, but it grew fairly rapidly thereafter, and it diversified its markets and its sources of imports in preparation for the more startling growth of the late seventeenth century.[46] Internal trade undoubtedly increased greatly, assisted by the organization of regular carriers on the main roads, the growth of specialized markets, and a proliferation of peddlers and hucksters operating out of inns.[47] The main industrial activity of England remained the manufacture and processing of cloth, catering for large domestic and export markets, but there were also some significant new developments in the century after 1540. Coal-mining in the Newcastle area became the first really large-scale bulk-producing industry in the western world, while in a host of other industries, from wire-making to soap-boiling, England took the technological lead from Germany. The result of this new industrial activity in terms of capital invested, the value of goods

[45] Victoria County History, Leicestershire (London, 19?) 3:137–42; J. Thirsk, The Agrarian History of England and Wales, vol. 4 (Cambridge, 1967), pp. 593–609.

[46] F. J. Fisher, "Commercial Trends and Policy in Sixteenth-Century England," in Essays in Economic History, ed. E. M. Carus-Wilson, vol. 1 (London, 1954); idem, "London's Export Trade in the Early Seventeenth Century," Economic History Review, 2d ser., vol. 3 (1950); R. Davis, "English Foreign Trade, 1660–1700," in Essays in Economic History, ed. Carus-Wilson, vol. 2.

[47] Thirsk, Agrarian History, 4:466–592; J. Crofts, Pack-Horse, Waggon, and Post (London, 1967).

produced, and labor employed was small in relation to the economy as a whole, and theories of a "first industrial revolution" can therefore hardly be taken seriously.[48] England in the seventeenth century remained what it and the rest of Europe had always been, an underdeveloped society, but there can be no doubt that it was much more market oriented and much richer than it had ever been before, more so than any other contemporary society, with the probable exception of the United Provinces.

Just as important as this absolute increase in wealth, and the changes in the way it was earned, were the changes in the distribution of the national income between the various orders of society.[49] Landed property passed from the Church to the laity (via the crown) and from the crown to the laity, mostly gentry, in a series of massive sales to pay for unprofitable wars. In the late sixteenth century it passed from the greater aristocracy to the gentry, and from many copyholders and all laborers, squeezed between inflated prices and rents and stagnant wages, to the freeholders and landlords. It flowed to merchants and particularly to tradesmen because of widening profit margins under inflation, and to the richer merchants through their hold on lucrative monopolies of trade. There was also a striking growth in the numbers and wealth of the more successful practitioners of law. In short, what occurred was a massive shift of relative wealth away from Church and crown, and away from both the very rich and the very poor toward the upper middle and middle classes. The shift was caused primarily by political acts of a government hard pressed to pay for war, by the inflation of prices, by improvident expenditure patterns maintained by the old rich, and by the entrepreneurial activities of the new rich. Given this changing socioeconomic situation, there was bound to be friction between the traditional wielders of power—the crown, courtiers, higher clergy, and aristocracy—and the growing but far from homogeneous forces of gentry, lawyers, merchants, yeomen, and small tradesmen. The problem that faced

[48] J. U. Nef, "The Progress of Technology and the Growth of Large-Scale Industry in Great Britain, 1540–1640," in Essays in Economic History, ed. Carus-Wilson, vol. 1; D. C. Coleman, "Industrial Growth and Industrial Revolutions," ibid., vol. 3.

[49] L. Stone, "Social Mobility in England, 1500–1700," Past and Present 33 (1966):23–29. For the debate over the gentry, see the extracts and bibliography in L. Stone, Social Change and Revolution in England, 1540–1640 (London, 1965), pp. xi–xxvi, 1–80, 179–83.

the state was how to bring the latter into fruitful and coopera-
tive participation in the political process.

Men of wealth and property allowed this friction to reach the
stage of open conflict between Parliament and the King in the
early years of the seventeenth century primarily because they
were no longer afraid, or rather were no longer as afraid as
they had been. During the last half of the sixteenth century the
ruling elites had been held together by the triple fear of a
jacquerie of the poor, a civil war over a disputed succession
linked to religious divisions, and invasion by foreign enemies.
By the early seventeenth century, however, these fears had subsided considerably. The last peasant revolt serious enough to
send the gentry fleeing from their homes in terror had been in
1549, when risings had taken place all over southern England.[50]
Brutal repression had quickly snuffed out these fires of rebellion in all areas except the County of Norfolk, but memories of
this alarming experience died hard and were almost certainly
a stimulus to the enforcement, such as it was, of anti-enclosure
legislation.

By 1640 two generations had passed since the great fear, and
memories had grown dim. Moreover, the threat of a renewed
outbreak, although certainly possible, now seemed fairly remote.
Population growth had eased off, real wages had stabilized or
even risen a little, the burden of taxation was very light or
nonexistent, labor-saving enclosure for pasture had been replaced by labor-intensive enclosure for arable, and a national
poor-relief system was in operation, along with massive private
charity, to take care of the old, the sick, and the growing numbers of unemployed. Minor risings had taken place recently in
old forest areas like Wiltshire, but they were severely localized.[51]
In 1642, men of property talked of the threat of popular uprising in order to discourage each other from taking up arms,
but they did not take it sufficiently seriously to deter them.[52]
This stands in contrast to the situation in 1688, when mob vio-

[50] Jordan, *Edward VI*, chap. 15.
[51] C. S. L. Davies, "Les Revoltes Populaires en Angleterre (1500–1700),"
Annales 1 (1969); D. C. Allen, "The Rising in the West, 1628–31," *Economic History Review*, 2d ser., vol. 5 (1952); E. Kerridge, "The Revolts
in Wiltshire against Charles I," *Wiltshire Archaeological Magazine* 57
(1958–59).
[52] Salisbury MSS, 131 f. 182 (Northumberland to Salisbury), Hatfield
House, Hertfordshire, England.

lence was quite widespread, and was clearly influential in persuading the men of property to close ranks and to unite rapidly behind William III.[53]

The second fear which persisted throughout the reign of Elizabeth was that her death would unleash a civil war over a disputed succession complicated by religious rivalries. This fear was a very real one, and it haunted politicians and Members of Parliament for forty-five years. It receded a little after Mary Queen of Scots had been executed, but it lay just beneath the surface of the Cecil-Essex feud in the 1590s, and was still thought to be a serious danger when Elizabeth lay dying in 1603. Londoners frantically bought weapons and hoarded food, while one enterprising scholar prepared himself to be the historian of a civil war which never happened.[54] The peaceful accession of James I finally put these anxieties to rest, but it should be remembered that his son Charles I was the first monarch since Henry VIII to ascend to the throne with a fully undisputed title.

Elizabeth's policy of masterly inactivity and politic temporizing was a brilliant success insofar as it staved off the civil wars which were tearing apart large areas of contemporary Europe, most notably England's nearest neighbors, France and the Low Countries. But none of the problems facing English society were resolved. They were merely postponed, to come to a head in a more dangerous form later, while Elizabeth's success had the paradoxical result of making civil war more rather than less likely in the future. The successful avoidance of an explosion for more than a century lulled the English elites into a false sense of security, and they were therefore willing to risk armed confrontation in 1642.

The third fear was that of invasion from abroad, but by the early seventeenth century this too had greatly diminished, and indeed had all but vanished. With the peace of 1604 the danger of invasion from Spain, which had been so real under Elizabeth, finally disappeared. The possibility that Ireland could be used as a staging point for invasion by Spanish forces seemed to have

[53] W. L. Sachse, "The Mob and the Revolution of 1688," *Journal of British Studies* 4, no. 1 (1964).

[54] J. Clapham, *Elizabeth of England*, ed. E. P. and C. Read (Philadelphia, 1951), pp. 27–28; G. Goodman, *The Court of King James I* (London, 1839), 2:57.

been eliminated by the planned genocide of the Irish population by starvation in 1600–1601 [55] and by the subsequent plantation of English settlers and economic recovery. Scotland was eliminated as a staging point for invasion by French forces, once the Scottish nobility had been converted to Protestantism and the two crowns had been united under James I in 1603. France had been so weakened by the Wars of Religion that it no longer appeared as the menace it once had been under Francis I, and would be again under Louis XIV. Men undoubtedly worried about the progress of the Catholic forces in the Thirty Years' War, but the victories of Gustavus Adolphus made a stalemate seem to be the most likely outcome, and few thought that England was directly threatened after the 1620s. By the 1630s, therefore, the three great pressures which might hold a congeries of ruling elites together and deter them from fighting among themselves were much less severe than they had been for more than a century, or were to be again for a long time indeed.

The most important cause, and symptom, of the decay of any establishment is the loss of prestige and respect among the public at large, and the loss of self-confidence among the leaders in their right and capacity to rule. A slow but inexorable erosion of this sense of trust may be observed in every sector of English governmental institutions in the late sixteenth and early seventeenth centuries. The credibility gap, as it is called today, manifested itself earliest in the Church, where the laity, from Queen Elizabeth downward, conspired to treat the clergy, and especially the bishops, with a contempt unparalleled before or since. There is no subsequent historical parallel to the simoniacal bargains with the crown and the courtiers by which Elizabethan bishops were obliged to alienate the hereditary property of their sees in return for their appointments. There is no previous or subsequent parallel to the Act of 1558, which gave the crown the power to seize valuable episcopal property in exchange for largely worthless bits and pieces of crown lands. There is certainly no parallel to the carefully baited sexual trap set by an eminently respectable Yorkshire gentleman, Sir Robert Staple-

<hr />

[55] C. Falls, *Elizabeth's Irish Wars* (London, 1950), pp. 255, 258, 264, 277, 284, 324, 326, 329, 335, 341; Edmund Spenser, "A View of the State of Ireland," in *Ireland under Elizabeth and James I,* ed. H. Morley (London, 1890), pp. 143–44.

ton, to catch the venerable Archbishop Sandys of York, any more than there is a parallel to the savagery of the Marprelate Tracts in the 1580s or to the scatological and scurrilous anti-episcopal pamphleteering of the 1630s.[56]

So affected was the clergy by this climate of opinion that many of the early Elizabethan bishops were willing, even anxious, to surrender their powers and their titles to become mere superintendents of a church administered in cooperation with well-to-do and zealous laymen. But Elizabeth, convinced of James's later aphorism, "no bishop, no king," would have none of these reformist suggestions, and so the bishops survived, their powers nominally unimpaired, but their wealth reduced and their prestige in decline. In 1573 Archbishop Sandys wrote despairingly that "our estimation is little, our authority is less, so that we are become contemptible in the eyes of the basest sort."

Nor were matters improved by the fact that in the late sixteenth and early seventeenth centuries the bishops were mostly men of lower-middle-class origin and of restricted outlook and experience. Before the Reformation many had been bright young men who had traveled Europe as ambassadors and had served in high positions at court, or were sons or relatives of squires and noblemen. But now, commented John Selden acidly, "they are of a low condition, their education nothing of that way."[57] They could no longer rely on the respect of the influential laity, which once had been inspired by the dignity of their office, by their political and administrative experience, or by their breeding.

Equally damaging to the prospects of the Anglican church in its early years was the legacy from its pre-Reformation past of a parish clergy which was incapable of meeting the changing needs of the laity. Moreover, the sharp decline in numbers entering the ministry during the disturbed period from 1540 to 1560 meant that in the first twenty years of its existence the

---

[56] Stone, *Crisis of the Aristocracy*, pp. 405–11; F. D. Price, "The Abuses of Excommunication and the Decline of Ecclesiastical Discipline under Queen Elizabeth," *English Historical Review* 57 (1942).

[57] P. Collinson, "Episcopacy and Reform in England in the Later 16th Century," *Studies in Church History* 3 (1966); J. Selden, *Table Talk*, ed. F. Pollock (London, 1917), p. 17; J. Hurstfield, "Church and State, 1588–1612: The Task of the Cecils," *Studies in Church History* 2 (1965); P. Collinson, *A Mirror of Elizabethan Puritanism* (London, 1964), p. 20.

Anglican church suffered from an acute shortage of manpower of any sort, much less of men of high caliber. As emphasis on ritual in the church service declined, the laity increasingly came to expect the parish clergy to be resident, well-educated, respectable preachers who were morally above reproach. These were standards which the sixteenth-century clergy were ill-equipped to meet. It was not until late in the century that numbers became adequate, educational levels improved enormously, and the clergy began by and large to fulfill most of the new requirements. But this improvement came too late to prevent the formation of powerful dissenting elements, particularly since many of the most energetic among the new clergy harbored strong reformist sentiments.[58] This change for the better, coupled with the construction by Hooker and others of the intellectual underpinnings that the Church hitherto had lacked, was sufficient to secure the ultimate triumph of Anglicanism at the time of the Restoration, but neither did anything to solve the serious economic problems of the Church; indeed, they may even have encouraged the further fragmentation of religious loyalties by splitting the ranks of Protestant enthusiasts into Puritans and Anglicans.

The failure of so many of the Anglican bishops and clergy to match up to the expectations of the laity in the early Elizabethan period led to a search by many conscientious men and women for a more inspiring and convincing religious experience and a more responsive religious organization. A vacuum of religious zeal was created by the non-preaching, non-proselytizing, absentee clergy of the Church established by Elizabeth, and it was filled by two groups of dedicated and determined men who differed utterly in their religious loyalties and beliefs but were very similar in the intensity of their faith and missionary enthusiasm. The first group was the seminary priests, who flooded back into England and built up a wholly new, firmly entrenched, Catholic minority of influential noblemen and gentlemen, to-

---

[58] F. W. Brooks, "The Social Position of the Parson in the Sixteenth Century," *Journal of the British Archaeological Association*, 3d ser., vol. 10 (1945–47); W. G. Hoskins, "The Leicestershire Country Parson in the Sixteenth Century," in his *Essays in Leicestershire History* (Liverpool, 1950); Hill, *Economic Problems of the Church*, chap. 9; P. Tyler, "The Status of the Elizabethan Parochial Clergy," *Studies in Church History* 4 (1967).

gether with their servants and tenants.[59] This new Catholic community was constructed on the ashes of the old pre-Reformation Church, but it owed far less to a continuity of faith and loyalty than to the absence of a respect-worthy alternative in the Anglican church and to the powerful moral force of the missionary priests.

On the other flank arose a group of dedicated Puritan ministers and preachers, many of them Marian exiles. They enjoyed the support of a significant number of influential peers, courtiers, and gentry who were pressing for purification of the Anglican church from within, and who used their patronage of church livings to protect the ministers from official persecution. Elizabeth's obdurate refusal to compromise with this moderately reformist group was the greatest blunder of her career, and one that was to have momentous consequences for English history. Not only did it exacerbate relations with her parliaments for many years, but it also drove many moderate Puritan reformers to formulate demands for radical changes in church organization. Although she successfully stamped out the Presbyterian movement in her time, Puritanism as a dissident force survived unimpaired and burst forth again in 1603 with the Millenial Petition. Compromise was once more rejected, mainly by the bishops, and the stage was set for a still more violent confrontation after the death of the easy-going James and the retirement of the sympathetic Archbishop Abbott.[60]

The chance of rallying opinion around a unified national church admittedly was not very great in 1558, but, such as it was, it had probably disappeared altogether by 1610. As a result, the Established Church did not even enjoy the loyalty of all its ministers at a time when it was trying to fight a war on two fronts—with Catholics on the right and Sectaries on the left. Many contemporaries doubted whether a state could survive if the religious loyalties of its subjects were divided, and the historical record tends to support them. Until ideological passions

[59] J. Bossy, "The Character of Elizabethan Catholicism," *Past and Present* 21 (1962).
[60] Collinson, "Episcopacy and Reform in England"; *idem, The Elizabethan Puritan Movement*, pp. 191–207, 243–48, 432–67; I. Morgan, *The Godly Preachers of Elizabethan England* (London, 1965); P. Seaver, *The Puritan Lectureships* (Stanford, Calif., 1970); Rosenberg, *Leicester*, chap. 6; M. H. Curtis, "The Hampton Court Conference and Its Aftermath," *History* 46 (1961).

subsided in the late seventeenth century, a population which was deeply split on religious issues tended to be extremely difficult to keep at peace.

If the prestige of the Anglican episcopacy and clergy was in decline, so also, though at a slower pace and at a later stage, was that of the titular aristocracy.[61] Their military power was the first to go. The gigantic estates of the old medieval magnates were broken up, and with them went control of large numbers of potential soldiers. At the same time, loyalties began to shift, the influence of nobles over client gentry and tenantry being weakened by increasing landlord absenteeism and by the trend toward economic rents, which severely reduced the service element in landlord-tenant relations. The noblemen were losing the military capacity either to fight against their sovereign or to serve him as military leaders in time of war. Devoted to court life, administration, or rural pursuits, they failed to acquire the technical competence and experience needed for military command in a Renaissance war. They were also losing their self-confidence as they became increasingly tied to the royal chariot by chains of hope, fear, and duty.

The aristocracy suffered a severe loss of their landed capital in the late Elizabethan period, primarily because of improvident sales made in order to keep up the life style they considered necessary for the maintenance of status. When they abandoned the sale of land and took to rigorous economic exploitation of what was left in order to maximize profits, they certainly improved their financial position, but at the expense of much of the loyalty and affection of the tenants. They salvaged their finances at the cost of their influence and prestige. This was particularly unfortunate because other factors were combining to reduce that influence and prestige. The most important of these was the granting of titles of honor for cash, not merit, in too great numbers, and to unworthy persons, which both lowered respect for the hierarchy of ranks and infuriated those who lost out in the scramble. As Tocqueville pointed out with reference to the causes of the French Revolution, the injustice of such a system of upward mobility generates even greater resent-

---

[61] Subsequent paragraphs about the aristocracy are a bald summary of the arguments presented in Stone, *Crisis of the Aristocracy*, chaps. 1, 3, 4, 10, and 14.

ment and hatred of the elite than a blocking of mobility channels altogether.

Other causes of the decline in respect for the aristocracy were the undermining of their electoral influence because of the rise of deeply felt political and religious issues; their increasing preference for extravagant living in the city instead of hospitable living in the countryside; and growing doubts about their attitudes, real or supposed, toward constitutional theory, the methods and scale of taxation, forms of worship, aesthetic tastes, financial probity, and sexual morality.

The third keystone of the establishment arch, along with the Church and the aristocracy, was the court, that ever-shifting group (some of them bishops or aristocrats) of advisers, servants, officials, and hangers-on who gathered in ever-increasing numbers about the Renaissance princes of Europe.[62] As local patronage became more and more concentrated in the hands of the crown, as tax revenues of the state increased, as the bureaucracy expanded, so the court became not only the monopolistic center of political power but also a market place for the disposal of an ever-increasing volume of cash, pensions, jobs, monopolies, and favors of all kinds. The successful operation of the court system depended on the maintenance of a delicate and extremely complicated political balance, by which no one faction was allowed to establish a grip on either the policy-making or the patronage-dispensing mechanism, and in which the favors distributed were sufficiently widespread to satisfy a majority of the influential supplicants, but not so inordinately lavish as to arouse the indignation of the taxpayers. The Early Stuarts failed on both counts. For eleven years they allowed policy and patronage to be placed at the disposal of a single favorite, George Villiers, duke of Buckingham; for three decades they dissipated royal resources in extravagant gifts and absurdly opulent court festivities; and they channeled the bulk of their

[62] For the role of the European court system, see H. R. Trevor-Roper, "The General Crisis of the 17th Century," in *Crisis in Europe, 1560–1660*, ed. T. H. Aston (London, 1965). For the English court, see Stone, *Crisis of the Aristocracy*, chap. 8; W. T. McCaffrey, "Place and Patronage in Elizabethan Politics," in *Elizabethan Government and Society*, ed. Bindoff, Hurstfield, and Williams; G. V. P. Akrigg *Jacobean Pageant* (Cambridge, Mass., 1962); J. H. Hexter, "The English Aristocracy, Its Crises, and the English Revolution, 1558–1660," *Journal of British Studies* 8 (1968): 57–69.

generosity into the hands of a favored few. This irritated many powerful nobles and courtiers who were left out in the cold, and it enraged the gentry in the House of Commons, providing them with legitimate grounds for the refusal of any more parliamentary grants of taxation. This refusal in turn obliged the King to auction off his powers for economic regulation, appointment to office, and the creation of new honors, actions which further heightened political tensions.

In the early and middle years of the reign of Elizabeth, the court successfully contained within a single political system of multiple checks and balances the representatives of a series of conflicting ideas and interest: Anglicans and Puritans, magnates and squires, gentlemen and merchants, court and country, hawks and doves in foreign and military policy, supporters of the prerogative and supporters of Parliament and the common law, and allies and clients of the Dudleys and the Cecils, the Devereux and the Cecils. What happened after 1600 was that this central political switchboard broke down, and many of these diverse and increasingly hostile groups began to organize locally and to band together, independently of the national political process at court and even in open hostility to it.

The growing political alienation of "court" from "country" was heightened by a parallel cultural and moral alienation, an ideological development which will be discussed later on. The composite result was a divorce of sensibility as well as a clash over policy. By the reign of Charles I, the concept of harmony and cooperation within the Commonwealth had almost completely broken down, the two words "court" and "country" having come to mean political, psychological, and moral opposites.

The English court contrived to arouse the same resentments that were felt on the Continent, but it failed to create a vested interest large enough to protect it against the legion of its enemies. It attracted all the odium of the vast tentacular institutions of France and Spain, without the compensating advantages of size and strength. When the crisis arrived, those on the inside were not sufficiently powerful or sufficiently conscious of their personal stake to resist the assaults from without.

Confidence in and respect for the bureaucracy were declining as fast as they were for the court and the courtiers. In the first place, corruption was growing rapidly at all levels of government, especially at the highest.[63] Inevitably there had been a great deal of corruption during the hectic years of seizure of church property and its disposal on the market between 1536 and 1551, but the more responsible administrators, such as William Cecil, had slowly reimposed some sense of order and responsibility.[64] The levels both of corruption itself and of protest against it seem to have subsided between about 1552 and 1588. But in the 1590s the crown found itself desperately short of money to finance the Anglo-Spanish War, and at the same time advancing age accentuated Elizabeth's temperamental instinct for avarice and meanness. As a result, the flow of favors, by which the greater officers of state normally were rewarded, was sharply curtailed at a time when inflation was reducing the fixed fees and salaries of all officials, greater and lesser, to derisory proportions in real terms. The officials were consequently forced into corruption, whether they liked it or not, with the inevitable result of deteriorating public services—the state of the navy in the reign of James is a classic case—and rising public indignation. The last twist to this screw was given by the duke of Buckingham in the 1620s as he frankly and cheerfully put everything up for auction, from a bishopric to a judgeship to a title of nobility.

The second development which undermined public confidence in the administration was the use made first by Elizabeth and then by the Early Stuarts of their powers for economic regulation, which had been pressed upon the government by an eager Parliament in the first half of the sixteenth century.[65] Designed to regulate trade and industry in the interests of national self-defense, the protection of the consumer, and other desirable social ends, these powers were now diverted into rackets oper-

[63] J. E. Neale, "The Elizabethan Political Scene," in his *Essays in Elizabethan History* (London, 1958); L. Stone, "The Fruits of Office: The Case of Robert Cecil, 1st Earl of Salisbury, 1596–1612," in *Essays in the Economic and Social History of Tudor and Stuart England*, ed. F. J. Fisher (London, 1961); J. P. Cooper, "The Fortune of Thomas Wentworth, Earl of Strafford," *Economic History Review*, 2d ser., vol. 11 (1958); Stone, *Crisis of the Aristocracy*, pp. 100–106, 489–95; M. Prestwich, *Cranfield: Politics and Profits under the Early Stuarts* (Oxford, 1966), chap. 9; A. J. Loomie, "Sir Robert Cecil and the Spanish Embassy," *Bulletin of the Institute of Historical Research* 42 (1969).
[64] J. Hurstfield, "Corruption and Reform under Edward VI and Mary," *English Historical Review* 68 (1953).
[65] Stone, *Crisis of the Aristocracy*, pp. 424–49.

ated by courtier grantees for their own financial benefit. Thus the monopolist became a stock figure of evil in the early seventeenth century. Efforts were made by Parliament to curb his activities by means of the Statute of Monopolies in 1624, but to no avail, and an important reason for the attack on so many administrative units and powers in 1640–42 was pent-up exasperation at the open perversion of economic controls.

Finally, the monarchy itself fell into disrepute. In the sixteenth century Henry VIII and Elizabeth were the foci of an adulation which evidently sprang to some degree from a deep ground swell of popular nationalist feeling, even if much of it today seems nauseating in its jingo ideology and its sycophantic flattery. But James I and Charles I had little personal charisma, and they were never much loved or feared either by those who were fairly close to them or by the people at large. As a hated Scot, James was suspect to the English from the beginning, and his ungainly presence, mumbling speech, and dirty ways did not inspire respect. Reports of his blatantly homosexual attachments and his alcoholic excesses were diligently spread back to a horrified countryside, while his pro-Spanish foreign policy and his close association with Gondomar exposed him to the (wholly unjustified) accusations of popish sympathies and a betrayal of England's national interests.[66] Charles I was more respectable in his personal habits, but he had a cold, arrogant, yet furtive manner which aroused both hostility and suspicion. Moreover, his devotion to his Catholic Queen and his employment of Catholic ministers exposed him to far more serious and widespread suspicions of popery. By 1640 there was not much left of "the divinity that doth hedge a king."

The counterpart of the erosion of confidence and trust in all elements of the Establishment in the Church and state was the growth in aggressive self-consciousness of the opposition to that establishment. It was in Parliament, and particularly in the House of Commons, that the opposition built its institutional base. An important reason why this national representative body continued to play so important a role in English political life is that, unlike the situation in France, the administrative subdivisions, the counties, were too small to serve as foci for politi-

---

[66] D. H. Willson, *James VI and I* (London, 1956), chaps. 20 and 21; Stone, *Crisis of the Aristocracy*, pp. 662–71.

cal activity, except on a very limited scale. As a result, the central institution had no rivals and gained steadily in prestige and power until men actually fought and even paid to be members of it, instead of having to be paid as an inducement to serve. With its control over taxation, especially for war, and its control over legislation, especially concerning religion, it was strategically placed to demand redress of grievances.

During the course of the middle and late sixteenth century many things happened to increase Parliament's powers and to diminish the capacity of the crown to control it. Its numbers grew from about three hundred to about five hundred, and the relative gentry component also grew, despite the fact that most new seats were borough seats.[67] The members gained experience and a sense of continuity owing to the enhanced frequency of parliamentary sessions between 1590 and 1614. They developed an efficient committee system, which freed them from manipulation by a crown-appointed Speaker, and by the early seventeenth century parliamentary leaders had begun to emerge, men who built their careers on playing a key role in debates and in committees of the Commons. The crown had serious trouble with this body at all times in the late sixteenth and early seventeenth centuries, but slowly the nature of the trouble changed and became far more menacing. In the early years of Elizabeth's reign there were quarrels over specific issues—religion, taxation, or foreign policy—but by the early seventeenth century the first signs of a formal opposition appeared, men who came to Parliament with a set determination to challenge the crown on a wide range of issues. Loosely calling themselves "the country," they developed a distinct ideology, tactics, and strategy.[68]

At the same time that these developments were taking place in the House of Commons, the same persons, in their role as Justices of the Peace, were gaining increased experience in local administration. In response to the growing burden of enforcing legislation about social control and social welfare, there was a

[67] J. E. Neale, The Elizabethan House of Commons (London, 1949), chaps. 7 and 15.
[68] Judson, The Crisis of the Constitution, chap. 7; W. M. Mitchell, The Rise of a Revolutionary Party in the House of Commons, 1603–29 (New York, 1957), chap. 5; W. Notestein, The Winning of the Initiative by the House of Commons (London, 1924); J. R. Tanner, Constitutional Conflicts of the 17th Century (London, 1928); F. D. Wormuth, The Royal Prerogative, 1603–49 (Ithaca, N.Y., 1939).

striking increase in their numbers and their experience, and consequently in their power to paralyze the workings of any government of which they seriously disapproved.

An important cause of the gentry's growing self-confidence was the striking improvement of their education. The period saw a great increase in enrollment in grammar schools, universities, and Inns of Court, in large part caused by the desire of the propertied classes to train their sons for their new responsibilities. In terms of the formal attendance of its members at an institution of higher learning, the House of Commons of 1640 was the best educated in English history before or since. Nor was this zeal for learning confined to the gentry. The electorate of yeomen, smallholders, artisans, tradesmen, and shopkeepers was becoming increasingly literate, and therefore more independent and articulate.[69] Moreover, both the gentry and their electorate were being educated at grammar schools, private schools, and colleges of the university, many of which were in the hands of ideological dissidents—Puritan schoolmasters and dons. More and more it looks as if this educational expansion was a necessary, but not sufficient, reason for the peculiar and ultimately radical course the revolution took.

At the same time that the members of the House of Commons were flexing their muscles in wrestling with the crown, friction was developing between legal officials and judges in the various courts of law. At the outset this quarrel, which around the turn of the century led the two common-law courts to challenge most of the so-called Prerogative Courts, had little or nothing to do with politics, and everything to do with professional jealousies over jurisdictions, litigants, and fees. But the crown came to the defense of the Prerogative Courts, and, with Sir Edward Coke's dismissal from the Chief Justiceship in 1616 because of his interference with Chancery and the Court of High Commission, and his emergence as an opposition leader in the Commons in 1621, the legal quarrel was absorbed into the broader political conflict. The common-law officials were very conservative persons who had no real quarrel with the crown

[69] L. Stone, "The Educational Revolution in England, 1560–1640," *Past and Present* 28 (1966):54–64, 69; *idem*, "Literacy and Education in England, 1640–1900," *ibid.* 42 (1969):98–102; J. H. Plumb, *The Origins of Political Stability in England, 1675–1725* (Boston, 1967), pp. 27–28, 34–38.

and were mainly concerned in the first instance with pursuing a private vendetta against their legal colleagues. But they were a dangerous group to antagonize, and the marriage of convenience between common lawyers and opposition gentry was one which a wiser government would have tried to avoid.

A true revolution needs ideas to fuel it—without them there is only a rebellion or a *coup d'état*. The intellectual and ideological underpinnings of the opposition to the government are therefore of the first importance. In England the most far-reaching in its influence on men's minds, although very difficult to pin down in precise detail, was Puritanism, here interpreted to mean no more than a generalized conviction of the need for independent judgment based on conscience and bible reading. In practical terms this took the form of a desire to purify the Church and to improve the quality of its ministers, to reduce clerical authority and wealth, and, most significant of all, to moralize Church, society, and state. These views were held by some nobles, many influential gentry, some big merchants, and many small tradesmen, artisans, shopkeepers, and yeomen. The sociological roots of Puritanism are still obscure, but in England, as elsewhere, there was some correlation between cloth-working and religious radicalism. The spread of Puritanism among the lower middle class must therefore be related to the unusual size of England's prime industrial activity.[70] The spread of Puritanism among the landed classes is more difficult to explain on economic grounds and must be related in part to its association with national independence, in part to the popularity of its Erastian anticlerical component, and in part to the congruence of aspects of the Puritan ethic with the aspirations of a ruling class in search of a moral justification for its existence.

If the causes of Puritanism are obscure, its consequences are plain to see. It provided an essential element in the revolution, the feeling of certainty in the rectitude of the opposition cause and of moral indignation at the wickedness of the Establishment. It also helped to construct the theoretical justification for a challenge to the existing order. What if the Elect of God are not identical with the leaders of society? What if the Anglican

[70] J. F. Davis, "Lollard Survival and the Textile Industry in the South-East of England," *Studies in Church History* 3 (1966); C. Hill, *Society and Puritanism in Pre-Revolutionary England* (London, 1964), chap. 4.

church is not part of the Covenant? Are there limits to the obedience a godly person owes to a sinful magistrate? Lastly, it provided the opposition with the necessary organization and leadership. The Puritan lobby in the House of Commons in the days of Elizabeth has been described as the first organized political party in English history, and the Puritan ministers played a decisive part as propagandists and links which bound the various opposition elements together.[71] For it was not only ideas and moral conviction that Puritanism offered; it was also direction and organization. Puritans were the clerical and secular leaders of the opposition (in and out of Parliament) to Elizabeth's religious and foreign policies. They were the leaders of the attack on Buckingham's character and policies in the 1620s. It was because of their association first as Feoffees for Impropriations and then as directors of the Providence Island Company that they could lay the plans for the overthrow of Charles's government in the 1630s.[72] It is as safe as any broad generalization of history can be to say that without Puritanism there would have been no revolution at all.

The second intellectual basis of the revolution was the common law.[73] It is noticeable how much of the debates in Parliament in the early seventeenth century was conducted in terms of law and with reference to legal precedents. The great constitutional issues of the day were fought out in test case after test case—the *Bates* case, the *Five Knights* case, the *Ship Money* case—and it was only when the opposition had lost them all that it took to radical legislation to change the legal ground rules. This intensive legalism was as pervasive as Puritanism in its effect on the mental set of the early seventeenth century. Increasing numbers of gentry rounded off their education at the Inns of Court, and even if it is still not clear quite what they did there, there is a *prima facie* case for supposing that they read some law, and certainly they rubbed shoulders and ate

[71] Walzer, *The Revolution of the Saints*, chaps. 4, 5, and 7; *idem*, "Puritanism as a Revolutionary Ideology," *History and Theory* 3 (1963); Neale, *The Elizabethan House of Commons*, p. 251; *idem*, *Elizabeth I and Her Parliaments*, 1957, 2:141; Collinson, *The Elizabethan Puritan Movement*, pp. 278–79, 303–6.

[72] Hill, *Economic Problems of the Church*, pp. 252–67; A. P. Newton, *The Colonising Activities of the English Puritans* (New Haven, 1914), chap. 10.

[73] Ogilvie, *The King's Government; The Crisis of the Constitution*, chap. 2; E. W. Ives, "Social Change and the Law," in his *The English Revolution, 1600–1660* (London, 1968).

meals with actual and prospective barristers and judges.[74] Even after this short period of fairly intimate exposure to the law had come to an end, a gentleman was still involved in legal affairs, whether he liked it or not, thanks to the maze of litigation in which every man of property was entangled; the experience may or may not have increased his affection and respect for the legal profession, but it certainly improved his knowledge of the law.

From the Middle Ages lawyers had inherited a set of rules and conventions which they could, and eventually did, use to erect barriers for the protection of private property, private interests, and private persons against the encroachment of a centralizing state. These defenses were based on the medieval concept of liberties, of private vested interests, but they were not less effective for that. From these particularist positions they developed a whole field of antiquarian research which they used to buttress the concept of the Balanced Constitution, using—or abusing—the myth of Magna Carta as the foundation stone. James I remarked that "ever since his coming to the Crown the popular sort of lawyers have been the men that most affrontedly in all Parliaments have trodden upon his Prerogative." The importance of the lawyers in the leadership of the opposition in the House of Commons is best exemplified in the career of Sir Edward Coke in the 1620s,[75] but he was only the most outstanding among many. It is no coincidence that the only solid achievement of the Long Parliament in its first year of existence was the abolition of the old rivals of the Common Law Courts, the Prerogative Courts, an issue on which gentry, Puritans, and lawyers were united.

The third component in the mentality of the opposition was the ideology of the "country." Spread by poets and preachers, and stimulated by newsletters disseminating scandalous gossip about the goings-on at court, it defined itself most clearly as the antithesis to this negative reference group.[76] The country was virtuous, the court wicked; the country was thrifty, the court

[74] W. Prest, "Legal Education of the Gentry at the Inns of Court, 1560–1640's," Past and Present 38 (1967).
[75] Ives, "Social Change and the Law," p. 126; C. Hill, Intellectual Origins of the English Revolution (Oxford, 1965), chap. 5; Holdsworth, A History of English Law, 5: 425–93; J. G. A. Pocock, The Ancient Constitution and the Feudal Law (Cambridge, 1957).
[76] Stone, Crisis of the Aristocracy, pp. 392–94; Zagorin, Court and Country, chap. 3.

extravagant; the country was honest, the court corrupt; the country was rural, the court urban; the country was chaste, the court promiscuous; the country was sober, the court drunken; the country was nationalist, the court xenophile; the country was healthy, the court diseased; the country was outspoken, the court sycophantic; the country was the defender of old ways and old liberties, the court the promoter of administrative novelties and new tyrannical practices; the country was solidly Protestant, even Puritan, the court deeply tainted by popish leanings. By the early seventeenth century England was experiencing all the tensions created by the development within a single society of two distinct cultures, cultures that were reflected in ideals, religion, art, literature, the theater, dress, deportment, and way of life.

The last and most difficult intellectual movement to handle, or even to document, is the spread of skepticism, which was slowly corroding belief in traditional values and traditional hierarchies. The new scientific attitudes and discoveries, of which Bacon was so strenuous a promoter, were important less in themselves than for what they did to shatter old certainties. Once it was discovered that the earth was not the center of the solar system, it immediately became questionable whether man was God's choice creation. As Donne put it in a much-quoted passage:

> And new Philosophy calls all in doubt
>
> .   .   .   .
>
> 'Tis all in peeces, all cohaerence gone,
> All just supply and all Relation.
> Prince, Subject, Father, Son are things forgot.[77]

The last line is the key in this passage, with its suggestion of the collapse of old authority patterns, both in the state and in the family. Attempts to show a direct association between Baconian optimism about the potentialities of scientific innovations on the one hand, and political radicalism during the revolution on the other, have not been very convincing.[78] What is much more plausible is the contribution of scientific discoveries to a mood of doubt and questioning.

---

[77] J. Donne, *Poems*, ed. J. C. Grierson (London, 1912), pp. 237–38.
[78] Hill, *Intellectual Origins of the English Revolution*, chap. 3, and the articles and notes in *Past and Present* 28–31 (1964–65).

This corrosion of authority was not confined to secular affairs but also spread to religion. The mere existence within a society of a number of actively competing religious sects and churches inevitably raised the question: What is the right road to salvation? To this the answer might be: Any; or perhaps even none. Toleration is bred of indifference, and indifference is bred of religious pluralism. As the religious fanatics on all sides shouted louder and louder, so more and more sober men began to adopt a latitudinarian attitude of watchful skepticism. The result of this two-pronged attack on established beliefs was a real crisis of confidence in the early seventeenth century. As Drayton wrote in 1625, "Certainly there's scarce one found that now knows what to approve or what to disallow." [79] The effect on the historical process of this mood of generalized anxiety and confusion cannot be neatly documented; but a reasonable supposition is that it played its part in undermining confidence in the established institutions of the Church and state.

To sum up this survey of preconditions, one can see that by the 1620s England was moving into a condition of multiple dysfunction. Both the government and the Church were demonstrating an inability to adapt to new circumstances, to the demands of new social forces and new intellectual currents. They were failing to satisfy the political, religious, and social aspirations of important sectors of opinion among gentry, merchants, lawyers, lesser clergy, yeomen, and artisans. These men were seeking a larger voice in political affairs and the right to consent to taxation, a reform of court morals (financial and personal), an overtly Protestant foreign policy, and a moderate purification of church ritual and a diminution of episcopal authority. The response they got from the Establishment was increasingly strident and irrelevant lectures on the Divine Right of Kings; the promotion to power of a group of clergy whose aim was to increase the importance of church ritual and to increase the authority of the episcopacy; the obstinate pursuit of the chimera of the Spanish marriage as the central objective of foreign policy; and even more blatant corruption, extravagance, and incompetence at court under the leadership of George Villiers, duke of Buckingham, the youthful darling of

[79] Hill, *Intellectual Origins of the English Revolution*, p. 8.

the doting and drink-sodden old King, and the bosom friend of his austere young heir. Enemies of the regime were subjected to half-hearted and intermittent persecution, than which nothing is better calculated to strengthen the resolve and unite the loyalties of an opposition. Men could rally behind an earl of Bristol or a Sir John Eliot and enjoy the pleasures of communally shared moral indignation without running much risk of personal danger.

Moreover, as time went on, there appeared that sinister precursor of a time of political troubles, the alienation of the intellectuals.[80] The Puritan ministers and lecturers in the cities and villages, the dons behind the graying walls of their colleges, and the common lawyers at the Inns of Court all increasingly felt themselves cut off in spirit and in reality from the central institutions of government. In so highly literate a society as that of early seventeenth-century England, this alienation of the most articulate segments boded no good for the regime.

The social structure itself was under great strain as a result of what most contemporaries regarded as an excessive degree of mobility among nearly all groups. As always, this mobility was confined to one or two dimensions among many, and as a result the individual, whatever the direction of his movement, suffered a sense of status inconsistency. The highly plausible theory of "status crystallization" has it that the more frequently acute status inconsistencies occur within a population, the greater will be the proportion of that population which supports programs of social change.[81] In the early seventeenth century, families and individuals were moving at an unprecedented pace both upward and downward on the social scale, and geographically from village to village and from countryside to town.[82] The result was deeply unsettling. Another disturbing development was the realization that the numbers of the leisured class and their children were increasing faster than suitable job opportunities in government, the army, the Church, or the law.

[80] M. H. Curtis, "The Alienated Intellectuals of Early Stuart England," Past and Present 23 (1962).

[81] Lenski, "Status Crystallization," p. 411.

[82] P. Laslett, "Clayworth and Cogenhoe," in Historical Essays, 1600–1750, ed. H. E. Bell and R. L. Ollard (London, 1963), p. 177; E. A. Wrigley, "London's Importance, 1650–1750," Past and Present 37 (1967): 46; R. H. Tawney, "The Gentry, 1540–1640," in Essays in Economic History, ed. Carus-Wilson, 1:192.

Consequently, frustrations were building up among unemployed and resentful younger sons. Finally there occurred a deepening split between two cultures, one represented by the bulk of the political nation, the other by a minority at court. It was a split symbolized by the emergence of clearly antithetical myths and ideologies: obedience versus conscience; the Divine Right of Kings versus the Balanced Constitution; the beauty of holiness versus Puritan austerity; court versus country.

This analysis of the various features in a deteriorating situation conceals one very important point, which is that the very success of the Elizabethan policy of cautious compromise and artful procrastination was an important source of trouble to the Stuarts. In the first place, Elizabeth's success in avoiding a war bred in the propertied classes an overconfidence in their ability to steer a steady course between the Scylla of docile obedience to the demands of the crown, and the Charybdis of the unleashing of civil war. In the Church, the policy of studied indifference to spiritual matters allowed the Puritan lecturers and the Catholic priests to capture the hearts and minds of some of the best and most educated elements of the population. In finance, the policy of turning a blind eye to widespread tax evasion by the landed classes, and gross under-assessment of customs by the merchant community, led directly to a constitutional crisis as soon as the Stuarts tried to remedy an intolerable situation. In Parliament, Elizabeth thoughtlessly allowed the numbers in the House of Commons to increase alarmingly. She fought a rearguard action for her prerogative inch by inch and step by step, but her very intransigence in matters which should and could have been compromised or conceded—such as the succession problem, moderate Church reform, and monopolies—encouraged the parliamentary gentry to formulate ever more aggressive demands for constitutional change. She has been well described as "the splendid though involuntary betrayer of the cause of monarchy."[83] At the same time, the pressure of the Elizabethan government on the Justices of the Peace to enforce an ever-increasing mass of legislation for social control led to a growing sense of political identity among the gentry of the

[83] J. E. Neale, "The Commons' Privilege of Free Speech in Parliament," in *Tudor Studies Presented to A. F. Pollard*, ed. R. W. Seton-Watson (London, 1924), p. 286.

county. They began to form corporative political institutions which could paralyze government if they came into conflict with the central authority at Westminster.[84] Some of the problems of the Stuarts were thus directly caused by the very success of Elizabeth's policies. She won many battles but died before losing the war.

If one were to single out the most important elements in the manifold preconditions which have been described, the principal three would be the failure of the crown to acquire the two key instruments of power, a standing army and a paid reliable local bureaucracy; the rise of the gentry, in terms of relative wealth, status, education, administrative experience, and group identity in county government, and also of political self-confidence in the House of Commons as the representative of a "country" ideology; and third, the spread throughout large sectors of the propertied classes of a diffuse Puritanism, the most important political consequence of which was to create a burning sense of the need for change in the Church, and eventually in the state. The most important secondary factors were the independent power of the common lawyers and their "Magna Carta" ideology; the progressive transformation of the economy, which came with the commercialization of agriculture and rural social relationships, the growth of overseas trade and industry, and the doubling of the population; the false sense of security caused by the initial success of Elizabethan compromise; and the increased size and cost, coupled with the deterioration in efficiency and repute, of the central organs of government and the court. It must be stressed that none of the developments here listed made the collapse of government—much less the outbreak of civil war or the rise of a genuinely revolutionary political party—inevitable. They did make almost certain some redistribution of political power, and very probable a reform of the Church, but whether these changes would come about by peaceful evolution, political upheaval, or force of arms was altogether uncertain, dependent upon the wisdom, or lack of it, of the governmental authorities, and the moderation, or lack of it, of the opposition.

[84] J. Gleason, *The Justices of the Peace in England, 1558–1640* (Oxford, 1969). I owe this insight to Mr. Victor Morgan. See also Stone, *Crisis of the Aristocracy*, p. 157.

THE PRECIPITANTS, 1629–39

During the decade before the crash in 1640, a series of developments took place which may be regarded as precipitants of crisis, bringing the collapse of governmental institutions from the realm of possibility to that of probability. The main emphasis must be placed on the folly and intransigence of the government, on its blind refusal to respond constructively to criticism, and on its obstinate departure on a collision course. It associated itself wholeheartedly with a vigorous religious reaction, guided and driven furiously forward by Archbishop Laud. The latter worked for recovery of the political power and prestige of the bishops after decades of neglect and contempt; for recovery of the economic resources of the Church through a revision of urban tithe assessments and a counterattack on lay impropriations after decades of robbery by the laity; for increased orderliness and ritualistic adornment of the Church and its services, taking what to a Puritan was the most offensive form of organs and altar rails, kneeling before the altar, and the use of the cross in baptism; and for a more relentless harrying of the Puritans than they had ever experienced before, even under Whitgift and Elizabeth.[85]

Worse still was the influence exerted over Charles by his Catholic Queen, the employment of Catholic laymen in high ministerial offices, the amiable relations established with the papacy, and the pursuit of a foreign policy which seemed blatantly pro-Spanish and anti-Protestant. Popular perceptions are often more important than reality, and given the hysterical fears of the time the suspicion that the administration was indelibly tarnished with popery had catastrophic effects on public confidence in the regime. A royal supporter remarked in 1640 that "the people being persuaded or of opinion that their leaders and service were Popish has done his Majesty more disservice than any one thing," a judgment escalated by a radical M.P. to the charge that "the root of all our grievances I think to be an intended union between us and Rome."[86] This was the main

[85] H. R. Trevor-Roper, *Archbishop Laud, 1573–1645* (London, 1940); Hill, *Economic Problems of the Church.*
[86] G. Albion, *Charles I and the Court of Rome* (London, 1935), chap. 14; *Calendar of State Papers Domestic, 1640,* pp. 493, 38.

cause of the troops' refusal to fight the Scots, which led directly to the downfall of the regime.

Parallel to this reaction in religion was a reaction in politics, in the degree of participation in government by the political nation of freeholders and gentry. Charles dismissed Parliament, proclaimed his intention of ruling without it, and proceeded to raise taxes without consent by juggling with the letter of the law and by perverting residual prerogative powers for emergency action in moments of national danger. This policy aroused formidable opposition, not because royal taxation in the 1630s was particularly bothersome to any class of society—indeed, it was almost certainly lighter than anywhere else in Europe—but because the money was levied in an unconstitutional and arbitrary manner and was used for purposes which many taxpayers regarded as immoral. Moreover, Charles inflamed the fears of the landed classes by encouraging Strafford to use Ireland as a laboratory for a large-scale experiment in authoritarian rule, an experiment which many Englishmen regarded as a prelude to the introduction of similar political methods at home.[87]

Thirdly, Charles attempted to enforce a social reaction, to put the lid on the social mobility he found so distasteful. He abruptly ended the sale of titles, he drove the gentry and nobility out of London back to their rural retreats where he thought they belonged, and he did all he could to bolster noble privilege and to reinforce the hierarchy of ranks.[88] He increased the proportion of second-generation noblemen in the Privy Council, he severely punished anyone who insulted aristocrats, he restricted access to the Privy Chamber according to rank, and some of his advisers considered the idea of attaching political and financial privilege to title on the continental model. The logical culmination of this attitude was the summoning of a medieval Great Council in 1640 to advise the King of how to deal with the crisis caused by defeat in the Scottish Wars. The noblemen themselves were busy writing or commissioning family histories, elaborating their coats of arms, and pushing their genealogies

[87] H. F. Kearney, *Strafford in Ireland, 1633–41* (Manchester, 1959); T. Ranger, "Strafford in Ireland: A Revaluation," *Past and Present* 19 (1961).
[88] Stone, *Crisis of the Aristocracy*, pp. 34, 117–19, 397–98, 751; H. F. Kearney, *The Eleven-Years Tyranny of Charles I* (London: Historical Association, 1962).

farther and farther back into a remote and improbable antiquity, while at the same time many were instructing their agents to exploit to the full the financial profits to be derived from a revival of long-forgotten feudal dues. Taken together, crown policies and the behavior of the nobility strongly suggest the beginnings of an aristocratic reaction which in time might have developed into something comparable to the more self-conscious and comprehensive movement in France in the decades before the French Revolution. The latter reaction is now thought to have played an important part in heightening the social tensions that finally led to the explosion of 1789, and it seems reasonable to suppose that the admittedly less well-developed reaction in England aroused similar resentments among the gentry. It played its part in stimulating among the members of the lower house that hostility to, and suspicion of, the House of Lords which is so evident a feature of even the early sessions of the Long Parliament.

Lastly, Charles got himself involved in economic reaction. Guild organization was imposed from above on numerous crafts and trades; the City of London was harried because of its involvement in Irish land settlement and the sale of crown lands; offensive and useless monopolies were strictly enforced, and attempts were made to tighten regulations governing the quality of cloth; the East India Company was infuriated by the cynical licensing of interlopers in the trade; the squirearchy was infuriated by the imposition of fines for distraint of knighthood and for violations of the anti-enclosure laws, by the revival of medieval forest laws, and even scutage, and by the transformation of ship money into an annual national levy.[89] Every aspect of economic life suffered from the feverish interference of a bureaucracy whose sole objective seemed to be the extraction of money by the imposition of a multitude of petty and irritating regulations, many of which were of dubious legality.

In short, the policy of Thorough was one of no concession to

[89] G. D. Ramsay, The Wiltshire Woollen Industry (London, 1943), chap. 6; G. Unwin, Industrial Organization in the Sixteenth and Seventeenth Centuries (Oxford, 1904), pp. 142–71; V. Pearl, London and the Outbreak of the Puritan Revolution (Oxford, 1961), pp. 79–91; R. Ashton, "Charles I and the City," in Essays in the Economic and Social History of Tudor and Stuart England, ed. Fisher; G. Hammersley, "The Revival of Forest Laws under Charles I," History 45 (1960).

the opposition; no co-option of potential opposition leaders; actions and statements which gave the maximum offense to the sensibilities and interests of important individuals and groups; and a persecution which created martyrs in dozens and exiles in thousands, but the main result of which was to arouse the opposition to greater fury and to win for it more support, rather than to stamp it out.

While these policies were being implemented, the ruling elites began to split apart, so that the reaction had to be carried out by a regime already half at war with itself. In the administration, "Thorough" fought "Lady Mora," Protestant Privy Councilors fought Catholic Privy Councilors, Laud and his supporters fought Weston and the Queen. The loyalty of a host of minor officials was undermined by the activities of the Commission on Fees, which threatened their livelihood.[90] The aristocracy split apart as more and more were ejected from, or refused to come to, court. The episcopal bench was split, as Laud and his Arminian allies fought Bishop Williams and his friends. Even the merchant oligarchies in the cities, and especially in London, were split by different religious affiliations and by growing irritation at the cavalier ill-treatment they were receiving from the crown.[91]

During the 1630s the royal strategy and tactics at last succeeded in welding together the naturally disparate forces of opposition. The most important development of all was the enormous increase of Puritan sentiment as moderate Anglicans were increasingly alienated by Laudian policies and were driven to adopt a more radical stand. Laud may justly be regarded as the most important single contributor to the cause of Puritanism in the early seventeenth century. His policies provide a classic example of the way in which so often in history concrete results do not merely fall short of the objectives of political actors but are actually the diametrical opposites. Similarly, the gentry, who harbored intensely ambivalent feelings toward the lawyers, were thrust into alliance with them by royal use of the courts of law

[90] H. R. Trevor-Roper, "Archbishop Laud," *History* 30 (1945); Aylmer, *The King's Servants*, pp. 193–201; *idem*, "Office Holding as a Factor in English History, 1625–42," *History* 44 (1959).
[91] R. Howell, *Newcastle upon Tyne and the Puritan Revolution* (Oxford, 1967), chaps. 2 and 3; Pearl, *London and the Puritan Revolution*, pp. 304–5.

to crush opposition and to impose taxation.[92] To break the electoral hold of the courtiers and officials, the gentry were obliged to encourage yeomen and artisans to claim their voting rights and to exercise them independently of the great political patrons. At the same time, leadership was provided first by Sir Edward Coke and Sir John Eliot, and later by Pym, Hampden, Say and Sele, and Warwick, and coherent organization at the top was achieved by the Providence Island directorate. The government in its folly gave the opposition its needed martyrs: Eliot, with his corpse resting in the graveyard by the Tower instead of with his ancestors, and Burton, Bastwick, and Prynne, with their cropped ears and long imprisonments. It also gave the opposition inflammatory popular slogans, "No Popery" and "No Taxation without Consent of Parliament." The final stroke was to focus all the different grievances of every malcontent in the kingdom into a personal hatred of the persons and policies of two men, Wentworth and Laud. The destruction of these two would, it was believed, purge the Commonwealth of the evils which were crushing it and open the way to a better state and a better Church.

One of the most surprising recent discoveries about the English Revolution is that the radical Parliamentary leaders, both at Westminster and in the shires, were significantly older, by a median of eleven years, than the loyal Cavaliers.[93] This generation gap in reverse can best be explained by the fact that it required personal experience of Buckingham's corruption in the 1620s and the tyranny of Charles, Laud, and Strafford in the 1630s to drive men to revolution. Both experiences were necessary, but neither by itself was sufficient, which is why the revolution did not occur in the 1620s and why the generation of the 1630s was more tolerant of royal folly than were its seniors.

The final contribution to the erosion of consensus and the deterioration of political control was the fact that this conflict over fundamental constitutional and religious issues took place against a background of serious economic difficulties.[94] The

[92] H. E. I. Phillips, "The Last Years of Star Chamber," *Transactions of the Royal Historical Society,* 4th ser., vol. 21.
[93] D. Brunton and D. H. Pennington, *Members of the Long Parliament* (London, 1954), pp. 15–16; Everitt, *Kent and the Great Rebellion,* p. 118.
[94] E. J. Hobsbawm, "The Crisis of the Seventeenth Century," in *Crisis in Europe, 1560–1660,* ed. T. H. Ashton (London, 1965); B. Supple, *Commercial Crisis and Change in England, 1600–1642* (Cambridge, 1964), pt. 1, chaps. 3–6.

main export trade in cloth was dealt a shattering blow in the crisis of 1620–21, and the European markets never really recovered. Moreover, the 1630s were generally a period of poor harvests, beginning with the catastrophic year 1630 and continuing thereafter. There was only one good harvest in the decade, a situation for which there was only one parallel in the next one hundred and twenty years.[95]

The early seventeenth century therefore pursued the familiar "J curve" of a fairly long period of prosperity, which arouses expectations of continuing improvement, followed by a sharp downward turn. The reactionary royal policies of the 1630s were pursued at a time of frustrated economic expectations for many sectors of society. Deteriorating financial conditions were definitely *not* a factor in arousing discontent among the landlord class, which was the main actor in the later drama. Rents were soaring in the 1620s and 1630s, and, taken as a whole, the gentry, who with their London allies would topple the government in 1640 and so set in motion the train of revolution, had probably never had it so good.[96] But the economic downswing probably helped to heighten tensions in the towns between the old established monopolistic merchant oligarchies and the pioneers in new markets, the interlopers in old markets, and the smaller traders, all of whom were excluded from the magic circle of power and privilege. The stagnation of the cloth trade must have helped to radicalize cloth-workers, just as the high price of food must have helped to drive urban apprentices, especially in London, into political action.

It should be emphasized that it is only within the insular context of Whiggish English historiography that Charles's policy can be labeled reactionary rather than forward looking. Seen from continental Europe, the objectives and methods of Charles, Laud, and Strafford were precisely those in which the future lay. The strengthening of the links between the Church and state, the suppression of dissidents on all fronts, the creation of an overwhelmingly powerful court, the acquisition of extensive financial and military powers—these were the basis of the all but universal growth of royal absolutism in Europe. If the trend

---

[95] W. G. Hoskins, "Harvest Fluctuations and English Economic History, 1620–1759," *Argicultural History Review* 16 (1968):17, 20.

[96] E. Kerridge, "The Movement of Rent, 1540–1640," *Economic History Review*, 2d ser., vol. 6 (1953); Stone, *Crisis of the Aristocracy*, pp. 324–34.

of the times led anywhere, it was in the direction marked out by Charles and his advisers. Thus it is only in the strict context of English historical development that "Thorough" can be called both reactionary and anachronistic. And even here a good deal of *ex post facto* rationalization goes into these judgments. It is possible that a personally more charismatic king, with an irreproachably Protestant reputation and more cautious and far-sighted advisers, might have continued for quite a long time to pursue rather similar policies, at a much slower pace and using greater tact, without running into serious trouble. Yet nothing could compensate for the lack of control over local government, the absence of religious unity, the lack of a standing army, and the lack of some independent supply of money. The necessary military and financial aid could come only from one of the Catholic powers, help from which would immediately alienate almost all the propertied classes, as James II was to discover at his cost. Thus, in the long run, the traditional view is correct, and Charles's policy was as doomed to failure as was that of his son half a century later. Under these conditions it seems legitimate to continue to describe Charles's policies as both reactionary and unrealistic.

THE TRIGGERS, 1639–42

The precipitants of the 1630s turned the prospects of political breakdown from a possibility into a probability. But it was a sequence of short-term, even fortuitous, events which turned the probability into a certainty. Chalmers Johnson has observed that "revolution is always avoidable if only the creative potentialities of political organization can be realized."[97] Those potentialities were never even noticed by the King and his advisers in the years 1639–42. The governmental collapse of 1640 followed directly from the decision of Laud and Charles to try to impose on the Scottish clergy the English system of worship and church organization at the same time as they threatened the Scottish noblemen with the loss of their ex-monastic estates. This drove the Presbyterian ministers and the nobility into an alliance and provoked a full-scale war. Defeat in the war, caused largely by the unwillingness of the English troops and their lead-

[97] Johnson, *Revolutionary Change*, p. xiv.

ers to fight, in turn led to the crown's loss of control over its armed forces, which is the first and most necessary prelude to revolution. A partial taxpayers' strike, the cost of the war, and the reparations demanded by the Scots combined to empty the royal treasury and led to financial collapse. The only way to raise the money necessary to carry on the government was to appeal to Parliament, which meant surrender to the now fully aroused forces of opposition to all aspects of royal policy.

The parliamentary election of 1640 was more bitterly and widely contested than any that had gone before it, and the supporters of the court everywhere went down in defeat. Courtiers and officials comprised 28 per cent of the Parliament of 1614 but only 11 per cent of the Long Parliament, a smaller proportion than in any previous Parliament of which we have record. Moreover, not only were official candidates rejected, but the old aristocratic patronage system showed signs of breaking down, regardless of political sympathies. The earl of Salisbury could no longer get his nominee into even one seat at St. Albans, and Lord Maynard was frustrated in Essex, although both were to side with Parliament. The latter complained furiously—and ominously—that "fellows without shirts challenge as good a voice as myself."[98]

When the Long Parliament met in 1640, Charles found himself almost alone. Of his four natural allies, the aristocracy was weakened by decades of economic and then status decline, and was deeply divided in its religious and political loyalties; the Church hierarchy was isolated, despised, and even more deeply split; the central administration and court were demoralized and untrustworthy; and the armed forces were shattered by defeat, and if forced to choose were liable to side with the enemy. Allied against him was a temporarily united band of enemies—gentry, nobles, merchants, and lawyers—inspired by such powerful ideals as a Reformed church, a godly Commonwealth, the Magna Carta, the Ancient Constitution, and the "country." But these were slogans rather than a concrete program, and it would be foolish to suggest that the opposition arrived at Westminster

[98] T. L. Moir, *The Addled Parliament of 1614* (Oxford, 1958), pp. 56–57; M. F. Keeler, *The Long Parliament* (Philadelphia, 1954), p. 23; L. Stone, "The Electoral Influence of the Second Earl of Salisbury, 1614–68," *English Historical Review* 71 (1956): 390–91; C. A. Holmes, "The Eastern Association" (Ph.D. diss., Cambridge University, 1969), p. 90.

in 1640 with much more in mind than a desire to preserve and increase the political influence of their class, to rid the Church of the popish innovations introduced by Laud, to put domestic and foreign policy on a forthrightly Protestant tack, and to reduce the political influence of the bishops. But to achieve these objectives they had to tear down institutions like the Prerogative Courts, which were more than 150 years old, to arrogate to themselves the power of determining the term of their own dissolution, to execute a minister of the crown, and to throw the Archbishop of Canterbury into the Tower. In fact, if not in theory, the first session of the Long Parliament dismantled the central institutions of government without erecting anything in their place. As yet, however, no one thought in terms of civil war, if only because the King had no one to fight for him except a handful of extremist Cavaliers. What changed the situation, and made war first possible and then inevitable, was a series of accidents and personal decisions inspired by folly, hypocrisy, and fear.

The most revealing symptom of a deteriorating situation was the increasingly hysterical rhetoric of the Puritan preachers, who were busy arousing the members of the Commons to a mood of high religious exhaltation which could lead directly to bloodshed. In his famous and much-quoted sermon, *Meroz Cursed*, delivered before the Commons on 23 February 1642, Stephen Marshall bitterly denounced all waiverers and neutralists, and called for whole-hearted support of the Puritan cause. He interpreted the biblical text "Cursed is everyone that withholdeth his hand from shedding blood" to mean encouragement to his hearers "to go and embrue his hands in the blood of men, to spill and pour out the blood of women and children, like water in every street." He told them that "he is a blessed man that takes and dashes the little ones against the stones."[99] His prospective victims were Irish, but it clearly would not be too great a step to divert this fanatical hatred toward any opposition group, whether English Protestant Royalists or Irish Catholic rebels. Once aroused, emotions of this depth are hard to direct and control.

The unexpected death of the moderate leader, Bedford, shattered plans for a kind of coalition government of Royalist sup-

[99] S. Marshall, *Meroz Cursed* (London, 1641), pp. 10–12.

porters and Parliamentary dissenters. With hindsight one can see that the Irish situation had been becoming more and more explosive for a decade, but to contemporaries the Irish Rebellion came like a bolt from the blue. Its timing could not have been more unfortunate, because the need to crush it made necessary the ressurrection of central power in its most extreme and dangerous form, an army. Ever since the collapse of the government in 1640, there had been a vacuum of power at the center, a situation which, had it not been for the Irish Rebellion in 1641, might have been allowed to continue until the political crisis had been settled. But the necessity of raising an army forced the opposition to demand control over the military forces.

It was at this point that personal factors came into play. Charles's record of duplicity and his persistent, if inept, attempts to resort to violence convinced some of the Parliamentary leaders that he was not to be trusted. They now genuinely feared for their lives; after all, it was they who had spilled the first blood—that of Strafford on the scaffold—and they knew that Charles had sworn revenge. They therefore felt themselves obliged for their personal safety, and to protect the constitutional gains they had won during the previous eighteen months, to demand both control over the armed forces and control over the appointment of ministers. But these demands went far beyond the limited objective of restoring the hypothetical Balanced Constitution, and as a result large numbers of former opponents of the King swung reluctantly back to the royal side. By the summer of 1642 King Charles had acquired what did not exist a year before, a large, if none too resolute, body of influential supporters. He could now risk a civil war with a reasonable chance of winning.

On the other hand, this forced shift to the left by the basically moderate Parliamentary leaders brought them new and vitally important allies, namely, the radical new governors of the City of London, who had seized power from the Royalist old guard by means of a peaceful political revolution in 1641. This combination of the City, that part of the Parliamentary gentry which stayed with the leadership, and a substantial minority of powerful noblemen was strong enough to oppose the King by force of arms, but the alliance inevitably threw the weight of influence in the direction of the more extremist wing from the City.

Similarly, on the Royalist side, although it was the shift of the more conservative gentry back to the King which gave him the army and the political support he needed, it was nevertheless the extreme Cavaliers who continued to exert the greatest influence over royal policies. Thus by 1642 the stage was set for civil war over demands which had become non-negotiable to many of the leaders, if not to the followers, on both sides.

CONCLUSION

This essay is not concerned with the causes of the further stages of the revolution. The war began with a fissuring of the traditional elites, but there followed the capture of the Parliamentary leadership by the hard-line proponents of military victory; the emergence of a radical, lower-middle-class political ideology and party in the Levellers; the destruction of the three old landmarks, Monarchy, House of Lords, and Episcopal Church; the replacement of the Commonwealth by a barely disguised military dictatorship; and the final collapse of the revolutionary regime and the restoration of the old order in 1660. The scope of this essay is limited to defining the long-term factors that made some modifications of the political and religious institutions very probable; the short-term factors, mainly errors of policy, that made it likely that the change would take the form of confrontation rather than adjustment; and the immediate events and decisions which caused first the central government to collapse, and then the victors to fall out over fundamentals, so that the country drifted unhappily into war two years later.

What was so distinctive about the English Revolution was the intellectual content of the various opposition programs and achievements after 1640. For the first time in history an anointed king was brought to trial for breach of faith with his subjects, his head publicly cut off, and his office declared abolished. An established church was abolished, its property seized, and fairly wide religious toleration for all forms of Protestantism was proclaimed and even enforced. For a short time, and perhaps for the first time, there came on to the stage of history a group of men proclaiming ideas of liberty not liberties, equality not privilege, fraternity not deference. These ideas were to live on and to revive in other societies, in other ages. In 1647 the Puritan John Davenport forecast with uncanny accuracy that "the light which is now discovered in England . . . will never be wholly put out, though I suspect that contrary opinions will prevail for a time."[100]

Although the revolution ostensibly failed, there survived ideas about religious toleration, limitations on the power of the central executive to interfere with the personal liberty of the propertied classes, and a policy based on the consent of a very broad spectrum of society. They reappear in the writings of John Locke and find expression in the political system of the reigns of William and Anne, with well-developed party organizations, the transfer of far-reaching powers to Parliament, a Bill of Rights and a Toleration Act, and the existence of a surprisingly large, active, and articulate electorate. It is for these reasons that the English crisis of the seventeenth century can lay claim to being the first "Great Revolution" in the history of the world, and therefore an event of fundamental importance in the evolution of western civilization.

[100] Hill, *Puritanism and Revolution*, p. 152.

J . H . ELLIOTT

3 | Revolts in the Spanish Monarchy

For the Spanish Monarchy the 1640s were a decade of revolt and of rumors of revolt. Rebellion in Catalonia in the spring of 1640 was followed by the secession of Portugal in December. A few months later, a conspiracy was unearthed which might have ended in the installation of that great magnate, the duke of Medina Sidonia, on the throne of an independent Andalusia. Then, in 1647–48, came a new wave of troubles. In the Spanish peninsula itself, these troubles were localized, and not perhaps very dangerous: an ill-organized plot centering on the unstable personality of an Aragonese noble, the duke of Híjar, and a number of popular outbreaks in the cities of southern Spain. But in Spanish Italy there was justifiable cause for alarm, as reports of rebellion and of strange popular upheavals flowed in from Sicily and Naples. If the Monarchy weathered these storms with greater success than might have been anticipated, there were certainly moments when its position could justifiably be regarded as critical; and the British ambassador in Madrid, Sir Arthur Hopton, was not far wrong when he wrote home in the summer of 1641: "I am induced to think that the greatness of this monarchy is near to an end. . . ."[1]

In spite of all the gloomy prognostications, one of the most remarkable features of this decade was that the heart of the Monarchy, Castile, held firm. For all the burdens and misfortunes of war, there was no *Fronde* in Madrid. Whereas France had its revolt at the center, Spain had its revolts on the periphery, and this peripheral character of the movements of unrest undoubtedly helped to avert a total catastrophe. But there is no

[1] Hopton to Vane, 26 July/4 August 1641, State Papers 94.42, f. 192, Public Record Office, London.

109

denying the supreme gravity of events, and it is natural that
the four major revolts in the Spanish Monarchy during this
decade—those of Catalonia, Portugal, Sicily, and Naples—
should have aroused great contemporary interest, and have been
discussed at considerable length. The word "revolution" (but
used in the plural, in the sense of "popular tumults") appeared
in the titles of contemporary narratives of the movements in
Catalonia, Sicily, and Naples.[2] This contemporary usage does
to some extent help to distinguish their character from that of
the fourth rising, the Portuguese, which was notable for the
absence of social upheaval. Of these four movements, the Portuguese was incomparably the most revolutionary in its long-term
consequences, but it remains the least revolutionary in character
if we adopt the modern criterion of a strong social orientation
as an essential element of revolution. But the word "revolution,"
as used today, tends to be misleading as a description of any of
these risings; and all of them would be better classified under
the more neutral heading of "revolts."

To search for the "preconditions" of revolution in the Spanish
Monarchy, then, is to search for something rather grander than
the revolts themselves appear to warrant. In particular, events
in Sicily seem to be so fortuitous and haphazard that, here at
least, the "precipitants" of revolt seem considerably more important and deserving of study than any long-term "preconditions." There was, after all, one permanent and universal precondition for revolt in every society in early modern Europe: the
pressure of population on food resources, and the ever-present
threat of harvest failure and starvation. Because of this threat,
the possibility of popular uprisings was built into every society,
and only a sudden tax increase or a rise in the price of bread
was needed to precipitate a tumult. Events in Sicily, and to a
lesser degree in the city of Naples, hardly extended beyond this
classical category of hunger riots; and it was perhaps only the
acute weakness of the Spanish Monarchy at this particular junc-

---

[2] A. Giraffi, *Le Rivolutioni di Napoli* (Venice, 1647); Luca Assarino,
Le Rivolutioni di Catalogna (Bologna, 1648); Placido Reina, *Delle Rivolutioni della città di Palermo* ... (Verona, 1648), cited by H. G. Koenigsberger, "The Revolt of Palermo in 1647," *Cambridge Historical Journal*
8 (1946):129. On page 44 of his *Mercurio* (1644) Vittorio Siri speaks
of the "revolution" of Portugal (in the singular), by which he presumably
intended to imply Portugal's restoration to its former state of independence.

ture which gave them their importance, although the colorful personality of the rebel leader Masaniello certainly helped to direct the eyes of Europe toward the strange events in Naples.

If we look at the pattern of revolt in the Spanish Monarchy— or indeed in early modern Europe as a whole—we are likely to find a constant recurrence of two types of unrest which may or may not make common cause. There is, on the one hand, popular revolt—mass insurrections born of hunger and misery, which often acquire religious and millenarian overtones, and sometimes escalate into a violent protest against the whole ordering of society. There is, on the other hand, the revolt which occurs within the political nation—a protest by a faction, or by the majority of the political nation, against an unpopular regime. Either of these revolts may occur without the other; or both may occur simultaneously; or one may provide conditions conducive to the outbreak of the other. A popular movement may, for instance, encourage a section of the political nation to challenge the regime—a possibility to which Bacon alluded when he wrote: "Then is the danger, when the greater sort do but wait for the troubling of the waters among the meaner, that then they may declare themselves."[3] Conversely, a division within the political nation may create a situation in which popular demagogues can seize the upper hand.

Of these four revolts, two—the Sicilian and the Neapolitan— appear to belong to the first category, that of popular movements accompanied by little or no elite participation. The Portuguese revolt was essentially an elite movement, although it enjoyed popular support. The Catalan revolt, however, is best seen as a combination of elite and popular movements, working sometimes in harmony but more often in disagreement, and precipitating a convulsion far more considerable in scale than anything experienced by Portugal, Sicily, or Naples. Indeed, the nearest equivalent in the Spanish Monarchy to the Catalan revolt was the revolt of the Netherlands eighty years earlier. The affinities between the Dutch and Catalan revolts are marked, and, indeed, were noted by contemporaries. "Holland is not more rebellious than Cerdanya," wrote one of the Spanish army commanders in northern Catalonia a few months before the out-

---

[3] Francis Bacon, "Of Seditions and Troubles," *The Works of Francis Bacon*, ed. J. Spedding, vol. 6 (London, 1858), p. 411.

break of the revolt. "Only the preachers are missing, to make them lose their faith along with their obedience."[4] The pamphlets produced by the Catalans to justify their rebellion suggest that they were conscious of following a path which the Dutch had trodden before them. It is perhaps not one of the least important of the preconditions for revolt that there should exist precedents and examples—a tradition of protest to which the discontented can turn in their time of need. Such a tradition was provided both by the example of the Dutch and by Catalonia's own long record of resistance to its princes.

In early modern Europe a revolt stood some chance of success only if it could count on the active participation of at least a section of the traditional governing class, and on the neutrality, if not the good will, of the greater part of the political nation. It was because the governing class either participated in the movement of revolt, or failed to rally to the crown and the agents of royal authority at the moment of crisis, that the Catalan and Portuguese risings were potentially far more dangerous to Madrid than the insurrections in Spain's Italian possessions. When analyzing the preconditions for revolt in the Spanish Monarchy, it seems reasonable, then, to begin by examining the phenomenon which made events in Catalonia and Portugal so disastrous for the government of Philip IV: the alienation of the ruling class from the crown. This in turn can help to illuminate the pattern of events in Naples and Sicily, where the absence of effective aristocratic participation suggests either that the preconditions for the alienation of the political nation did not apply in those territories, or that they were counterbalanced by other forces working to hold crown and political nation together.

Throughout the sixteenth and seventeenth centuries, movements of protest among the governing classes of the different kingdoms and territories of the Spanish Monarchy inevitably conformed to a certain common pattern because these territories shared a common relationship to the crown and the central government. The number, the disparity, and the widely differing historical antecedents of the various dominions subject to the king of Spain had imposed on the Spanish Monarchy a consti-

[4] Cited by J. H. Elliott, *The Revolt of the Catalans* (Cambridge: Cambridge University Press, 1963), p. 368.

tutional and administrative structure in which the demands of central government were checked and counterbalanced by the necessary recognition of provincial diversity. The traditional system by which the Monarchy was governed in theory, if not always in practice, was summarized by the seventeenth-century jurist, Solórzano Pereira, who wrote that "the kingdoms must be ruled and governed as if the king who holds them all together were king only of each one of them."[5] Unfortunately, this maxim concealed a fiction which goes far to explain the uneasiness and discontent of the dominant social groups in the territories concerned. The assumption was that, in spite of the incorporation of a kingdom into the wider unit of the Spanish Monarchy, nothing had really changed—that its life would continue much as before. In practice, this assumption proved to be false.

The first and most obvious sign of change was that the prince no longer lived among his people. All but one of the kingdoms of the Spanish Monarchy—Castile—were kingdoms without a king. An attempt was made to palliate the deficiency by appointing viceroys; but a viceroy (generally some Castilian grandee) was a poor exchange for a king, just as a viceregal court was a poor exchange for the royal court, established since 1561 in Madrid. The fact of absentee kingship was of incalculable importance as a source of discontent, and it was a fact on which the kingdoms and provinces constantly harped as they compiled their long lists of complaints. The king was the fountainhead of justice, administration, and patronage. How could he see that the laws were executed, the guilty punished, and the good rewarded, if he did not live among his vassals and know at first hand what was happening among them? This was a cause of constant bewilderment and distress, which found forceful expression among the aristocracy of the Netherlands in the 1560s, in Aragon during the early 1590s, and in Catalonia and Portugal on frequent occasions during the opening decades of the seventeenth century. Perhaps it was never better put than in a Catalan petition of 1622: "How fitting it is that Your Majesty, as king, father and lord of all your states and kingdoms, should come personally to see all that you have in this Principality, and

[5] *Ibid.*, p. 8.

to console your most loyal vassals. We cannot but be jealous of the good fortune of others who enjoy the royal presence at first hand, and we beg the King's Majesty to come and acquaint himself in person with the affairs of this province so as to improve its government. . . . In thirty-seven years, only twice have your vassals seen their king and lord, and it is this long absence which is responsible for the violation of their laws. . . ."[6]

Royal absenteeism, then—the absence of a father figure in essentially patriarchal societies—played an important part in disorienting these societies, although its exact psychological significance is not easy to determine. In some ways, it may have helped to increase popular veneration for the king, since a monarch who was so far away could not possibly be held responsible for the villainous acts of his local ministers and officials, and would surely bring them to book if he could see for himself what was happening. It is not therefore surprising to find the mobs in Catalonia, Naples, and Sicily all crying "Long live the king!", sometimes coupled, as in Catalonia, with "Down with bad government!" On the other hand, the king's permanent absence also tended to prompt a search for a compensating object of loyalty; and this object was likely to be the *patria,* or fatherland.

The concept of the *patria* was hesitant and uncertain in sixteenth- and seventeenth-century Europe. The word was probably more often used of a local than a national community; and, insofar as it betokened a national community, its command over loyalties was insecure. But the dominant social groups in Catalonia and Portugal possessed a conception of their own national communities which gave them a yardstick by which to measure the actions of the royal government. This conception was no doubt unrealistic and idealized. In Catalonia it was based essentially on memories of a magnificent, if now increasingly remote, past, and on the survival from that past of a constitutional system built on the firm foundations of law and representation, and on a binding contractual relationship between the prince and his subjects. In Portugal, it drew strength from the recent fact of national sovereignty and independence, which had come to an end almost within living memory. It was also inspired by a deep pride in the epic achievements of a small nation whose

[6] *Ibid.,* p. 153.

global conquests hinted at a providential mission which had been momentarily interrupted, but certainly not terminated, by the misfortune of union with Spain. There was undoubtedly an element of wish fulfillment, and a blindness to certain unpleasant realities, in the images which the Catalans and the Portuguese possessed of themselves. But it was precisely this idealization of their own communities as historical, national, and legal entities which made them scrutinize so closely the actions of Madrid. And in the disparity between the ideal and the reality—a disparity which would increase sharply in the 1620s and 1630s—there lurked a danger which Madrid would be unwise to ignore.

It was not only history which gave the dominant groups in Catalan and Portuguese society a sense of the distinctness and coherence of their own communities. This sense was also kept alive by the very nature of the constitutional system under which they lived. Since it remained official doctrine that "the kingdoms must be ruled and governed as if the king who holds them all together were king only of each one of them," they retained their traditional laws, institutions, and forms of government. This meant not only that they still preserved a high degree of autonomy but also that they possessed agencies and institutions which might be used as vehicles for collective protest. Each country had its Cortes, although the effectiveness of these assemblies was limited by the fact that they were dependent upon the personal attendance of the king. But the Catalans possessed in their *diputació* a permanent standing committee of the Cortes, which was designed to represent and to further the interests of the community as a whole. The Portuguese, while less fortunate institutionally, held a trump card in the presence among them of the duke of Braganza, a member of the native nobility whose royal blood made him an obvious focus of national loyalty as an alternative to the king of Spain.

It is extremely difficult to know how deep this community consciousness ran in Portugal and Catalonia. There is clear evidence that many Catalans felt themselves excluded from the contractual society which was a source of such constant self-congratulation to the governing class, and that they looked on the *diputació* as an institution for perpetuating the interests of a closed and selfish oligarchy. But collective traditions of liberty, independence, and past achievement appear to have lurked beneath the surface. The parish clergy were the ideal guardians of this collective memory—close enough to the people to enjoy authority among them, and sufficiently educated in the national traditions to be able to transmit them to the populace and to urge from the pulpits that they should be defended to the last drop of blood. There was, too, an instinctive sense of hostility to the outsider, which was heightened by differences of language. The fact that Catalonia and Portugal preserved their individual languages was not, of itself, decisive. Indeed, Castilian had already made significant inroads among the Catalan governing class by the middle of the seventeenth century. But linguistic differences did help, at every level, to sharpen the sense of distinctiveness and to increase the community's sense of inner coherence in its relationship to the outer world.

Neither the Catalans nor the Portuguese, therefore, had much reason to identify themselves with the regime in Madrid. In this sense, there was a long-standing alienation between provincial community and central government, which must be regarded as an essential precondition for revolt. This alienation may not have seriously worried the mass of Catalans or Portuguese, for whom there was not much to choose between a government based in Madrid and a government in Barcelona or Lisbon. But its impact on the dominant social groups in both countries was deeply felt. Nobles regarded themselves as excluded from patronage and from opportunities of employment in the royal service; urban oligarchies believed that an absentee ruler neglected their economic and social interests; and the political nation as a whole resented a government which was either heavy-handed or inefficient, and frequently both, and which was conducted at the behest of a faraway Madrid.

Friction between provincial community and central government was no doubt a universal fact of life in seventeenth-century Europe, although it was clearly at its most serious in those territories which, like Catalonia and Portugal, had succeeded in preserving a strong sense of their own identity together with laws and institutions to safeguard it. To understand why this friction reached a level that came to be regarded as intolerable, we must look more closely at the major political developments of the two decades preceding the risings of 1640.

Here we find that the years around 1620 mark an important change in the relationship between the Madrid government and the dominant social groups of Catalonia and Portugal. This change may be summarized as a transition from neglect to intervention, from an excessive degree of indifference to an excessive degree of interest in Catalan and Portuguese affairs.

Much of the reign of Philip III can be characterized as a period when the central government was in retreat. A regime which feared complications and embarrassments above all else, was happy enough to let local communities lead their own lives, as long as they caused no trouble. This permissive approach to the problems of government and administration provided opportunities which local aristocracies could not have been expected to overlook. The Catalan gentry, for instance, could aid and abet the activities of bandit gangs with a reasonable degree of impunity. But Madrid's attitude also provided opportunities for forceful viceroys, who no longer felt themselves unduly inhibited by their instructions from the king. Sicily, during the viceroyalty of the duke of Osuna (1611–16), and Catalonia, during the viceroyalties of the dukes of Alburquerque and Alcalá (1616–22), were endowed with just such viceroys—men who were determined to restore order and provide firm government, and who were not unduly worried about the methods they employed. Inevitably their high-handed behavior made them influential enemies and provoked a general uneasiness about the infringement of traditional liberties.

Consequently, for Catalonia at least, the reign of Philip IV opened in 1621 in an atmosphere of suspicion and mistrust. The character of the new regime, and particularly of the principal minister, the count of Olivares, did nothing to dispel these feelings. It quickly became clear that the Olivares regime was the antithesis of the Lerma regime, which had ruled the monarchy for most of the reign of Philip III. It was energetic instead of indolent, active instead of passive, interventionist instead of abstentionist. Partly this reflected the character of Olivares himself, but it also reflected the overpowering needs of the moment, as Spain returned to war. The demands of foreign warfare, together with the crippling economic weakness of Castile, effectively imposed a new policy on the government in Madrid, irrespective of the ministers' personalities. This policy was aimed at mobilizing all the resources of the Spanish Monarchy for war; and this mobilization implied a vigorous attempt to exploit the reserves of wealth and manpower of every kingdom and province, regardless of its rights and privileges.

From the early 1620s, then, Madrid had embarked on a policy which was bound to subject provincial communities to increasing pressure from the central government as the strains of war began to tell. This pressure was all the more intolerable because it was inevitably associated by the governing classes of Catalonia and Portugal with the aggressive intentions of Castile. The dominant position of the Castilians in the Monarchy, and the arrogance with which they asserted themselves, had built up a strong pressure of fear and resentment in the non-Castilian kingdoms. The Castilians had monopolized the royal person; they had taken for themselves the most lucrative posts and offices; and they were suspected of wanting to impose their own laws, customs, and institutions on kingdoms and provinces which had as much right to an independent existence as Castile. As Olivares' plans for the mobilization of the Monarchy began to unfold, it was natural enough that they should be seen as designs to further this process of Castilianization.

In 1625 and 1626 the rumor swept through the Monarchy that Olivares' aim was to establish "one king, one law, one coinage."[7] The one king was already, to all intents and purposes, a Castilian. It was reasonable to assume that the one law and the one coinage would be Castilian, too. In fact, the rumor represented a reasonably accurate assessment of Olivares' long-term intentions. If he were to mobilize the Monarchy for a supreme military effort, he somehow had to undermine the laws and liberties which preserved the autonomous status of the various provinces and shielded them from the heavy demands for taxes and soldiers which were regularly imposed on Castile. In the circumstances of the time, uniformity was likely to mean conformity—conformity with Castile, the most easily exploited kingdom in the Spanish Monarchy. The policies of Olivares therefore heightened the congenital suspicion of Castilian intentions and strengthened the determination of the Catalan and Portuguese ruling classes to preserve the independent identity

[7] *Ibid.*, p. 213.

of their own communities, increasingly threatened by an alien power.

In practice, the legal and institutional barriers with which the Catalans and Portuguese shielded themselves made it difficult for Olivares to implement his plans for establishing any general uniformity of contribution to the war effort throughout the Spanish Monarchy. The pressure from Madrid, however, was intense, particularly during the 1630s. Constant threats, demands, and harassment did succeed in extracting significant sums from the cities of Lisbon and Barcelona, but only at the cost of a rapidly rising mutual exasperation. Olivares needed, and was determined to obtain, fixed regular fiscal contributions from the Portuguese and the Catalans; and his difficulties only increased his determination. For their part, the Portuguese and Catalans resented the ruthless persistence of Olivares and his unwillingness to acknowledge the great services they felt they had rendered. Two events in 1637 might have served as warning signals of the dangers that lay ahead. In Portugal, there were riots in Evora and other cities against a new contribution which Olivares was attempting to levy, while in Catalonia the population displayed a marked reluctance to participate in a campaign against France launched from their territory. Although the Portuguese nobility remained passive in 1637, it was becoming clear that the alienation of the Portuguese and Catalan political nations from Madrid was by now almost complete.

I have tried to suggest that the sources of this alienation can be traced far back into the past, but that they were compounded by Madrid's policies in the years after 1620—by the ruthlessness and persistence of its demands and by the Castilian nationalist overtones which accompanied them. By 1640 the dominant social groups in both Catalonia and Portugal were angry and afraid. In many respects their fear was selfish, for they were threatened with the loss of privileges which they had tended to exploit and abuse; but for many of them it was fear enhanced by an awareness, whether conscious or subconscious, of the wider implications of the policies which Olivares was pursuing. They saw the historical identity of their national communities jeopardized. They saw, too, how grossly the Castilians had mismanaged their own affairs, and they were, not unnaturally, alarmed at the prospect of being overwhelmed in the general catastrophe which threatened to engulf Castile.

By 1640 the ruling classes of both Catalonia and Portugal were sufficiently alarmed and sufficiently exasperated to accept, or connive in, a decisive break with Madrid. When they acted in this way, were they acting from a position of economic strength or weakness? Unfortunately, we simply do not possess sufficient information to provide a clear-cut answer. From the late 1620s, plague, famine, and war seem to have depressed the Catalan economy, although there are signs of continuing resilience, especially in the agrarian life of eastern Catalonia. Portugal, too, suffered severely from the war, and especially from the loss of rich overseas possessions to the Dutch. But here, also, there were signs of resilience and vitality, particularly along the Atlantic coastline. By 1640 it may be said that, while both countries had known better times, both were uneasily aware that they might soon be faced with worse; for, while the degree of prosperity of Catalonia and Portugal is impossible to measure in absolute terms, there can be no doubt that both were highly favored in relation to Castile. Perhaps the most obvious and striking contrast lay in the state of their currencies. The years 1604–40 were years of great monetary stability for Portugal, while the Catalan coinage had been stable since 1617.[8] The dizzy fluctuations of the Castilian currency during the same period make the alarm of the Catalans and Portuguese at the idea of "one coinage" easy to understand.

For the Catalan commercial classes, no particular advantage was to be gained from breaking free from the Monarchy: it was enough to keep Castile at arm's length. But, for those Portuguese merchants who were not actively involved in the Spanish crown's finances, the story was rather different. Portugal had gained valuable advantages from its union with Castile in 1580. It had secured access to the American silver which it so badly needed for its own commercial transactions; it had been able to draw on the resources of the Spanish Monarchy for the defense of its overseas empire; and Portuguese merchants had managed to infiltrate Spain's American territories. But by the 1630s these

[8] F. Mauro, *Le Portugal et L'Atlantique au XVII⁰ Siècle* (Paris: S.E.V.-P.E.N., 1960), p. 417; Pierre Vilar, *La Catalogne dans l'Espagne Moderne*, vol. 1 (Paris: S.E.V.P.E.N., 1962), p. 616.

advantages had either disappeared or were on the point of disappearing. American silver remittances to Seville were dwindling; Castilian military assistance had failed to keep the Portuguese empire intact; and the authorities in Spanish America were clamping down on the activities of Portuguese businessmen. With the economic benefits of union vanishing before their eyes, Portuguese mercantile interests had good grounds for believing that their country might once again fare better on its own. Indeed, by the late 1630s it was hard to imagine that an independent Portugal would fare any worse than a Portugal which was tied to, and dragged down by, Castile.

Insofar as they existed, therefore, the economic preconditions for revolt may have been based more on expectation than on reality. Catalonia and Portugal enjoyed a reasonable degree of prosperity in comparison with Castile; but it was a prosperity which may have been dwindling and which was certainly under attack. If they remained united to Castile, both countries could look forward to progressive impoverishment, until they found themselves reduced to the misery which had already overtaken Castile. Through its participation in the Atlantic economy, an independent Portugal was likely to possess opportunities for recovery and expansion which were not open to Catalonia, as a Mediterranean state. In this sense, the Portuguese ruling nation had positive economic incentives to revolt which were lacking for Catalonia. But, insofar as economic considerations guided the decisions of either the Catalan or the Portuguese ruling class, the dominant consideration was probably a negative one: to save themselves from the economic disaster which stared them in the face.

There is a world of difference, though, between disenchantment with a regime and the willingness to rise against it, or at least to remain neutral when it is attacked. The final, and most important, precondition for revolt by the ruling class, or by influential sections of it, is that it should have the opportunity to act with a reasonable prospect of success. This opportunity was provided by the weakening of the Spanish Monarchy in 1639–40. During these two years it became increasingly apparent that the balance in the Thirty Years' War was tilting against Spain. Defeats on land and sea—particularly the great naval defeat at the Battle of the Downs in October, 1639—had undermined the prestige of Spanish arms, and hence, also, the authority of the Spanish crown. This growing weakness of Spain abroad was accompanied by growing pressure by the central government at home, as it desperately attempted to extract more men and money from the provinces of Spain.

In Catalonia in the opening months of 1640, the behavior of the royal army billeted in the principality provoked a spontaneous peasant uprising which swept everything before it. The king's army disintegrated before the eyes of the Catalans, and as this happened the impotence of Castile was devastatingly revealed. The collapse of royal power in the principality, together with the great upsurge of popular protest, pushed the supreme representatives of the Catalan nation, the *diputats*, into deciding whether they would take command of events or be commanded by them.

In assuming the leadership of the movement of protest, the *diputats* were enormously strengthened by Catalonia's inheritance of contractualism, which provided them with a cast-iron justification for breaking with the king if he defaulted on his obligations to his vassals. But, in any event, they had judged the national mood correctly. Because the crown's authority had sunk so low, and because the Catalan political nation had been so deeply alienated from the Madrid regime by the events of the past two decades, the governing classes either supported the *diputació* in its assertion of independence or stood watching passively as the drama unfolded before them.

For the Portuguese political nation, six months later, the decision was more easily reached. Madrid had failed to suppress the Catalan revolt, and, in failing, had displayed its weakness to the world. There was no royal army in Portugal, and the immediate dangers of action were minimal, whereas the dangers arising from inaction might be great, especially as Olivares had ordered the Portuguese nobility to join the military campaign against the Catalans. Moreover, the French had made it clear to the Portuguese conspirators, as they had made it clear to the Catalans, that they would be ready to come to their help. This time, unlike 1637, the Portuguese political nation, headed by the duke of Braganza, was prepared to take the plunge. The events of the next few days fully justified the risk. December, 1640, was a *coup d'état*, not a revolution.

During 1640, therefore, the ruling classes in Catalonia and Portugal showed themselves willing to countenance, or to participate in, a revolt against royal authority. The preconditions for this willingness seem to lie both in the constitutional structure of the Spanish Monarchy, with its uneasy combination of centralized government and absentee kingship, and in the policies pursued by Madrid over the preceding twenty years. But these preconditions were not peculiar to Catalonia and Portugal: they applied to the Monarchy as a whole. Yet the Sicilian and Neapolitan aristocracies signally failed to follow the example of their Catalan and Portuguese colleagues in the next great year of revolt, 1647.

There were, certainly, some intimations of a vague aspiration after independence in Sicily and Naples during the 1640s. In Naples, especially, a few nobles entered into intrigues with the French. But in neither territory does one find that deep alienation of the political nation from the crown which made it possible for a few determined leaders in Catalonia and Portugal to strike out in a new political direction. Nor did the political nation in Sicily and Naples seem to possess any clear sense of an ideal community or *patria* which might serve as an alternative focus of loyalty. Compared with Catalonia and Portugal, Spain's Italian possessions enjoyed only a limited degree of autonomy. The institutional barriers against royal power had been eroded during the sixteenth century. The parliaments of both Sicily and Naples were easily managed by the viceroys; and the Sicilian deputation, so far from behaving like the Catalan *diputació* as the watchdog of the community's liberties, met weekly in the viceregal palace and required viceregal ratification for its proceedings.[9]

This weakness of the representative institutions reflected, and helped to encourage, an absence of communal spirit on any national scale. Regional rivalries were acute. The feud between Palermo and Messina, for instance, made united action impossible in Sicily in the revolt of 1647.[10] This lack of any real feeling of political coherence in Naples and Sicily seems to have deprived them of what proved to be an essential precondition

[9] Denis Mack Smith, *Medieval Sicily, 800–1713* (London: Chatto & Windus, 1968), p. 132.
[10] Koenigsberger, "The Revolt of Palermo in 1647," p. 144.

for an effective movement of protest by the governing classes of the kind achieved in Portugal and Catalonia.

Sicily and Naples, then, lacked both the communal spirit and the institutional defenses enjoyed by the Portuguese and the Catalans. The implications of this lack for their economic and social life were far-reaching. Because they were unable to protect themselves from fiscal demands by the crown, they were systematically exploited by Madrid to a degree that would have been unthinkable in Catalonia and Portugal. From the 1620s, as the crown demanded more and more money for its war effort, this exploitation became intense.[11] In particular, enormous sums were extracted from Naples in the decade before the rising of 1647, in spite of the protests of successive viceroys that Madrid was demanding the impossible. But, in order to secure its Italian remittances, the Madrid regime was forced to concur in a long series of local concessions, which ended by drastically altering the balance of power in the viceroyalty of Naples.

This change in the balance of power, which has recently been brilliantly analyzed by Rosario Villari,[12] may be summarily described as a gradual abandonment of the state's functions and their assumption by the local aristocracy. During the sixteenth century, the viceregal government in Naples had to some extent been able to keep the Neapolitan baronage at arm's length, and to hold a balance between the nobles and the communes. But, from the 1620s, in Naples, as in Sicily, the viceroys could meet the fiscal requirements of Madrid only by selling offices and rights of jurisdiction and by alienating royal demesne in increasingly large quantities. At the same time, the viceroys needed the assistance of the aristocracy in raising taxes from an impoverished countryside. Under the pressure of fiscal necessity, therefore, the viceregal administration in Naples sold out to the aristocracy. The nobles were able to restore family fortunes which had foundered at the end of the sixteenth century. They extended their control over the countryside; they encroached increasingly on the shrinking rights of the communes, which had traditionally looked to the viceroy for protection; they ac-

---

[11] See Mack Smith, *Medieval Sicily*, pp. 206–8, and R. Villari, "Baronaggio e finanza a Napoli alla vigilia della rivoluzione del 1647–48," *Studi Storici* 3 (1962):263; see also G. Coniglio, *Il Viceregno di Napoli nel Sec. XVII* (Rome: Edizioni di Storia e Letteratura, 1955), pt. 3.
[12] *La Rivolta Antispagnola a Napoli* (Bari, 1967).

quired an increasing influence in the city of Naples itself; and they infiltrated the viceregal administration. As a result, royal authority, and indeed state power itself, virtually collapsed in Naples in the early 1640s. The nobles were in control.

This aristocratization of public life in Naples, and to a lesser degree in Sicily, virtually destroyed the possibility of a Portuguese-style movement for independence among the political nation. The governing class in Spain's Italian possessions was heavily dependent upon the crown—for titles, for posts, for concessions of jurisdiction—and at the same time satisfactorily independent of it, in the sense that it was now powerful enough to behave more or less as it pleased. In these circumstances, there was no incentive to revolt.

In Naples and Sicily, then, the commanding position achieved by the nobles with royal assistance in the 1630s and 1640s drastically reduced the possibilities of serious political conflict with Madrid. It was true that Madrid was exploiting their homelands; but they lacked a sense of communal loyalty, and in any event they were enjoying more than their fair share of the plunder. The relative absence of *political* conflict, however, was more than offset by the acute *social* conflict which such excessive aristocratic dominance ensured. From the early years of the seventeenth century there was, in effect, permanent civil war in the Neapolitan countryside—a civil war developing out of a bandit movement which was partly an expression of baronial feuds but also a reflection of deeply felt rural demands for social justice and a more equitable distribution of wealth.[13]

Aristocratic oppression built up strong resentments, which inevitably spilled over from the countryside into the towns, as the nobles encroached increasingly on municipal rights and tightened their grip on municipal government. The cities themselves seethed with unrest, for rural misery in Sicily and Naples had driven more and more countrymen into the towns, and Palermo and Naples were among the largest European cities by the middle of the seventeenth century. Urbanization on this scale brought acute problems of food supply and employment. This in turn meant that there was a large urban population which was restless, hungry, and insecure—ready material for revolt.

[13] See the program of Marco Sciarra, *ibid.*, p. 67.

As popular passions reached explosion point, a leader would emerge from among the populace. In Palermo, it was first a miller, Antonio La Pilosa, and then a gold-beater, Giuseppe d'Alesi. In Naples, it was Masaniello, a fisherman, and then, after his murder, Gennaro Annese, an illiterate blacksmith. These men were the symbols, the heroes, and sometimes the victims of the popular movements they led; and at times, as with Alesi and Masaniello, they were even more potent in death than in life. Legends gathered around them, for they embodied the aspirations of a populace which saw in their meteoric careers the fulfillment of impossible dreams. Masaniello, raised from rags to riches, and appointed captain general by the viceroy, symbolized the triumph of the people over their traditional oppressors, the nobles. He symbolized, too, the fulfillment of another popular dream—the restoration of what was assumed to be a traditional and historic alliance between the king and the people. For in Naples and Sicily there survived in folk memory the blurred image of a time when the people had participated in government, before the nobles took away their rights. Among the literate sections of urban society there were men, especially lawyers and clerics, who were ready enough to sharpen these memories and to articulate popular grievances. Behind Masaniello stood Genoino, the aged lawyer who had devoted his life to the study and advocacy of the people's historic rights.

At the popular level, therefore, just as much as among the upper ranks of society in some parts of the Spanish Monarchy, an idealized history helped to provide both a program for action and theoretical justification for movements of revolt. But, where aristocratic revolt was directed against the power of the crown, popular revolt was directed against the power of the aristocracy, and aspired to restore a golden age in which social justice was maintained by the joint action of the king and his people.

Urban revolt, when it came, was therefore likely to take the form of an attack on the socially dominant groups rather than on the government of the viceroy, although the latter was often to blame for the immediate causes of distress. In Naples and Palermo in 1647 the *precipitants* of revolt were rising food prices, forced up by dearth and taxes. But the *preconditions* were to be found in social and economic grievances, which united town and country in a great movement of protest against a social system that had become more inequitable and oppressive as the result of Madrid's policies during the preceding two decades. This discontent at once determined the character and limited the possibilities of the Italian risings. Because they were directed primarily against the existing social system, they could not expect the elite participation that was indispensable for any lasting degree of success. Confused in their leadership, uncertain in their aspirations, they died away as dramatically as they had flared up—anguished and spontaneous outbursts which were doomed to disappointment.

There was, then, a paradox about the revolts of Sicily and Naples. Madrid's policies had created a situation conducive to revolt, but it was the type of revolt which was least likely to endanger Spanish control over the Italian territories. Threatened by social upheaval, the local elites could be expected to support the royal government in suppressing a rising directed primarily against themselves. In these circumstances, Madrid's only real cause for alarm lay in the possibility of effective French intervention. A French presence, strong enough to stamp out social unrest, might have deflected the loyalty of the Neapolitan ruling class from the king of Spain. Failing this presence, Naples would not become another Portugal.

In Naples and Sicily, therefore, we have a popular movement, but no serious movement by the dominant social groups. In Portugal we have a movement by the political nation, but no popular movement, except insofar as the populace showed itself to be solidly behind the action taken by its governing class. We are left, then, with Catalonia as the one example among these four revolts of action by the political nation in conjunction with a popular uprising. But if we approach this popular uprising expecting to find preconditions, in the sense of Professor Stone's "long-run, underlying causes," we are likely to be disappointed. There were, admittedly, serious social tensions in seventeenth-century Catalonia. Sporadic banditry pointed to unrest in the countryside, where the rural gentry often exercised a tyrannical control over their vassals, and where the stabilizing presence of a solid and substantial class of landed peasants was to some extent offset by the chronic instability of the landless laborers. There were tensions, too, in the towns, where the oligarchical control of urban government and the exclusiveness of the guilds had created widespread bitterness. But the discontent of the lowest groups in rural and urban society probably ran less deep in Catalonia than in Naples or Sicily, and it would be misleading to see a "revolutionary situation" developing during the 1630s, so far as popular revolution is concerned.

The popular revolution, when it came in 1640, was provoked not by unbearable internal pressures but by an extraneous element—the king's army, billeted in Catalan homes and living off the wealth of the Catalan countryside. It was the behavior of the troops, and the extortions of royal officials, desperately attempting to ensure that the army had enough to eat, which drove the Catalan peasantry to revolt. This revolt spread from the countryside to Barcelona and the other towns of the principality, and was directed in the first instance against the troops and against royal officials and collaborators. The very fact that these were the prime targets of attack indicates the character of the uprising in its early stages—a vast and spontaneous outburst of popular anger against the men who were destroying the Catalans' homes and their country. Once the soldiers had been driven out of the country, and the royal officials had been tracked down and killed, the popular uprising began to change its tune. The collapse of authority enabled discontented elements to seize the initiative and to pay off old scores. The oligarchs and the rich replaced royal officials as the objects of popular wrath. Social upheaval thus followed in the wake of the popular uprising until the political nation, with French assistance, again recovered a degree of control over a restless principality.

It would seem, therefore, that, for all the elements of social discontent which colored the Catalan revolt after its first euphoric moments, events in Catalonia bore a much closer resemblance to those in Portugal than to the Italian insurrections. In both Portugal and Catalonia in 1640, anti-Castilian sentiment was sufficiently powerful at all levels of society to provide at least a temporary basis for action on a national scale. The Catalan and Portuguese revolts were "nationalist" uprisings, in the sense that all classes of society were momentarily drawn together in a common movement of protest against the threat posed to the community's survival by the agents of royal authority. In Sicily and Naples, on the other hand, heavier royal pressure at an earlier stage had helped to undermine such community consciousness as existed, and sectional divisions precluded corporate action. It is true that sectional divisions ran deep in Catalonia also. But for a few months in 1640 the community reasserted itself over individual and sectional interests; and during those months the official representatives of the community, the *diputats*, provided leadership which showed itself uniquely responsive to the popular mood.

Yet, if the Iberian and the Italian insurrections assumed different characteristics and moved in different directions, the preconditions for revolt in Italy and the Spanish peninsula were fundamentally similar. Catalonia, Portugal, Naples, and Sicily were all societies governed by remote control from Madrid, and more immediately by viceroys who could not fully compensate for the absence of the royal person. All of them fell victim to the fiscal and military demands of the Spanish crown, which was gradually succumbing beneath the weight of a disastrous war. This pressure from Madrid involved an increasingly indiscriminate and ruthless exploitation of every available source of wealth. Catalonia and Portugal were sufficiently strong to prevent this exploitation from becoming excessive, but Naples and Sicily were not. Hence the differences in their revolts. The Sicilian and Neapolitan risings were born of distress—the distress of an exploited population venting its anger on a governing class which had found that its most profitable line of action lay in cooperating with Madrid. The Catalan and Portuguese risings were born of fear—the fear that their societies would soon go the way of Naples and Sicily, and, most of all, of Castile. In one instance, misery proved a precondition of revolt; in the other, a relative prosperity. But behind all four revolts the same phenomenon was to be found: the relentless fiscal pressure exerted by an alien government which was facing defeat in war.

A Note on Further Reading

The four revolts discussed in this lecture have not, to the best of my knowledge, been taken together and examined on a comparative basis by earlier historians. R. B. Merriman, in his *Six Contemporaneous Revolutions* (Oxford: The Clarendon Press, 1938), devoted a chapter apiece to the Catalan, Portuguese, and Neapolitan rebellions, but neglected the Sicilian rising. His accounts of the revolts were narrative rather than analytical, and he was more concerned with the relationship between the various revolts than with their similarities and differences. In attempting a comparative survey I have therefore had recourse to studies of the individual revolts, and some of these studies are patently inadequate for answering the kind of questions which historians tend to ask today. In particular, the Portuguese revolution badly needs a detailed modern analysis. Although F. Mauro's *Le Portugal et L'Atlantique au XVIIe Siècle* (Paris: S.E.V.P.E.N., 1960) is an important examination of certain aspects of Portuguese economic life, neither our knowledge nor our understanding of the background and origins of the events in Portugal has made much progress since the publication of L. A. Rebello da Silva's *Historia de Portugal nos seculos XVII e XVIII*, vols. 3 and 4 (Lisbon, 1867–69); and the clearest account of Olivares' Portuguese policy is still to be found in A. Cánovas del Castillo's *Estudios del Reinado de Felipe IV* (Madrid, 1888). The revolt of Catalonia, on the other hand, has received considerable attention, of a revisionist nature, in the past few years. Pierre Vilar's *La Catalogne dans l'Espagne Moderne*, vol. 1 (Paris, 1962), is a superb study of the Catalan economy and society which sets the revolt firmly in the context of earlier developments in Catalonia. J. H. Elliott, in his *The Revolt of the Catalans* (Cambridge: Cambridge University Press, 1963), examines in detail the evolution of Madrid's Catalan policy and the nature of the Catalan response. The story of events after 1640 is carried on by J. Sanabre in *La Acción de Francia en Cataluna en la pugna por la hegemonía de Europa (1640–1659)* (Real Academia de Buenas Letras, Barcelona, 1956).

Study of the Italian revolts has also been patchy, although some interesting and important work has been done in recent years. The most accessible approach to Sicily for English readers is provided by Denis Mack Smith, whose *Medieval Sicily, 800–1713* (London, 1968), contains a chapter on the Palermo revolt of 1647. This uprising is more closely analyzed by H. G. Koenigsberger in "The Revolt of Palermo in 1647," *Cambridge Historical Journal* 8 (1946): 129–44. A useful but limited introduction to the troubles in Naples is to be found in M. Schipa's *Masaniello* (French translation, Paris, 1930). It is now possible to obtain a clearer idea of Spanish fiscal policy and its consequences thanks to G. Coniglio, whose *Il Viceregno di Napoli nel secolo XVII: Notizie sulla vita commerciale e finanziaria* appeared in 1955. But the most exciting new approach to the revolt is provided by R. Villari in his *La Rivolta Antispagnola a Napoli* (Bari, 1967). This volume, however, is primarily concerned with rural developments, and it is greatly to be hoped that a sequel will appear which will offer an equally illuminating account of events in the city of Naples itself.

4 | The Fronde

The purpose of this essay is not to describe the "precipitants" of that major revolt, the *Fronde* (1648–53), not to consider, that is, the events which directly provoked the acts of rebellion and the government's reaction to them. Rather, it is to expose, through an analysis not only of the revolt itself but also of the struggles and interactions among the many diverse groups within French society, the fundamental tensions and clashes of social and political interests which can be traced back through the first half of the seventeenth century and seem to be almost permanent features of French society. An understanding of these "preconditions" is necessary to any explanation of the revolt and reveals the extent to which the *Fronde* was the expression of a deeply troubled society and state.

The first and most important precondition of the *Fronde* was war. From 1614 to 1629 civil war troubled France, and beginning in 1624 she was for the next several decades deeply involved in the Thirty Years' War. Between 1624 and 1635 she participated in that war indirectly, supporting the enemies of the Habsburgs. She supplied the Netherlands, Sweden, and the Swiss Grisons with money, seizing fortresses in Lorraine, Alsace, Switzerland, and Germany, particularly on the Moselle and Rhine rivers, and others in Italy, such as Pignerol. In this manner, France cut the military roads used by the Spanish government to send troops, weapons, and money to the rescue of their brothers, the Austrian Habsburgs, and to the Spanish Netherlands. The French also seized the "gates" and "avenues" through which the Spanish and the Austrians could have invaded

France. This was the so-called *guerre couverte,* the "cold war." But the Habsburgs defeated their adversaries one after the other. After the Swedish disaster at Nordlingen (1634), Richelieu decided to attack the Habsburgs openly and directly. In 1635 Louis XIII declared war on the Spanish, and after 1635 France was officially at war with the Habsburgs of both Austria and Spain and their allies. This was the *guerre ouverte,* the open war. The Peace of Westphalia in 1648 did not end the war for France. Mazarin continued the war with Spain until the Peace of the Pyrenees in 1659. Although some Frenchmen thought of European hegemony, of conquests including all the left bank of the Rhine and of extending France's borders to match those of ancient Gaul, the aims of the royal government were limited to maintaining France's independence, ending Habsburg claims to world hegemony, and securing those territories necessary to France's defense against invasion.

But not all Frenchmen understood the royal policy. Many of them, the "good Catholics," the old *Ligueurs,* even those close to the king at his court—the mother of Louis XIII, Marie de Medicis, for instance, and the Keeper of the Seals, Michel de Marillac, the Queen Mother's *créature*—supported the Spanish "Catholic king." They believed that the Habsburg policy was only a struggle against heresy, an effort to re-establish Catholicism, and they blamed the royal council for the war and alliances with Protestant adversaries of the Habsburgs. They were prepared to resist royal demands and even to revolt and ally with Spain. At the very least, they pleaded for peace and resisted a major war effort. Still others, willing to take part in the struggle against the Habsburgs, believed that the French government could have concluded peace earlier and prolonged the war only to justify abuses of power and extortion of money. The government was partly responsible. Richelieu often claimed that peace was at hand, and Mazarin declared on several occasions that peace depended on his taking unilateral action.

These long and difficult wars demanded a major national effort and placed a heavy strain on French resources. The royal government was obliged to adapt to the war, to become a war government, resembling a dictatorship or monocracy rather than a kingship or monarchy. It became increasingly necessary to compel everyone, especially the royal family and royal officials, to obey immediately and completely. It became necessary to stop defeatist or enemy propaganda by any means and to foster patriotism and a military frame of mind. Above all, it was vitally important that the government find money for the troops; clothe and feed them; buy weapons, guns, and powder; arrange transportation; repair and build some fortresses and destroy others; and supply allies, such as the rebellious Dutch, Portuguese, Catalans, and Hungarians. The government greatly increased all kinds of taxes. It not only established new ones but even imposed some of them on towns or corporate bodies traditionally exempt from ordinary taxes. Thus it repeatedly violated provincial and local liberties and privileges in order to find money and it even created a sort of revolutionary administration—staffed by tax farmers, *traitants* or *partisans,* supplemented by royal commissioners, *intendants,* and soldiers— which replaced the ordinary officials in the execution of royal power.

Let us look, for example, at the financial district, the *généralité,* of Bordeaux. The most important tax, the *taille* extracted one million French livres tournois from 1610 to 1632, but it rose to more than two million in 1635, three in 1644, and almost four million in 1648—a fourfold increase in sixteen years at a time when prices stagnated and then fell. But along with the *taille* the people paid other taxes, most of them for the army: the *taillon* for the heavy cavalry and provisions for the regular troops at the Spanish border, in garrisons, winter quarters, and the like. Soldiers had the right to quarters and food in private homes, including the so-called *ustensile*—that is, "bed, linnen, dish, bowl, glass, and a place near the fire and the candle." The population had to furnish food, and, even though the soldiers did pay, the money they used was drawn from a special tax levied by the province or by the municipality. The local inhabitants claimed that the provisions were equal to another *taille.* In fact, the soldier took what he needed, and the burden was even greater. To these exactions were added various *aides* and demesnial taxes, which were placed on an increasing number of daily necessities. In a few years hundreds of new taxes came into being. To these taxes, one must add the levies of men. Each year the militia furnished to the army a troop of soldiers, complete with uniforms, equipment, and weapons and paid for by the municipalities or rural communities. The armies thus drew labor from agriculture and handicrafts at a time when most productive work was manual. Rural communities and town municipalities were obliged to send men, horses, and carts for the demolition of noble châteaux which Richelieu had ordered or for wall construction and trench digging. They were obliged to supply food to the men and horses and to pay for the workers and for transportation. In some parishes these expenses reached two or three times the *taille*. Finally, the financial officials were paid in proportion to the taxes levied. In some cases these extra sums increased taxes by two-thirds.

Moreover, this deluge of taxes fell on the French people at a time when their ability to pay had declined because of the prolonged economic recession of the seventeenth century. Commerce with Spanish America had become less and less active, and imports of gold and silver had diminished every year to the point that these metals were very scarce by 1650. As far as one can determine, the secular increase of prices was slowed down until about 1630; prices as a whole stagnated from 1630 to 1640 and then fell. As a result, both peasant and artisan had smaller profits and less money with which to pay their taxes.

The seventeenth century was also a period of extensive atmospheric calamity; winters were very hard, seed froze in the ground, and heavy summer rainfalls prevented the crops from ripening. Harvests were bad and consequently the price of bread, the principal food, was high. Scarcity of food, epidemics, plagues, and a high death rate followed the classic pattern. Contemporaries referred to these collectively as *mortalités*. The most serious *mortalités* occurred between 1630 and 1632 and led to the disorganization of the entire French economy. They reached another high in 1648–53, at the time of the *Fronde*.

Consider the Province of Guyenne. In 1627 there were heavy floods, followed in 1628 by abnormal cold. Food became scarce. The winter of 1629 also was severe. In March, 1629, torrential rains flooded the crops; there was no harvest in 1630; in 1631 there was famine. The scarcity of food was felt even more in the lower Garonne valley, where wine had become almost the only produce of the land. Crops were relegated to unfloodable pastures. In the Bazadais there was almost no arable land at all. Nor did the country quickly recuperate these losses; from

1629 to 1639 hailstorms destroyed the vineyards in the middle Garonne and along the Charente. Spring rainfalls ruined the soil in Armagnac, Lomagne, and Condomois. As a result, the inhabitants of Guyenne were miserable.

This hungry population easily fell victim to plagues. About 1625 a serious plague spread throughout Europe. It struck Burgundy in 1626. From there it spread to the Loire valley, then to the center of France, reaching Languedoc in 1628, Agen and the Garonne valley in 1629, then La Rochelle, and finally all of Saintonge. The summer of 1631 was the worst. Thereafter the disease abated, but reappeared in sudden bursts. In 1652–53 there was another epidemic as deadly as that of 1631.

The first consequence of these epidemics was the loss of productive labor—artisans and farm workers died in greater numbers than the members of other social groups. In Moissac about twenty-three people died every year, but during the summer of 1629 there were 55 deaths. At Caprais de l'Herme, where one counted 4 deaths in a normal year, there were 118 in 1631. Frequently, one-third of the inhabitants were lost in a single *mortalité*. The second consequence was the cessation of commerce. Well-to-do persons fled to their country houses. Municipal governments forbade strangers to enter the towns or *bourgs,* suspended fairs and markets, and refused goods from other regions. These actions created an economic crisis.

By prolonged hunger and epidemics the provinces were impoverished. After two or three bad harvests, many of the inhabitants of the rural parishes, usually small landowners, became paupers. Houses and villages were deserted. In 1634 only six inhabitants remained in the village of Espaignet. A large number of the population became vagrants. They went from Limousin and Auvergne to Angoumois and Périgord, from Quercy and Rouergue to the Garonne, from the provinces devastated by the armies—Lorraine, Champagne, Picardie—to the Ile de France and Paris, thus spreading the diseases. They went from the poorest regions to the less poor and from the country to the towns, which were better stocked and protected. In 1628 six thousand vagrants from Limousin crowded at the gates of Perigueux, flooding the suburbs of the town. The land was not cultivated. Prices fell. The small owners sold out for a pittance to the large. Between 1632 and 1648 the land survey (the *cam-*

poix), in Guyenne, which had been drawn up from 1598 to 1612 to serve as a tax base, had to be redone several times. Municipalities and rural communities went into debt to treat the sick and feed the hungry. The dire consequences of one *mortalité* were not over before another one came, and after 1630 France underwent increasingly serious economic and social difficulties, which at times reached catastrophic proportions.

The result was a permanent state of unrest. Disturbances grew more and more frequent, and revolts ripened. Cases of bodily assault became more frequent before the judicial courts. These included attacks on tax collectors, privileged people partially exempt from taxes, sergeants-at-arms and other officials attempting to enforce tax collection, as well as on inhabitants of neighboring villages accused of not paying their proper share of the financial burden. Some noblemen, barons, and chevaliers were put under arrest for such assaults and for having led their peasants against the financial officers of the king. In other cases one finds the classic riots aimed at preventing the sale of grain outside the province or town, protesting the high price of bread, or pillaging the grain stocks of the Church. In a number of cases there were spontaneous riots against soldiers. On 8 July 1640, a company of light cavalry passed at sunset near the village of Les Granges. Convinced that the cavalrymen intended to quarter in their houses, the peasants attacked them with pikes and muskets. Isolated riots could easily lead to organized revolt.

The regions most affected by these events were situated to the west and south of a dividing line running roughly from Rouen to Geneva. Generally speaking, north and east of this line were the large, open, rectangular fields, the large-scale farms (*grande culture*) of the eighteenth-century French agronomists; west and south of the line were the small, irregular, enclosed fields, where small-scale farming was practiced. The open fields existed in agricultural areas organized for the grain trade, where large farmers (*gros fermiers*) with capitalistic means cultivated extensive areas, using salaried *valêts*, servants, and day laborers. These men had the means to withstand bad harvests and to recover after them. They were interested in maintaining the social order and in disciplining the poor, to whom they gave work and wages. Generally speaking, although this northeastern region might be ravaged by the armies of rebellious princes and foreign powers, it did not participate in the rebellions to any great extent. There were more tensions and disturbances in the regions of enclosed fields, where modest sharecroppers, with the help of their families and one or two hired hands, cultivated small or medium-sized farms for their own subsistence. They usually had only small grain reserves, and two successive bad harvests brought them to the brink of poverty. Under these circumstances royal taxes and seigneurial dues easily became too heavy for them and they revolted. But usually they revolted against the financial officials of the crown, and if they burned houses or châteaux, they were the houses and châteaux of the financial officials, not those of the *gentilshommes*, the local military nobility. Only rarely did they attack individual *gentilshommes*, and never the seigneurial system. In fact, *gentilshommes* often protected their peasants from the royal financial agents. Recall also that the French seigneurial system in the seventeenth century admitted that the peasant *censitaires* were real owners of their tenure and that the law protected them from eviction by the seigneurs.

Members of the royal family and the great noble families of the realm, the so-called *grands*—the dukes, marquis, counts, and barons—revolted frequently during the period from the death of Henri IV (1610) to the *Fronde* (1648). A series of conspiracies revolved around the princes of the blood and especially around Marie de Medicis and Gaston d'Orleans, respectively the mother and brother of Louis XIII, as they and their antagonists sought to foment uprisings and civil strife in a bitter struggle for influence and power at court and in the country. There was the uprising of 1615–16, involving the princes of the blood; the uprising of Marie de Medicis in 1618–20; the conspiracies of Ornano and Chalais in 1626; the plotting of Marie de Medicis; the "Day of the Dupes" of 10 November 1630; the disgrace of the Queen Mother; the exile of the king's devoted keeper of the seals, Marillac; the arrest and condemnation of his brother, marshall of France and commander-in-chief of the armies, executed at Rueil on 8 May 1632; the desertion in Lorraine, a foreign and enemy country, of Gaston, whose companions were declared guilty of high treason in a royal proclamation on 30

March 1631; the uprising of Henri de Montmorency in Languedoc, crushed in 1632; new conspiracies of Gaston, the other
princes of the blood, and the *grands*, who allied with the Spanish during 1636 and 1637; the conspiracy of Gaston d'Orleans,
the count of Soissons, the duke of Bouillon, the duke of Guise,
and other princes and officials of the crown, defeated in 1641;
the conspiracy of the king's favorite, Cinq-Mars, *grand écuyer*
of France, and Gaston, duke of Bouillon, with Spain in 1642,
which ended with the decapitation of Cinq-Mars; the conspiracies after the death of Louis XIII; and finally, the uprising of
Gaston d'Orleans, the princes of Condé and Conti, and other
grands during the *Fronde*.

The revolts of the princes and the *grands* certainly involved
selfish interests, but they also had a constitutional basis.
Although the kingdom of France had no written constitution
similar to those which later appeared during the revolt of the
British colonies in North America, it possessed a customary constitution, "inscribed in the heart of every Frenchman," composed
of royal edicts registered by the parlements and of certain habits
and customs, all of which constituted the so-called fundamental
laws of the kingdom—a *de facto* constitution. The princes
claimed that these fundamental laws had been violated by the
king and that their revolts were legitimate because they were
an attempt to re-establish the customary constitution. Although
it was vested in one king, since the time of Hughes Capet, government had been considered the business of the entire royal family. The kings recognized the right of the members of their
families to participate in the government, and royal edicts and
ordinances were prefaced by the statement that the king had
consulted his mother, his brothers, and the princes of the blood.

One consequence of this theory was that when the king was
a minor (Louis XIII until 1614, and Louis XIV until 1651, at the
time of the *Fronde*), the government was in the hands of a
council headed by the senior uncle of the king, Monsieur, duke
of Orleans, and composed of the princes of the blood and of
other princes and *grands* personally loyal to him. By an edict
of Charles V, the king attained legal majority at the beginning
of his fourteenth year. Thereafter, the decisions of his government were represented as his personal decisions. No one had the
right to disobey a decision of the king himself. However, the
publicists writing for the princes insisted that, although he was

legally adult, the king was still a minor in age until he was at least twenty-one. They also added that, in fact, he was the tool of confidants and tyrants, a prisoner of their wishes. Hence the princes agreed that until 1621 (in the case of Louis XIII) and until 1658 (under Louis XIV) the princes should have made government policy in the name of the king. Because these conditions had not existed, the princes claimed that they had both a right and a duty to revolt.

Furthermore, when the king came of age, he was supposed to govern by himself. It was generally agreed by everyone that the king should be a ruler, acting personally, deciding policy, and giving orders himself. His obligations were, first of all, to take the advice of his natural councilors—the princes of the blood, the other princes, the *grands*—and of all persons who had become councilors of state through high office, such as the officers of the crown, the chancellor of state, or the constable. The king could not compose his council at will. Secondly, he was morally obliged to observe the ordinances of God, the oath at his coronation, which constituted a sort of contract between king and people through which he obliged himself to protect their lives, property, religion (against any kind of heresy), and liberties and privileges. He was obliged to observe the fundamental laws of the kingdom, such as the *lex salica,* for without these laws he would not have been king. His royal prerogative came from the fundamental laws: they preceded him, were beyond his power, and served as the legal basis of his kingship. Finally, he was obliged to observe the ordinances of his predecessors and his own, and if it became necessary to change them he could do so only with the consent of his council of state and, in very important cases, only with the consent of the Estates-General of the realm. But neither Henri IV, nor Louis XIII, nor Louis XIV acted in this way, even when Henri IV and Louis XIII were mature men. Especially the sickly Louis XIII and the boy Louis XIV left the government to their *créatures,* their favorites, in times when so many difficulties arose on all sides. Some of these "prime ministers of state" were mere adventurers who had fraudulently obtained the king's confidence or that of the Queen Mother—Concini or Luynes, for example; sometimes they were able statesmen such as Richelieu or Mazarin, devoted to the person of the king.

Formally, the king governed through a council of state, filled with his personal *créatures* or the *créatures* of his prime minister, all of whom were considered favorites of the king. He appointed such *créatures* as secretaries of state, financial superintendent, or chancellor. These men in turn suggested to the king their own *créatures* for appointment as royal commissioners to promulgate the royal orders everywhere and to compel everyone to execute them. Such were the members of some extraordinary judicial courts who judged certain *traitants* and *partisans* accused of theft, or certain governors of towns who had capitulated too easily before the enemy, or some noblemen suspected of treason. Among them were the famous *intendants*, men supervising the armies at the front and dispatched to the provinces to subject everyone to the royal will. The *intendants* brought with them terror not unlike that of 1793. A chain of *créatures* entirely devoted to their protector, their master, their patron, extended from the king to the humblest peasant, exacting obedience from everyone.

The maxim of all these men was "reason of state." The welfare of the state, the greatness of the state as a condition for the welfare of all the people and for their happiness, was the supreme goal and the supreme law. To reach this goal the king and his ministers were free to ignore existing laws, liberties, privileges, and rights. They were entitled to change every law, violate every privilege, encroach on every liberty, reject every right. They were not even bound to their promises or oaths. *Salus publica* was the supreme law, and the king and his ministers were the only judges of the means to procure this common welfare. Even if the subjects of the king disapproved of his policy and acts and judged him absolutely wrong and his acts absolutely bad, the king, as God's lieutenant and inspired by Him, obliged them by their conscience to obey his orders without delay.

Although the princes would have used the same absolute power and the same reason of state had they been masters in the council of state, they and their publicists severely criticized this policy and advocated the old customary constitution. In doing so, they gained the general sympathy of the inhabitants of the kingdom. For most of them, this dictatorial government was a tyranny. And the tyrannicide theory of the religious wars had not been forgotten: when a king became a tyrant it was the duty of the princes and magistrates to correct him. If he did not change his ways, it was their duty to seize and depose him. And a simple citizen, if moved by the spirit of God, could kill him. In this case, killing was not murder. Even those who thought it was their duty to obey the king and who understood the necessity of the wartime dictatorship were not entirely at ease and hoped that the new measures would be temporary. Many followed the princes, believing that they were right and that it was morally necessary to renew the customary constitution.

When they revolted the princes used their faithful followers. One of the bases of this society was personal loyalty, *fidelité*. Some men gave themselves entirely to a superior. They served him with everything at their disposal: counsel, sword, pen, speech, propaganda, intrigue, treason—even, if necessary, offering their lives to their master and following him in revolt against king and state or allying themselves with a foreign enemy against their own country. The superior was their master, their protector, their patron. They were his faithful, his devoted, his *créatures*. The *créatures* wanted and obtained from their master favor, protection, confidence, friendship, clothing, food, lodging, a place in the army or in the officer corps, an honorable marriage, and social advancement. Voluntary mutual affection and devotion were the basis of this fidelity, a personal link between two men. This was not feudalism, because the inferior did not render to the superior *foi et hommage* and did not expect a fief in return. This was a social relationship *sui generis*—fidelity. Not only were there some noblemen—military or civil officials—among the faithful, but commoners as well, most of them officials, lawyers, attorneys, and other members of the *petite robe*. The king himself could not have governed without his *créatures*, who served him faithfully more because of their special oath of fidelity to him as their patron than because he was the legal head of state. When the state collapsed during the *Fronde*, the king and kingship were saved by a few thousand *créatures* of the young king who remained faithful to him because they were his men, his devoted. The princes also had *créatures*, and these *créatures* had their *créatures* in turn. Because of these chains of fidelity, when the princes revolted they were followed by thousands of people throughout the kingdom, and even by whole provinces.

The war government of the king's favorites, ministers, and commissioners encountered the bitter opposition and frequent revolt of the corporate bodies of officials. The most important bodies of ordinary judicial officials were the courts of the *bailliages* or *sénéchaussées*, the *présidiaux*, and the sovereign courts —parlements, *Chambres des Comptes*, and *Cours des Aides*. There were also courts of justice for financial affairs, exercising both a judicial and an administrative power, the bodies of the *elus*, and above them the *trésoriers généraux de France*, who were considered members of the sovereign courts. The *Greniers à Sel* were primarily courts of justice for all affairs concerning the royal salt monopoly. The *Maîtrises des Eaux et Forêts*, the *Monnaies*, and other minor courts completed an elaborate hierarchy. Most of these added the quality of *conseiller du roi* to their office, which should not be confused with the office of *conseiller d'état*. All of these magistrates had the same conception of their duties: they owed the king fidelity, that is to say, obedience. But they also owed respect to the dignity of their offices, that is to say, respect for justice, equity, moral and positive laws, and for a kind of constitutional balance between the king and his subjects. Thus they owed the people in their jurisdictions protection against the absolute power of the king. These last two obligations often caused them to delay the execution of royal orders which did not seem to them to meet the conditions of equity and justice and to request new ones. They also felt obliged to respect the legal forms, which constituted protection for the king's subjects. In 1630, for instance, the *trésoriers de France* received the order to levy the *taille* and the *crue de garnisons* before the royal edicts had been registered by the Parlement of Bordeaux and the *Chambre des Comptes*. The *trésoriers* refused to proceed, because previous royal edicts prohibited them from levying any tax ordered by the absolute power of the king without an edict registered by the sovereign courts.

When they believed a royal order was wrong, these *conseillers du roi* had the duty and the right to present a remonstrance to the king, pointing out the ways in which these orders were erroneous or apt to lead to unfortunate consequences. This right of remonstrance sometimes resulted in amendments or withdrawal of royal orders or in the confirmation of the king's will. It was the duty not only of the sovereign courts but of all corporate bodies of officials. The remonstrances of the parlements were significant. By acting in such a manner corporations of officials delayed the execution of royal orders, but parlements could do even more. The officials of the lesser courts, for example, could send remonstrances only once, and, if the king persisted, they had to execute his orders. The parlements, on the other hand, could renew remonstrances six, seven, or even eight times, despite royal order of execution (*lettre de jussion*). Often the officials, instead of directly refusing to obey, waited so long that their procrastination amounted to disobedience and the beginning of rebellion. Such procedures were unacceptable in wartime, and such different conceptions of public function compelled the king to employ special commissioners, among them the so-called *intendants;* Richelieu did not like them, but they enforced the king's authority and mobilized resources for the war. The king also employed tax farmers, the so-called *traitants* or *partisans*. The corporate officials reacted to the use of commissioners and *traitants* as an offense to their dignity, a violation of past ordinances, and an act of tyranny.

Furthermore, the king's actions threatened their material interests and social influence. They were privileged persons and as such were exempt from the *taille* and many other taxes. But in these times of emergency the king found other means to make them contribute to the expenses of the state. The king gave them higher salaries (*gages*) and permitted them to charge higher fees for their professional services. But in exchange he forced them to advance him large capital sums. The operation was in fact a forced loan. The *gages* represented the interest on the capital sums advanced by the officials. In 1648 the *trésoriers de France* as a corporate body claimed to have remitted more than thirty million livres tournois to the royal treasury during the preceding sixteen years. The *elus* claimed to have paid more than two hundred million livres since 1624 and more than sixty million livres since 1640. To meet these obligations the officials were often obliged to borrow money at high interest rates and to tie up their capital. To make matters worse, after 1640 the destitute royal government began to reduce the *gages* and fees of the officials. The *elus,* for example, lost a quarter of their *gages* in 1640, that is, their income for three months from each year. Then there was another reduction, and then another, and finally in 1647 their *gages* were frozen altogether. The government also claimed three-quarters of their private fees. No wonder the officials were heavily indebted to their relatives and friends. The *trésoriers de France* lost the most important part of their *gages* and fees after 1643. It was the same for almost all the officials.

The government also employed other methods which greatly irritated the old officials. It created new offices and sold them, so that the number of officeholders continually increased. There were ten *trésoriers de France* in every *généralité* in 1610; there were twenty-five in 1648. The parlements were also altered. For example, in 1641 Richelieu created a fourth chamber, the *Chambre des Requêtes,* in the Parlement of Provence, which added two presidents, fourteen councilors, two substitutes, twelve attorneys, and a host of clerks, controllers, and *huissiers.* The government also created entire new bodies of officials, a new *élection* in Agenais in 1623, more *présidiaux* in Guyenne and Provence in 1648. However, for the royal treasury the most profitable of these measures was the creation of a new "semester" for each parlement. The operation consisted of requiring the "old officials" to exercise their duties during only six months of the year and creating another group of officials equal in number to the old officials for the other six months. Thus, in October, 1647, the Parlement of Provence adopted the new semester plan. The government created seven presidents, forty-five councilors, two attorneys for the king, one *procureur du roi,* and a number of lesser officials and clerks. The semester was supposed to bring one million livres to the royal treasury from the sale of new offices. The *traitant* Tabouret organized the sales and received his profit on the operation. The Parlement of Normandy had adopted the semester plan in 1641; abolished in 1643, it was re-established in 1645 to satisfy the *traitants.*

The consequences of these innovations were disastrous for the old officials. If they accepted them, they had fewer judgments to hand down, fewer operations to perform, and therefore smaller fees and less influence over the subjects of the king.

Their authority as well as their revenues were diminished. Often they bought the new offices from the king and either succeeded in having them abolished or combined with their own offices, thus receiving the corresponding *gages* and fees. But either way the operation was onerous. In the long run the old officials were unable to buy all the new offices and ended by requesting parlements not to register the edicts creating them. If the parlements were forced by the king to register the edicts, the officials tried to hinder the sale of the offices by threatening potential buyers, murdering some, refusing to receive the new officials, or preventing them from exercising their functions. Sometimes the officials provoked unrest among the populace and even took up arms in revolt. Such was the case in the Parlement of Provence in 1649.

The *intendants* had the same effect on the interests of the officials. After 1635 they had the task of supervising the officials; investigating their conduct and acts; holding them to their duty; rectifying their errors, defects, or misdemeanors; and informing the government of the situation in the provinces. In many cases the *intendants* were ordered to exercise permanently all of the regular functions of the officials, especially of the financial officials, using the most loyal as their commissioners and leaving to the others only the execution of simple legal formalities. The officials lost their reputation, their power, and their profits. They hated the *intendants* and demanded their suppression.

The hereditary nature of the offices led to other clashes between the government and the officials. Since 1604 each official had been permitted to pay a kind of annual insurance premium, amounting to a sixtieth of the estimated value of his office. When an official died, his family, and not the king, had the right to keep the office, assuming that a member of the family was able to exercise the function. Otherwise, the family could sell the office, keep the money, and the buyer would be accepted by the king as the new official. This insurance was called the *Paulette*, after the *traitant* Paulet. The *Paulette* guaranteed the heredity of the office or at least the capital invested in the office, but it was granted for only nine years. At the end of each nine-year period the government threatened not to renew it. In their search for security, the officials tried to obtain renewals. Capitalizing on the insecurity of the officials, the government asked the sovereign courts to register new financial edicts and to require all the officials who benefitted from the *Paulette* to make a heavy loan to the state in return for the nine-year renewal. After 1620 the government divided and weakened the officials by granting some categories of officials—the members of the sovereign courts, for example—attractive conditions for the *Paulette* while disfavoring other categories.

The *Paulette* gave the government a means of exerting financial pressure on the officials. But it also aroused the officials to opposition. In 1620, 1638, and 1647 the parlements strongly opposed the royal financial edicts and denounced the heavy taxes, the huge expenses of the court, and the insolent profits of the *traitants* and *partisans*. They denied that the necessities of war were a sufficient excuse for these edicts and claimed to defend the neglected welfare of the people. Long and difficult negotiations ensued, especially in 1647 and 1648. The permission to pay the *Paulette* expired on 31 December 1647. There was the usual commercial bargaining; the government waited as long as possible to grant a renewal, and the Parlement of Paris put forth the strongest opposition in order to obtain it on the best possible terms. When the government finally granted the renewal it was at a high price. The officials protested and became increasingly hostile. Then the government suppressed the *Paulette* altogether, claiming it was a royal favor and not a right of the officials. If the officials would not agree to the royal terms, then the king could refuse to grant it. Finally, after prolonged negotiations and many extreme claims, the government and the officials reached an agreement.

At first, things went as usual. When the Parlement seemed to give way, the royal council, by the declaration of 30 April 1648, granted the *Paulette* but suppressed all *gages* for four years. Only the Parlement of Paris obtained the *Paulette* unconditionally. Yet it did not forget how the king had divided the officials by favoring some and disfavoring others in 1621 and 1630. This time it presented a solid front with the other officials. The consequence of the royal *arrêt* of 30 April 1648 was the Parlement judgment of 13 May, the *arrêt d'Union*. This *arrêt* created the Assembly of the Chamber of Saint-Louis, a committee of all the sovereign courts in Paris. On 18 May the royal council abolished the *Paulette*. To regain it the Parlement of Paris disobeyed the verbal orders of the chancellor and the queen as well as the sentences of the royal council on 7 and 10 June, which annulled the *Arrêt d'Union*. It began to present more and more extraordinary demands in the hope of forcing the court to give way. On 31 July 1648, the queen accorded the *Paulette* on the same terms as had been arranged in 1604, which were very favorable to the Parlement. Now the Parlement could not turn back. It was afraid of losing its influence over the Parisian people, which it would if it became known that the Parlement had acted primarily in its own narrow interests. So it persisted in its rebellion. In actual circumstances, this parlementary opposition led to a general revolt.

The Parlement of Paris gave its actions a constitutional basis. It argued that this court of justice had grown out of the old *Curia Regis* of the Capetian kings and had been a part of the assembly of vassals obliged to serve as counsel to the king. From this *Curia Regis* a group of councilors had been progressively segregated and chosen by the king to judge in his place. They specialized in judicial affairs, formed a court, and established permanent functions about the time of Philipe le Bel in the *palais* at Paris. They were the only officials of the king who administered justice. Further, by interpretation and extension of the role of the king as supreme judge—because all his powers were derived from justice and because originally, in deciding to go to war, the king in fact "judged" the affairs of state—the Parlement of Paris pretended to be much more. It claimed to be a continuation, uninterrupted for eleven centuries, of the annual general assembly of the Francs in the Champs-de-Mars, which deliberated on matters of state and was called the *Parlamentum*, and it now insisted on the same authority and power. It stated that the resolutions of the *Parlamentum* on affairs of state were sovereign and that, consequently, its own resolutions in such matters also should be sovereign. It argued that at the time of Charlemagne's empire the Francs had become so numerous that it was impossible to convoke the entire assembly, and that it became necessary to assemble only the most notable Frankish warriors. The Parlement of Paris claimed that the *Parlamentum* had begun to judge disagreements between private parties only at the time of Saint Louis, four centuries later;

hence its function as a court of justice was accidental and de-
rivative, while its role as a council of state was fundamental. It
also claimed that all its power came from the absolute will of
the kings, that it was an emanation of the absolute power of
the kings, and that, exercised over so many centuries by the
will of so many kings, its authority was the authority of kingship. The Parlement of Paris was the temple of kingship, the
depository of kingship; no particular king had the right to dis-
possess it of its authority and power. Moreover, the decisions of
the king were the "real will" of the monarch, and not mere
whim or impulse, only when they were "received" by the Parlement. Royal declarations, edicts, and ordinances were law only
when verified and registered by Parlement. The king exercised
supreme authority, but this authority was greatest when he decided and passed laws while sitting in his Parlement, in a *lit de
justice*, which was his real throne, with the help and advice
of his sovereign court, which represented the *soul* of kingship,
the king being only its sacred embodiment.

The implications of these ideas were as follows. First, the
Parlement should at any time have access to all the affairs of
state and should be able to deliberate and make decisions about
them. Second, to this end, the Parlement should convoke the
king's vassals: the princes of the blood; the peers of the realm,
both ecclesiastic and lay; the high officials of the crown; and the
councilors of state, thus reconstituting in fact the old *Curia
Regis* and the old *Parlamentum*. Finally, the Parlement should
convoke the other royal officials, examine the affairs of state,
and deliberate about reforms of the state.

The king applied the ceremony of the *lit de justice* when he
came to sit in his Parlement to impose his will and to compel
the Parlement to register his laws. But the Parlement of Paris
claimed that on these occasions the king could only receive the
advice of the members of his Parlement. In order to thwart any
royal abuse of power, they claimed the right to deliberate on the
laws and edicts presented by the sovereign, to vote on them in
the absence of the king, and even to re-examine the laws already
registered in the *lit de justice*. It was not necessary to convoke
the Estates-General of the kingdom, because the Parlement of
Paris itself represented the three orders: clergy, nobility, and
tiers état. As for the provincial parlements, they had been insti-

tuted after the kingdom became larger and only to judge conflicts and crimes of private parties. They could lay no claims to
examining affairs of state.

Actually, the customary constitution stated that the king was
the head, the kingdom the body, and that the Parlement, even
if it had originally been a representative of the realm, could not
have existed at all or had any power without the king. The
presence of the king was not a violation of the *Parlamentum*,
because as the head of the assembly the king should come to
know, through the advice offered, the profound and real will of
the assembly and of the kingdom and should express it through
his personal decisions and orders, which were the law. This was
the "mystery" of the monarchy. The customary constitution also
stated that the Parlement should deliberate on the affairs of
state only when the king permitted it to do so, and Louis XIII
remembered this custom in the edict of 21 February 1641.

Thus the political theories advanced by the Parlement of
Paris were, in fact, revolutionary. They were the basis of constant opposition, which easily grew into rebellion in 1615 and
1648. Such political action was very dangerous. People had profound respect for the Parlement, the temple of justice. Its
sentence and judgments were considered of the highest authority, and many subjects of the king felt justified in refusing obedience to the government, or in openly revolting, on the basis of
the Paris Parlement's constant criticism of the royal government.
The parlements of the provinces advanced the same claims,
shared the same pretensions, and enjoyed the same authority
in their jurisdictions, where they were venerated as the "fathers
of the country."

The royal government aroused bitter resentment by violating
the liberties and privileges of the provinces. Many of them preserved their representation through the *états provinciaux*, provincial assemblies with deputies from the three orders. Although
the provincial estates of the center of the realm—Orléanais,
Anjou, Maine, Touraine, Berry, Marche, Limousin, Haute-
Auvergne, and Périgord—had disappeared, it was different in
the outlying provinces. The estates of Normandy, Brittany,
Rouerge, Guyenne, Quercy, Velay, Béarn, Labour, Basse-Navarre,

Nebousan, Quatre-Vallées, Bigorre, Soule, Comté de Foix, Languedoc, Provence, Dauphiné, and Bourgogne continued to function. Generally speaking, their privileges remained intact. They had the right to consent to taxes after a discussion with the envoys of the king; to apportion and levy taxes through their own officials; to propose and finance public works such as roads, bridges, and canals; to present requests to the king; and to solicit royal *arrêts*, edicts, and declarations.

Strained by the financial demands of war, the royal government encroached continually on the privileges of these provincial estates. The representatives could not assemble at their own will but had to be called by the king. In some provinces the king convoked the estates less and less frequently. That was the case in Dauphiné, Normandy, Basse-Auvergne, Quercy, and Rouerge. The Estates of Provence were not assembled after 1639. All of these estates disappeared after the *Fronde*.

Sometimes the king tried to impose taxes on the provinces, often appointing new royal officials to levy them. For instance, in 1628, during the siege of La Rochelle and the war in Italy, the Estates of Languedoc paid only part of the subsidy requested by the royal envoy. By an act of his absolute power the king raised the *tailles* of Languedoc by 200,000 livres and ordered the *trésoriers de France* at Toulouse and Béziers, rather than the agents of the estates, to levy them. In 1629 the king established royal *elus* in this province. These new officials were to levy the taxes. The financial agents of the estates were abolished. The consequence was not only the legal opposition of the Estates of Languedoc and of the Parlement of Toulouse but also an uprising led by a number of the bishops and nobles of Languedoc and followed by a certain number of artisans and peasants. They supported the joint rebellion of Gaston d'Orléans, the Queen Mother, and the duke of Montmorency, the last being finally defeated at Castelnaudary in 1632.

Such royal encroachments aroused the indignation of the people and sometimes united all levels of the population against the king. The inhabitants regarded the province as their "fatherland" and the members of the provincial estates as their protectors and the "fathers of the country."

The same was true for the municipalities. Most of them had received privileges and franchises from successive kings and, although these were royal grants, the inhabitants considered them as sacred rights. In many cases the government felt compelled to limit some of these liberties, and such limitations often led to opposition, rebellion, and uprising by a united cross-section of the population.

Let us consider the case of Angers in some detail. Since 1474 the town had been an immediate vassal of the king. It formed a small republic with its own government and administration; it possessed general assemblies composed of representatives of the sixteen parishes, the clergy, the royal magistrates, and the university. It elected twenty-four aldermen for life, a mayor for two years, an attorney general, and a town clerk, all of whom were made hereditary nobles by their municipal posts. The municipal body exercised political and judicial power, kept the town keys, defended the city wall, organized the town militia with the mayor as captain general, and levied the municipal taxes. All the inhabitants of Angers were exempt from the *taille*, the *gabelle*, the quartering of troops, the *francs-fiefs* (the tax paid by commoners who were fief-owners), and the *ban et arrière ban*.

At the end of the fifteenth century the most important families of the town—the royal magistrates who usually exercised municipal functions—gained a royal concession. The mayor was to be elected only by the aldermen and was himself to be an alderman. Henceforth the municipal government became the monopoly of a few families of royal magistrates who controlled other posts and offices as well, for Angers had a *sénéchaussée* court and later a *présidial*, an *élection*, a *prévôté*, a *grenier à sel*, and a *maréchaussée*. This was a small oligarchy which had its own pressure group, the Brotherhood of Saint Nicholas. It considered the town hall as its property and the municipal government as its inheritance.

This situation remained practically unchanged until 1601, when the parishes, the clergy, and the university once again obtained the right to elect the mayor and the aldermen. Because of their own local power and influence, however, the royal magistrates continued to be elected, along with a very few attorneys and merchants. Nevertheless, the competition for municipal office seriously divided the inhabitants of Angers. The descendants of the old municipal families, forced to submit

again to elections by the general assemblies, felt deprived of
what they believed to be their right. The other inhabitants, even
though they generally elected royal magistrates and members
of these old families, felt cheated and accused the members of
the municipal government of exempting themselves, their relatives, and friends from taxes and other municipal burdens. The
inhabitants charged the members of the municipal government
with proposing new taxes to the royal government and then
taking a percentage of this new revenue. They also accused them
of profiting from the municipal tax farms, of dividing among
themselves the funds for missions to Paris, and of forming trade
associations which gave them an illegal monopoly on the grain
trade.

Pitted against the royal magistrates who constituted the
municipal administration of Angers were the corporate bodies
of the liberal professions—attorneys, proctors, notaries, physicians, surgeons, and apothecaries. Above all, the attorneys
claimed that they, rather than the royal magistrates, should
hold the primary places in the town council. The liberal professions were allied with the merchants, who were very rarely
elected as aldermen; the merchants constituted five great *corps,*
which frequently united with those of Touraine and the Orléanais for the common protection of their privileges. They had
their own commercial justice and elected their own judges. But
here was another source of conflict with the municipal government, because they were obliged to elect their judges from a
list of fifty notable merchants chosen by the aldermen.

The municipal administration was also in conflict with the
artisans. The municipality was the special judge of the "manu-
factures," guilds, and brotherhoods of artisans at Angers, which
had twenty-seven guilds of artisans. These men were irritated
by the numerous and heavy consumption taxes and by the
alleged waste of municipal funds. They accused the magistrates
of theft and malfeasance in office. And it was true that the
aldermen refused to impose direct taxes proportioned to the income of the inhabitants, preferring indirect taxes on food and
town utilities, so that the poor paid proportionally more than
the well-to-do. Often artisans opposed constructive innovations
in town regulations simply because they had been proposed by
the royal magistrates and the municipal government.

The Catholic clergy also had daily conflicts with the royal magistrates. The ecclesiastics had sixteen seigneurial jurisdictions in the town of Angers. Appeals from these courts came before the royal justices. Both the bishop and the canons of Saint-Maurice also had their ecclesiastic justice, or *officialité*. Since ecclesiastic and civil matters were mixed in many a law case, some were appealed to the *officialités* and other to royal justice. As a result, during meetings of the general assemblies in the town hall or during municipal elections, there was a history of jurisdictional disputes behind the quarrel of the clergy with the royal magistrates.

Since 1484 the university had been under the legal tutelage of the civil lieutenant of the *sénéchaussée*. The university was overtly dissatisfied with the royal magistrates and accused them of tyranny. It followed the lead of the clergy and the attorneys against the municipal administration.

These clashes of interest created a very difficult situation. Because of their positions in the municipal administration, the royal magistrates usually were on the side of the royal government. And if they were sometimes forced into opposition, they never went so far as to revolt. During the *Fronde* they were Mazarins. By contrast, all the other *corps* of Angers not only were in opposition but revolted openly against the royal government. They were all ardent *Frondeurs*.

At Angers the revolts were caused by violations of municipal privileges and liberties. During the civil war of 1614–20 the town was ransomed several times; the people accused the judiciary aristocracy. The government appealed to the royal government for help. Richelieu intervened in the elections and after 1625 invalidated more than one. Through armed force he replaced the legally elected mayor with an unpopular one, suspended the functions of another, and obliged the town to elect his candidate. Subsequently, the mayor became some sort of royal agent. Beginning in 1635 Richelieu, and Mazarin after him, violated the financial immunities of Angers, levied the *gabelle* and other new taxes, and increased the older taxes regularly every year. The king found ways to extort three or four times more money from the town than it would have paid through the *taille*. In addition, Angers was made to pay for its immunities, such as its exemption from the *ban et arrière ban* and from the *francs-fiefs*. The well-to-do inhabitants of the town were increasingly heavily taxed. The town was now obliged to guard and feed hundreds of prisoners of war. It had to pay for army provisions every year.

Increasingly, the townspeople were unable or unwilling to pay these very large sums. Some of them were imprisoned by royal order. There were riots. Women and children attacked the houses where the clerks of the tax farmers had their offices. The resistance to taxes remained adamant. Finally, in 1648 the government lodged thirty-two cavalry companies in the town until the inhabitants agreed to pay. The soldiers extorted money from the townfolk; pillaged the houses; stole furniture, jewelry, and even the beds of the poor; stabled their horses in drawing rooms and bedrooms; and ruined the tapestries, woodwork, and carpets. The town was ready for an uprising.

One part of the nobility, the *gentilshommes*, sometimes from very old families of the *noblesse d'épée*, had become frustrated with their position in the state and the society. First of all, they felt they ought to exercise power—political, judiciary, and then administrative power. They felt that the realm had been created and cemented through the sword and the blood of the true nobility, the *gentilshommes*. The realm was maintained now, as always, by their sword and their blood. Their qualities came from this blood. And their blood, their race, as much as their services, gave them the right to command. The clergy was entitled to impose the laws of religion, but it fell to the true nobility to impose political laws. To command as military officers or magistrates was the very essence of the nobility and the *gentilhommerie*.

But the *gentilshommes* had been deprived of their right by the commoners, the *tiers état*. Through the venality of office simple burghers, vile merchants, monopolized royal offices. The *gentilshommes* hated the *Paulette*, which they saw as a means of keeping these offices in the hands of commoners. True, in order to exercise the most important of these offices, such as those of the sovereign courts or in the royal council, the commoners had to be ennobled to satisfy the customary constitution. But for the *gentilshommes* this civil nobility, this *noblesse de robe*, was not true nobility. The *robins*, even embellished with *fleurs-de-lys*, remained bourgeois. Moreover, they claimed to be social equals, even superiors, the true nobility! They claimed they were just below the king and commanded the "people" as his officials. And, for them, the "people" were composed of the clergy, the nobility, and the commoners. For the *gentilshommes* such pretensions were insufferable.

The *gentilshommes* complained of being judged in criminal cases by such royal officials, and even by the most humble, the *prévôt*. A simple priest could be judged only by ecclesiastic judges; a commoner was judged by commoners. But the *gentilshommes* were judged by persons below their social rank. They wished to be judged only by other *gentilshommes*. They laid claim to all the offices, not only the military ones, but the judicial and ecclesiastic dignities as well. They demanded that at least a third of the offices in the royal courts of justice be reserved for them.

The *gentilshommes* also protested that their financial immunities had been violated. They were exempt from the *tailles*, but the government taxed their tenants (*fermiers*), who were consequently obliged to ask the *gentilshommes* for a reduction in rent. The government also taxed the *censitaires* of the *gentilshommes*, and if, in a year of poor crops, the *censitaires* paid their royal taxes, there was not enough left to pay their seigneurial dues. By this reasoning the *gentilshommes* claimed that they too were being taxed, albeit indirectly. Furthermore, they were obliged to pay indirect taxes on food, wine, tobacco, and salt (the *aides et gabelles*). When the tax farmers of the *gabelle* obtained from the royal council the right to search for smuggled salt, the troops were also ordered to search the houses and châteaux of the *gentilshommes* and even to attack them if necessary.

The *gentilshommes* complained of not being permitted to enter commerce. They had always had the right to cultivate the lands of their domains directly, with the help of their domestics and *valêts*, without losing their noble quality or their privileges. But the royal financial officials claimed that the *gentilshommes* cultivated too much land; they wanted to impose the *taille* on them and their domestics. The *gentilshommes* thus felt dispossessed of all their rights, privileges, and liberties. As a result, they frequently joined the revolts of the princes of the blood and of the *grands* of the kingdom.

One aspect of the rivalry between the *gentilshommes* and the royal officials was the permanent struggle in many provinces between the governor and the local parlement, such as the conflict between d'Epernon and the Parlement of Bordeaux or that between Count d'Alais and the Parlement of Provence. Governors were *gentilshommes* of high birth and dignity; usually they were owners of large seigneurial domains in the provinces where they were appointed and were high-ranking members of the royal army. Commissioned to exercise the governmental power of the king in the provinces, they often attempted through their *créatures* to create principalities for themselves. They encountered the strong opposition of the parlements, which claimed to be the leaders, protectors, and administrators of the provinces. These clashes often led to popular riots and uprisings which were incited by both parties.

In their antagonism toward the royal financial officials and the royal council the *gentilshommes* incited and even led their peasants, with whom they had common interests. When the sergeants and *huissiers* came to seize cattle, furniture, and plows from the peasants who were unable or unwilling to pay their taxes, the *gentilshommes* hid people, cattle, and goods in their châteaux and manor houses and received the fiscal agents with musket shots. They advised their peasants not to pay taxes, and when the royal council sent companies of cavalry and infantry to enforce collection, the *gentilshommes* led troops of armed *créatures*, domestics, and *censitaires* to fight them. In some provinces, such as Normandy and Périgord, these skirmishes were not an occasional occurrence but a permanent social phenomenon. The letters of the *intendants* of the provinces to the chancellor and the secretaries of state are full of complaints about the *gentilshommes* and even about royal officials who owned fiefs and seigneuries in the province and acted like the *gentilshommes*. The *intendants* wrote that the parishes often were financially able to pay the taxes but that, encouraged by the *gentilshommes*, they refused to do so. Some of these parishes, such as Mantilly in Normandy, did not pay the *taille* for seven years. Many of the peasant riots, revolts, and uprisings were directly provoked by the *gentilshommes* or their officers and servants and sometimes were led and organized by them. All of the peasant uprisings were indirectly provoked by the *gentilshommes,* royal officials, the princes, parlementary criticism of the royal government and its policies, and the widespread propaganda against the government in general.

Things are not simple in history. Princes, *grands, gentilshommes,* officials, merchants, artisans, peasants, provinces, and municipalities—all had reasons to revolt, and some of them revolted often. But not all of them rebelled. In the final analysis, the rebellions and uprisings were the actions of minorities, sometimes small minorities. A great number of the inhabitants of the kingdom remained loyal to the king and obedient to the state. Many of them perhaps shared the feelings of the rebels, but other feelings prevailed. Even among the corporate bodies which rebelled against the king, such as the Parlement of Bordeaux, a great many of the councilors followed reluctantly, and near the end of the movement the so-called parlements were only rump parlements. Reasons for revolt—even excellent ones —do not necessarily lead to revolt. In each man there are inner conflicts of interest and feeling, and often we cannot know why one feeling prevails over another.

But we cannot avoid the fact that the division between loyal subjects and rebels, between Mazarins and *Frondeurs,* cut vertically through the hierarchy of French society. It was not a conflict of social strata, of orders, or of classes—if there were "classes" in seventeenth-century France. When we speak about noblemen, we should say not "the nobility" but "some noblemen"; about peasants, not "the peasantry" but "some peasants"; and so forth. During the *Fronde,* in the jurisdiction of Bordeaux many *gentilshommes* followed the royal governor, d'Epernon, despite their resentment of the royal government, and not all of those who followed were his *créatures.* But, despite their resentment of the officials, many other *gentilshommes* followed the Parlement of Bordeaux, not the princes of Condé or Conti. Despite their bitterness against the ministers, the royal magistrates of Angers remained loyal, and many other inhabitants, despite their anger, were not *Frondeurs.* There is no strict determinism in the matter of revolt and revolution, no logical sequence, no direct link between the set of circumstances explaining and justifying revolt and the act of revolt itself. The link is a psychological one, a very complex psychological one, and in most cases the historian is unable to enter into the psychology, conscious or subconscious, of the men he studies.

SUGGESTED READING

Bourgeon, Jean-Louis. "L'île de la Cité pendant la Fronde: Étude sociale." *Fédération des Sociétés historiques et archéologiques de Paris et de l'Île-de-France,* vol. 13. Paris and Île de France, 1962.

Boutruche, Robert. *Bordeaux de 1453 à 1715.* Bordeaux: Fédération historique du Sud-Ouest, 1966.

Communay, A. *L'armée à Bordeaux.* Bordeaux, 1887.

Debidour, Antonin. *La Fronde angevine.* Thèse de Lettres, Paris, 1877.

Deyon, Pierre. *Étude sur la société urbaine au 17e siècle: Amiens, capitale provinciale.* Paris: Mouton, 1967.

Durand, Yves. *Cahiers de doléances des paroisses du bailliage de Troyes pour les États Généraux de 1614–1635.* Paris: Presses Universitaires de France, 1966.

Durand, Yves; Labatut, J. P.; and Mousnier, R. *Problèmes de stratification sociale: Deux Cahiers de la Noblesse pour les États-Généraux de la Fronde (1649–1651).* Paris: Presses Universitaires de France, 1965.

Goubert, Pierre. *Beauvais et le Beauvaisis de 1600 à 1730.* Paris: S.E.V.P.E.N., 1958; 2d ed., Armand Colin, 1968.

Knachel, Philip A. *England and the Fronde.* Ithaca, N.Y.: Cornell University Press, 1967.

Kossmann, E. H. *La Fronde.* Leiden: Université de Leyde, 1954.

Le Roy Ladurie, Emmanuel. *Les paysans de Languedoc.* 2 vols. Paris: Imprimerie nationale, 1966.

Loublinskaya, A. D. *Documents pour servir à l'histoire de France au XVIIe siècle: Lettres et mémoires adressés au Chancelier Séguier (1633–1649) Languedoc, Provence, Dauphiné.* Leningrad: Académie des Sciences d'U.R.S.S., Institut d'histoire de la section de Léningrad, 1966.

———. *French Absolutism: The Crucial Phase, 1620–1629.* Cambridge: Cambridge University Press, 1968.

Merle, Louis. *La métairie et l'évolution agraire de la Gâtine poitevine de la fin du Moyen-Age à la Révolution.* Paris: S.E.V.P.E.N., 1958.

Mousnier, Roland. *La Vénalité des Offices sous Henri IV et Louis XIII.* Rouen: Maugard, 1945.

————. "Quelques raisons de la Fronde: Les causes des journées révolutionnaires parisiennes de 1648." *XVIIᵉ siècle,* 1949, pp. 33–78.

————. "Comment les Français voyaient la Constitution." *XVIIᵉ siècle,* 1955.

————. "Recherches sur les soulèvements populaires avant la Fronde." *Révue d'histoire moderne et contemporaine,* pp. 81–113. Paris: Presses Universitaires de France, 1958.

————. "État et commissaire: Recherches sur la création des intendants des provinces (1634–1648)." *Forschungen zu Staat und Verfassung: Festgabe für Fritz Hartung.* Berlin: Duncker und Humblot, n.d. (1958?).

————. "Recherches sur les syndicats d'officiers pendant la Fronde: Trésoriers généraux de France et Elus." *XVIIᵉ siècle,* 1959, pp. 76–117.

    The five preceding papers have been reprinted with others by the same author in *La Plume, la Faucille et le Marteau.* Paris: Presses Universitaires de France, 1970.

————. *L'assassinat d'Henri IV.* Paris: Gallimard, 1964.

————. *Lettres et mémoires addressés au Chancelier Séguier (1633–1649).* 2 vols. Paris: Presses Universitaires de France, 1964.

————. *Fureurs paysannes.* Paris: Calmann-Levy, 1968.

Pillorget, René. *Vente d'offices et journée des barricades du 20 janvier 1649 à Aix-en-Provence,* n.p., n.d.

Porchnev, Boris. *Les soulèvements populaires en France de 1623 à 1648.* Paris: S.E.V.P.E.N., 1963.

Ranum, Orest A. *Richelieu and the Councillors of Louis XIII.* Oxford: Clarendon Press, 1963; French translation, Pedone, 1966.

Venard, Marc. *Bourgeois et paysans au XVIIᵉ siècle: Recherches sur le rôle des bourgeois parisiens dans la vie agricole au Sud de Paris au XVIIᵉ siècle.* Paris: S.E.V.P.E.N., 1957.

MARC RAEFF

5 | Pugachev's Rebellion

In the eighteenth century Russia was undergoing a rapid transformation, albeit its rate varied from one aspect of the country's political, social, and economic life to another. Under the impulse of Peter the Great the over-all pattern of this transformation displayed those characteristics which we most readily associate with the modern absolute monarchies that emerged in Western Europe in the course of the sixteenth and early seventeenth centuries. Seen from this perspective, Russia seems about a century behind France and Spain, and perhaps half a century behind its neighbors Sweden and Prussia. Indeed, if such a chronological *décalage* is correct, we are justified in considering the popular uprising led by Emelian Pugachev in 1773–74 to have been the Russian counterpart of the sixteenth- and seventeenth-century West European revolts and revolutions that have shaped the other contributions to this volume.

The pace of change in Russia was most noticeable in the military and diplomatic fields, where larger expenditures of money and manpower were entailed, as well as in the area of administration, where the primary task was to mobilize the country's resources for political and military action. A glance at the share of the state's expenditures devoted to military and administrative purposes between 1725 and 1767 readily illustrates the point. Total expenditures for the military establishment rose from 6.5 million rubles to 9.6 million, even though they fluctuated, dropping below the 1725 level in 1767, only to jump rather steeply after the outbreak of the first Turkish war in 1768. The relative importance of administration and court costs, rose consistently in the same period, from 31.1 per cent to 41.5 per cent for general and fiscal administrative purposes and from 4.4

161

per cent to 10.9 per cent for the court.[1] At the same time, the expansion of the military establishment increased the burdens of conscription, borne exclusively by the peasantry, as after 23 August 1773 the call rose from 1 conscript for every 150 male "souls" to 1 for every 100.[2] It is true that part of the increase in taxation was absorbed by the rapid growth of the population. But the accompanying expansion of the empire's borders imposed more and greater administrative and military tasks on the government, and these in turn pushed up expenditures.[3]

It is rather difficult to assess adequately the rise in economic potential, which might have rendered the increased burdens more bearable. The industrial development introduced by Peter the Great did not maintain itself on the same level after his death, but during the reign of Elizabeth its pace quickened. This time it took place under the sign of individual enterprise, in the form of monopoly privileges granted to select individuals of Elizabeth's entourage, in particular the Shuvalovs. The pace of economic development was further stimulated by the abolition of internal duties in the 1750s and of *octroi* rights in 1762.[4] These measures also helped to involve the peasantry in local trade by encouraging them to take their goods to nearby town markets. After the death of Elizabeth the government fostered competitive entrepreneurial activity, especially on the part of the nobility, by abolishing the monopoly concessions granted in the previous reign and by giving to the owners complete discretion in disposing of the products grown or found on their estates as well as the products of their peasants' labor.[5] Carried out with the help of foreigners, especially settlers in the south and east, this promotion of economic activity increased the complexity of administration and opened the gates to many social,

[1] S. M. Troitskii, *Finansovaia politika russkogo absoliutizma v XVIII veke* (Moscow, 1966), p. 243.

[2] J. T. Alexander, "The Russian Government and Pugachev's Revolt, 1773–1775" (Ph.D. diss., Indiana University, 1966), pp. 15–16.

[3] Troitskii (*Finansovaia politika*, p. 215) gives the following figures:

	1719	1744	1762
Total pop. (in 1,000 souls)	15,578	18,206	23,236
Taxable male pop. (in 1,000 souls)	5,570	6,676	7,362

[4] *Polnoe Sobranie Zakonov Rossiiskoi Imperii*, 1st ser. (St. Petersburg, 1830), no. 10,164, 20 December 1753 (hereafter cited *PSZ*).

[5] *PSZ*, no. 15,447, 28 June 1782. The policy culminated in the privileges included in the Charters to the Nobility and to the Towns, *PSZ*, nos. 16,187 and 16,188, 21 April 1785.

ethnic, and religious conflicts between the indigenous population and foreign newcomers.

With respect to the dynamics of social structure we observe a double phenomenon: On the one hand, the nobility was coming closer to being a genuine estate (*Stand*), enjoying all cultural and social, as well as economic, advantages. The nobles were gradually, albeit incompletely, changing from a class of state servants into a privileged estate of leisured and landowning individuals who were free to pursue their private interests. On the other hand, the peasantry had become almost a closed caste whose members were no longer bound to the land, but tied to the person of their owner—in fact, mere chattel. In addition, they were barred from access to the source of political authority. The connecting links that had existed, albeit in diminishing form, between the peasant community and the czar were broken by the interposition of the serf owners—be they private lords or agents of the Church or state. The return of more and more nobles to their estates (after 1762) meant that individual serf owners could effectively impose their tyrannical whims on the peasants, controlling in minute and annoying fashion their daily routine and interfering in their personal lives. The lord's presence made recourse to any state agent or institution well nigh impossible. The peasants felt abandoned by the modern state. This transformation of their relationship to state and landlord had been in the making since before Peter the Great. Gradual as it had been, it bore the earmarks of inevitability, and the peasant masses, although far from reconciled, bowed to it as they bowed to the rigors of their natural environment.[6] More specific facts and conditions, however, helped to fashion the background of the Pugachev revolt.

[6] Soviet historiography stresses increasing "feudal" exploitation and the abuses to which the serfs were subjected. But usually this led only to individual outbreaks and localized acts of disobedience or revenge. On the peasantry of the eighteenth century in general, a decent introduction in English is J. Blum, *Lord and Peasant in Russia from the Ninth to the Nineteenth Century* (Princeton: Princeton University Press, 1961), esp. chaps. 15–24; see also M. Confino, *Domaines et Seigneurs en Russie vers la fin du XVIIIe siecle—Étude de structures agraires et de mentalités économiques*, Collection historique de l'Institut d'Études slaves, no. 18 (Paris, 1963). The classical work is V. I. Semevskii. *Krest'iane v tsarstvovanie imperatritsy Ekateriny II*, 2 vols. (St. Petersburg, 1881–1901); the Soviet classic is N. L. Rubinshtein, *Sel'skoe khoziaistvo Rossii vo vtoroi polovine XVIII v.: Istoriko-ekonomicheskii ocherk* (Moscow, 1957).

In Western Europe the increase in fiscal burden played a major role in paving the ground, or providing the spark, for popular revolts. We have mentioned that in Russia the total expenditures of the state rose sharply in the eighteenth century; consequently, taxation increased also. The basic item of direct taxation was the capitation (*podushnaia podat'*) introduced by Peter the Great, which applied to every adult male soul of the taxable population (i.e., mainly peasants, although other small social groups also were subject to it). Curiously, the rate of capitation did not increase dramatically in the course of the half-century preceding Pugachev's rebellion. Total receipts increased, but this was partly because of the population growth already mentioned.[7]

Was this relative stability of the rate of capitation evidence of the marginal character of Russian agriculture, or was it rather the result of the government's reluctance to burden the property of the nobility and thereby in fact reduce the serfs' contribution to their masters' revenue? To date, the available evidence has not provided a clear answer. In any event, the increase in the state's requirements was largely met by a sharp rise in indirect taxes, which naturally fell most heavily on the ordinary consumer—the peasant. Between 1724 and 1769 the share of direct taxes in the total revenue of the state dropped by 11.6 per cent, while that of indirect taxes rose by 10.6 per cent and of regalia by 1.4 per cent.[8] The tax burden of every male soul increased by 181 per cent between 1724 and 1769, and direct taxes rose by 146 per cent; indirect taxes rose by 242 per cent. Most indicative of the growing burden imposed on the common folk is the fact that revenue from such essential products as salt rose by 190 per cent and from vodka by 345 per cent, while *octroi* receipts (affecting local consumption) increased by 188 per cent.[9] In addition, a strong inflationary trend resulted in higher prices on all goods. The value of money dropped by an estimated 13 per cent between 1725 and 1767; it fell even more sharply after the start of the Turkish war in 1768 and eventually led to the introduction of paper *assignats* and still greater inflation in the second half of Catherine's reign.

[7] The total sum collected by the state rose by 239 per cent, while the taxable population rose 131 per cent (Troitskii, *Finansovaia politika*, p. 219).

[8] Troitskii, *Finansovaia politika*, p. 214.

[9] *Ibid.*, p. 219.

Naturally, the increase in prices affected grain trade as well. In the west, rising grain prices had often precipitated popular unrest and revolts, mainly in the cities. Soviet scholars make much of the rise in grain prices as evidence of increasing feudal exploitation and deepening crisis in the feudal economy. I confess that this reasoning does not strike me as convincing. Of greater significance, I think, are certain basic features of eighteenth-century Russian agriculture which are only indirectly tied to the price fluctuations of grain. In the first place, the marginal character of agricultural production throughout most of the empire should not be overlooked. A yield of three times the seed planted was considered a good average, and a yield of from four to five per unit of seed was considered very good and fortunate indeed. If we take into account the necessity of preserving seed for the next planting, for reserves, and for feeding an ever-increasing population, we discover the precariousness of the peasant's condition.[10] The low yield was accompanied by capricious and sharp seasonal and geographical fluctuations. Grain prices also fluctuated greatly because the peasants were forced to buy grain for food and seed in times of penury. Prices rose sharply in the 1760s and 1780s.[11] It should be noted, however, that the lion's share of high grain prices lay in the cost of transportation, which limited the possibility of shipping grain over long distances and prevented relief from reaching areas stricken by bad harvests, if they were remote from areas yielding good crops.

The needs and interests of the nobility may help to explain the great concern for high grain prices evinced in the second half of the eighteenth century. Indeed, before the great expansion of grain production in the Ukraine and its easy shipment to domestic and foreign markets, the nobles purchased grain for their own needs, for a rather large number of unproductive domestic serfs, and on occasion to help their own peasants. Paradoxically, therefore, the land-owning nobles (in service and away from their estates) were consumers and buyers of

[10] Rubinshtein, Sel'skoe khoziastvo Rossii, pp. 355–56; for some judicious comments on Russian harvest yields see A. Kahan, "Natural Clamities and their Effect upon Food Supply in Russia," Jahrbücher für Geschichte Osteuropas 16, no. 3 (September, 1968):353–77.

[11] Rubinshtein, Sel'skoe khoziastvo Rossii, pp. 413–14.

grain rather than its producers and sellers. At the same time, as an increasing number of peasants left the estates to work in cities or non-agricultural occupations on a permanent basis (*otkhod*), their lords gained the impression that the number of productive hands working the land was decreasing while the number of mouths dependent upon purchased grain was growing.[12] The latter stimulated the need for marketable grain, holding out hopes for more income from greater agricultural production. These hopes seemed particularly attractive because serfs who paid only quitrent (*obrok*)—the value of which was relatively low and stable—provided an inadequate and quite inflexible source of revenue. Interest in agriculture as the main source of wealth was in part stimulated by the popularization of fashionable western economic ideas (e.g., physiocracy) and the government's educational propaganda (competitions sponsored by the Free Economic Society). We can therefore readily understand that a psychological and cultural climate favorable to agriculture developed in the second half of the century and encouraged the nobility to seek an increase in their share of agricultural production.[13] The successful raising of quitrent payments above the inflationary decline of the currency's purchasing power seemed to demonstrate the peasantry's greater ability to pay and, by implication, offered more scope for the exploitation of serf labor.[14]

These factors explain what M. Confino has called the "rediscovery" of corvée (*barshchina*) on the part of the serf-owning nobles.[15] They account for the spread of corvée not only on large estates but also to smaller ones and, of particular significance for our topic, to those estates in the east and southeast which heretofore had been relatively immune to this form of servitude.

---

[12] The well-to-do nobles lived in the capitals or large cities surrounded by a crowd of domestic servants recruited from their serf peasantry. This represented in many cases a not insignificant drain of the productive rural population.

[13] Confino, *Domaines et Seigneurs en Russie*, esp. chap. 1; see also M. T. Beliavskii, *Krest'ianskii vopros v Rossii nakanune vosstaniia E. I. Pugacheva: Formirovanie antikrepostnicheskoi mysli* (Moscow, 1965), pt. 4.

[14] Rubinshtein, *Sel'skoe khoziastvo Rossii*, p. 156 (quoting calculations of Semevskii, *Krest'iana v tsarstvovanie Ekateriny II*, 1:49, 54). Possibly, too, as the Soviets stress, peasants were becoming more involved in local trade (bringing their produce to nearby town markets).

[15] Confino, *Domaines et Seigneurs en Russie*, pp. 198–201.

The *corvée* was more burdensome than the quitrent, not so much in terms of economic accounting as in human terms, which were immediately perceived by the serfs: stricter control and a regularization of peasant activities on the estate and a reduction of the land available to the serf for his own use. Little wonder that the system was resented and that its spread (or return) to new estates aroused those peasants who had become accustomed to greater leeway in their routine activities. It is of some significance that, in the rich agricultural region of Voronezh Province affected by the Pugachev rebellion, 384 of the 393 estates that fell victim to the rebels were on *corvée*, only 2 per cent being on quitrent.[16]

The 1760s and early 1770s showed greater concern for a livelier pace of economic activity, fuller exploitation of all available human and natural resources in the empire, and a gradual shift to a market orientation. The truly dramatic change, however, would come only in the 1780s and later, with the opening up of the agricultural potential of the south. But the discussions at the Codification Commission of 1767 and the competitions sponsored by the Free Economic Society gave expression to the growing realization that the old ways of economic life had to go and that new ones were needed.[17] This realization served to create a mixed atmosphere of hope and disarray among the nobles and peasants. The latter expressed their confusion in a restlessness and pervading discontent, a proneness to rumor and rebelliousness.

What aggravated the situation in Russia before 1773 was the persistence of a few conditions which had been sources of irritation and conflict since the beginning of the century. As the repeated complaints of deputies to the Codification Commission of 1767 testify, security and protection of property and person were woefully inadequate in the Russian empire. The complaints

[16] S. I. Tkhorzhevskii, *Pugachevshchina v pomeshchich'ei Rossii: Vosstanie na pravoi storone Volgi i v iune—oktiabre 1774 g.* (Moscow, 1930), p. 36.
[17] On the discussions at the Codification Commission of 1767 see Beliavskii, *Krest'ianskii vopros*, pts. 2 and 3; for a perceptive analysis of the nobility's economic attitudes see W. R. Augustine, "The Economic Attitudes and Opinions Expressed by the Russian Nobility in the Great Commission of 1767" (Ph.D. diss., Columbia University, 1969); and for a more superficial summary see P. Dukes, *Catherine the Great and the Russian Nobility: A Study Based on the Materials of the Legislative Commission of 1767* (New York: Cambridge University Press, 1967), chap. 3.

came mostly from nobles who had been spoliated and brow-
beaten by richer and influential neighbors, attacked by brigands,
and cheated by unscrupulous merchants. But anything that
worsened the condition of these nobles also directly affected
their peasant serfs, who in the final analysis had to make up
for their masters' losses and who bore the brunt of the brutality
directed at their owners.[18]

A major source of lawlessness and dissension was the frequent lack of set and recognized boundaries between estates,
peasant allotments, Church property, and state lands. Hence the
general demand for a comprehensive land survey. After a false
start under Elizabeth, it really got under way with the issuance
of revised instructions in 1765.[19] As badly needed as it was,
however, the survey did have undesirable consequences for some
groups of the population. Indeed, Catherine's instructions of
1765 directed that the surveyors register and validate all existing boundaries unless they were being contested in court by the
parties concerned. These instructions meant in effect that the
state acquiesced to previous seizures of state lands and empty
tracts, and ratified the spoliations of free peasants and petty
serf owners by rich and influential nobles.[20] Among the main
victims were the *odnodvortsy* (owners of one homestead), about
whom more will be said in connection with the Pugachev revolt
itself. Along the same lines, the third general census, begun in
1762, not only counted and registered the taxable population but
also immobilized it. As it had done since the sixteenth century,
the process of counting drove to flight those who did not wish
to be tied down permanently.

To round out the picture of disarray and insecurity which
contributed to the peasantry's forebodings of the traditional
world's crumbling and of worse times to come, we should note

---

[18] Augustine, "Economic Attitudes and Opinions," chaps. 2–3 and *passim;*
Dukes, *Catherine the Great;* Beliavskii, *Krest'ianskii vopros,* pt. 2.

[19] I. E. German, *Istoriia russkogo mezhevaniia,* 2d ed. (Moscow, 1910);
L. V. Milov, *Issledovanie ob "Ekonomicheskikh primechaniiakh" k general
'nomu mezhevaniiu: K istorii russkogo krest'ianstva i sel'skogo khoziaistva
vtoroi poloviny XVIII v* (Moscow, 1965), chap. 1.

[20] For example, the problem of "tilling soldiers" (*pakhotnye krest'iane*)
in Tsentrarkhiv, *Pugachevshchina* (Materialy no istorii revoliutsionnogo
dvizheniia v Rossii XVII i XVIII vv. pod obshchei redaktsii M. N. Pokrov-
skogo), vol. 2: *Iz sledstvennykh materialov i offitsial'noi perepiski* (Moscow-Leningrad, 1929), pp. 375–76; hereafter this document collection will
be cited as *Pugachevshchina.*

the frequent recurrence of crop failures, plagues, and epidemics. Among the latter the most dramatic was the 1771 epidemic in Moscow, which brought to the surface all the unconscious and unfocused fears and panics of the populace.[21] In a way, it was a prelude and dress rehearsal for the Pugachev revolt. That is why, on the eve of the rebellion, the report of drought in the Ural area sounded ominous indeed.[22]

Government policies with respect to Church matters further contributed to the unsettling atmosphere which permeated the Russian body social in the early 1770s. Since the sixteenth century the Muscovite state had followed a policy which aimed at putting under secular control all lands owned by the Church (monasteries, dioceses). Peter the Great pursued the same goal, but shifted the focus of attention to the political and fiscal control of the Church hierarchy. The latter was saddled with new obligations, while its administration was assimilated to a department of the secular state. But the Church's resources—or the means of collection—were inadequate to meet the new obligations imposed on it. As a consequence, its serfs were among the most exploited and poorly administered of the peasantry. Little wonder that discontent and unrest were endemic among Church peasants, so much so that Catherine II estimated that about fifty thousand were in open revolt at the time of her accession. Elizabeth had laid the ground for a new administrative setup by transferring Church (primarily monastic) peasants from the direct control of ecclesiastic institutions to that of local noblemen and tax farmers. However, this arrangement did not prove very successful either, because the tax farmers and local nobles used their new function to their exclusive personal advantage.

The legislation of Peter II with respect to the Church aroused some of those rumors and hopes which played no small part in

[21] N. N. Firsov, *Pugachevshchina: Opyt sotsial'no-psikhologicheskoi kharakteristiki* (St. Petersburg–Moscow, n.d.), p. 171; A. I. Dubasov, "Chuma i Pugachevshchina v Shatskoi provintsii," *Istoricheskii Vestnik* 13 (1883):113–35; see also R. E. McGrew, *Russia and the Cholera, 1823–1832* (Madsion: University of Wisconsin Press, 1965), for a general background on epidemics, and Kahan, "Natural Calamities," for a tentative chronology of epidemics and crop failures.

[22] P. Pekarskii, "Zhizn i literaturnaia perepiska P. I. Rychkova," *Sbornik stat'ei, chitannykh v otdelenii russkogo iazyka i slovesnosti imperatorskoi Akademii Nauk* 2, no. 1 (St. Petersburg, 1867):136.

the Pugachev uprising. Following perhaps his personal anti-
orthodox inclinations, as well as his unreflecting impetuosity,
Peter decreed on 16 February and 22 March 1762 that all Economy Peasants (i.e., serfs on monastic and diocesan lands) be
removed from the direct administration of the College of Economy and, in return for the payment of a yearly quitrent of one
ruble per soul, have the free use of all the land they worked.[23]
This act was naturally interpreted as a freeing of the Church
peasants and as the first step toward a general emancipation of
all serfs.[24] The peasants "interpreted" the decrees to mean that
they were free to discontinue their payments and obligations to
church authorities, and the government had to intervene with
clarifications restricting the implications of the law.

To assuage the Church hierarchy, as well as to provide a firm
basis for new legislation, Catherine II annulled the act of
Peter III upon her accession. This annullment aroused the peasants' suspicion of her as an evil, illegitimate ruler enthroned to
cheat them of the freedom granted by their "true" czar. Eventually, Catherine promulgated her own, more moderate act of
secularization in 1764, which eliminated any hopes for general
emancipation the peasants may have entertained.[25] The confusion and tergiversations of the government in this matter led
to rumors and disturbances, all of which came into the open
during the Pugachev uprising, when many Church peasants revolted in support of their own "true" emperor, who had given
them freedom, a freedom of which the evil nobles and unlawful
empress had robbed them.

Peter III had also made himself quite popular with the Old
Believers and other dissenters through a series of measures
which improved their status, permitted freer exercise of their
rites, and encouraged those who had fled beyond the borders of
the empire to return to Russia. The resettling of Old Believers
from Poland in the eastern provinces—e.g., the valley of the
Irgiz—made of Peter III's name a virtual password into the
ranks of that peculiar freemasonry which was the Old Believers

---

[23] PSZ, no. 11,481; see also M. Raeff, "The Domestic Policies of Peter III
and his Overthrow," American Historical Review, June, 1970.
[24] An impression perhaps reinforced by the promulgation of the manifesto on the nobility's freedom from service; see PSZ, no. 11,444, 18
February 1762.
[25] PSZ, no. 12,060, 26 February 1764.

and of which Pugachev made good use in the earlier stages of his career.[26]

Often we read in general histories that Peter III's granting freedom from service to the nobility led the peasants to expect a similar act freeing them from serfdom; and the failure of such an act to materialize was ascribed to the conspiracy of the nobility to which Peter himself fell victim. This interpretation is hard to document, and it is doubtful that such reasoning, if it did occur, played a decisive role in the *Pugachevshchina*. But, to the extent that Peter's manifesto of 18 February 1762 made it possible for many nobles to leave service and return to their estates, it resulted in increasingly closer supervision and greater exploitation of the serfs. The fact that this was indeed sometimes the case and a direct cause of peasant discontent and rebellion is well documented in our sources.[27]

With the peasants agitated by various rumors of freedom relating to the short reign and mysterious demise of Peter III, it is little wonder that the people believed he had not died, that he would return to complete the emancipation of his people. Hence the dozen or so pretenders—*samozvantsy*, familiar company in times of trouble in Russia—who are known to have appeared between 1762 and 1774.[28] Without going into the fascinating story of this phenomenon it may suffice to note here that the legendary pretender, *samozvanets*, appears as the suffering and wandering czar or prince-redeemer, the savior; the false Peter III also appeared in this saintly form.[29] In the case of the Old Believers the myth was reinforced by their mystical conceptions of the Second Coming of Christ. Thus the founder of the Skoptsy sect (castrators), Kondratii Selivanov, claimed to be both Christ and Peter III.[30] Nor was it an accident that Pugachev's claim to be Peter III was suggested to him and promoted by Old Believer hermits in the Iaik region.[31]

[26] P. Shchebal'skii, *Nachalo i kharakter Pugachevshchiny* (Moscow, 1865).
[27] This was also an explanation given by Pugachev, *Pugachevshchina*, 2:194.
[28] K. V. Sivkov, "Samozvanstvo v Rossii v poslednei treti XVIII v.," *Istoricheskie Zapiski* 31 (1950): 88–135.
[29] K. V. Chistov, *Russkie narodnye sotsial'no-utopicheskie legendy XVII–XIX vv.* (Moscow, 1967), chap. 1; M. Cherniavsky, *Tsar and People—Studies in Russian Myths* (New Haven, Conn.: Yale University Press, 1961).
[30] Shchebal'skii, *Nachalo i kharakter*, pp. 50–51.
[31] Firsov, *Pugachevshchina*, p. 117; N. Dubrovin, *Pugachev i ego soobshchniki: Epizod iz istorii tsarstvovaniia Ekateriny II 1773–1774*, vol. 1 (St. Petersburg, 1884), pp. 160 ff.

In summary, Russia was undergoing the travails and disarray that accompanied its adaptation to the innovations introduced by Peter the Great earlier in the century. With respect to social structure, the nobility and the peasantry had undergone a transformation that had changed their mutual relationship as well as the relation of each to the state; but their estate character still needed to be defined more clearly by legislation. The legislation had been promised but had not yet been fulfilled.[32]

To the population the role of the state appeared particularly ambiguous. On the one hand, it had spread its grip geographically and administratively: many areas and activities that earlier had been left to communal and individual action were now within its direct purview. On the other hand, the state aimed at promoting novel trends in the economy and society which would make for entrepreneurial modernity. At the same time it had also taken the seemingly paradoxical step of eliminating direct connection with the people by allowing the serf-owning nobles to become a barrier between peasantry and ruler. The decree of 1767, which completely prohibited direct petitions to the empress from the peasantry, was only the final act of a trend that had shattered the traditional concept of the sovereign held by the people.[33]

Let us now turn to an examination of the specific conditions that prevailed in the region where the Pugachev revolt took place—i.e., the middle Volga valley (the area between the Volga and the Ural watershed) and the open plains between the southern slopes of the Ural Mountains and the Caspian Sea. The mere enumeration of these constituent parts gives an idea of the area's variety, a variety of landscapes and economic resources which was reflected in the social makeup of the region.

[32] Catherine II had tried to work out a new code of laws and to this end called together deputies to inform her on conditions and needs. In a way, this effort culminated in the Charters of 1785. But the very process of electing and convening the deputies in 1767 had set the popular mind aworking; it may have contributed to the restlessness and sense of expectation, as has been correctly noted by R. Portal, *L'Oural au XVIIIe siècle: Étude d'histoire économique et sociale*, Collection historique de l'Institut d'Études slaves, no. 14 (Paris, 1950), pp. 315, 319.

[33] *PSZ*, no. 12,633. It is significant that permission for the nobles to petition the sovereign directly had to be clearly specified in the Charter of 1785.

We shall therefore describe and discuss the specific regional circumstances that formed the background of the rebellion, and were sometimes a direct cause of it, in terms of groups and classes of inhabitants.

In the absence of reliable detailed local studies, it is difficult to generalize about the conditions of Russian peasants in the areas of agricultural settlement, i.e., the provinces of Penza, Perm, Saratov, and the eastern fringe of Voronezh. Yet, on the basis of studies that treat this area roughly as a unit, the dominant impression is that the peasant was better off in this eastern frontier than in the central provinces around Moscow. An area of relatively recent settlement and development, the peasants' land allotments were not only adequate but even plentiful, although in truth much of it was not used to the full.[34] Balanced against these positive aspects was the fact that because of the recent date of their settlement the peasants were not quite attuned to the local geographical and climatic conditions, so that we observe greater fluctuations in harvest yields than occurred in the old central provinces.[35]

But, in the eighteenth century, land had not yet become the scarce commodity and sore spot of the peasants' economy which it was to be in the late nineteenth century. More vital to their prosperity were the serfs' dues and obligations to their masters and to the state. The quitrent payments had risen considerably in the course of the eighteenth century; yet from all evidence they had remained lower in the east than in the central agricultural regions of Russia.[36] On the basis of our present knowledge it is more difficult to determine the extent of conversions to *corvée*, which we have noted as one of the significant trends, during the second half of the eighteenth century. There are indications that it took significant proportions in the Province of Penza, which more and more produced for export beyond its own confines, taking advantage of transportation facilities offered by the waterways of the Volga system. A similar trend is to be observed in Saratov Province. As mentioned earlier, a

[34] See the table of land allotments compiled by Rubinshtein (*Sel'skoe khoziastvo Rossii*, pp. 434 ff.) for all of European Russia.

[35] *Ibid.*, pp. 361–62.

[36] Rubinshtein, *Sel'skoe khoziastvo Rossii*, pp. 156–58; see also A. I. Zaozerskii, "Buntovshchiki: Epizod iz istorii Pugachevskogo bunta," "*Veka*"—*Istoricheskii sbornik* 1 (1924):115–16.

change to *corvée* was perceived as a new, rigid, and particularly burdensome form of "exploitation"—even though in strict economic terms the *corvée* was not necessarily worse than the *obrok*. This feeling was especially strong in "new" areas of settlement, where the peasants had generally enjoyed greater leeway than their counterparts in the central regions.

The extent of the steady increase in hired help on noble and peasant lands and of social stratification within the village, emphasized by Soviet historians as a factor in rural ferment, is difficult to determine. The mere presence of landless agrarian workers naturally contributed to the lack of cohesion in the village and may have made for acute conflicts, but it need not have resulted in open revolt. Quite clearly, however, with its peasant organization and life resting on traditional forms and fixed customs, the village would react strongly to any sudden change, and such a reaction could take the form of disobedience, open revolt, and anarchy. For instance, a change in ownership might trigger a revolt if the new owner attempted to change— not to mention increase—the dues and obligations of the peasants. While not confined to Russia, such a situation was more frequent there in the eighteenth century—and the effects more dramatic—because the inheritance laws and customs led to a considerable redistribution and splintering of estates which radically transformed their character.[37]

All in all, the condition of the serfs and the state of agriculture in the areas of Russian settlement were no worse in the east than in the center; as a matter of fact, all things considered (including the greater likelihood of the landlord being far away in the capitals), it was probably better. Although it was no doubt idealized, the picture traced by S. Aksakov of his grandfather's estate on the Kama was not too far off the mark. But the circumstances of the other social groups reveal a few important differences from those of the Russian peasantry.

The Volga valley had for a long time been the haven for escaped serfs from the central provinces. Although gradually superseded by regions farther east (and south), in the eighteenth century the middle course of the "Mother River" still

---

[37] Zoazerskii, "Buntovshchiki"; E. S. Kogan, "Krest'iane penzenskoi votchiny A. B. Kurakina vo vremia dvizheniia Pugacheva," *Istoricheskie Zapiski* 37 (1951):104–24.

attracted many loose-footed elements of the Russian people.[38] These escapees (*beglye*) either established their own villages or joined existing households and estates. Most of them were runaways from state lands in the central provinces; only a minority had escaped from privately owned estates, because individual owners, or their agents, apparently managed to control their serfs better than did state officials. Beginning in the 1730s, however, a new trend may be discerned in the pattern of settlement of these escapees from the center. In the first quarter of the eighteenth century most of the peasants who had fled settled down in their own households, forming new villages of their own. After the 1730s they tended to become landless, hired agricultural help on the estates of local nobles (or Cossack elders) or in other peasants' households.[39] Obviously, this development meant that the more restless, as well as impoverished, element was on the increase in the region. The escaped peasants settling along the middle Volga were the object of a double squeeze. The free land they worked as squatters was coveted by estate-owning nobles (*pomeshchiki*) moving from the north and northwest who were grabbing all the land they could lay their hands on, by means fair or foul—state grants, purchase, or outright seizure. On the lands they acquired these nobles settled their own serfs, whom they moved from the old estates in central Russia, or they took in the landless laborers mentioned above and virtually turned them into their bondsmen. A similar squeeze was exercised from the south. The Cossack elders (*starshina*, i.e., officers) from the Don Cossack Host had become landowners (an act in 1775 was to equate them in status with the Russian service nobility) and were expanding their holdings beyond the territory of the Host, where their opportunities were restricted by the privileges of the Cossack Host

---

[38] A brief summary, although I do not share the interpretation, is found in V. V. Mavrodin, *Krest'ianskaia voina v Rossii v 1773–1775 godakh: Vosstanie Pugacheva*, vol. 1 (Leningrad, 1961), pp. 341–47; Semevskii, *Krest'iane v tsarstvovanie Ekateriny II*, vol. 1, chap. 12, esp. pp. 342–43.

[39] T. P. Bondarevskaia, "Beglye krest'iane srednego Povolzh'ia v seredine XVIII v.," in *Krest'ianstvo i klassovaia bor'ba v feodal'noi Rossii: Sbornik statei pamiati Ivana Ivanovicha Smirnova*, Akademiia Nauk SSSR, Institut Istorii, Leningradskoe otdelenie, Trudy, vyp. 9 (Leningrad, 1967), p. 395, gives the following figures: from 1700 to the 1730s, 51.9 per cent of the escapees lived in their own households, compared with only 21 per cent from 1740 to the 1770s; hired help rose in the same periods from 20.9 per cent to 42.1 per cent.

and the absence of serf peasants. They, too, settled their new estates with serfs moved from the central provinces or with landless *beglye,* whom they attached to the land. Thus from both north and south the formerly free "frontier" of the Volga valley was nibbled away by the advance of the estate (*pomestie*) using serf labor.

In the westernmost part of the region swept by the Pugachev rebellion, the right bank of the middle Volga (administratively part of Voronezh *guberniia*), were a number of *odnodvortsy* (single homesteaders).[40] These were the descendents of petty military servicemen who had settled on what in the sixteenth and early seventeenth centuries had been the military frontier (*liniia*) protecting Moscow from Crimean Tartars and Ottoman Turks. With the end of their military function, they had declined to the status of small, but free, peasants who tilled their own lands, in some cases with one serf family to help them out. A high proportion of them also were Old Believers, so that they felt particularly alienated from the state established by Peter the Great—an alienation which an extra heavy fiscal burden did nothing to relieve. Having lost their military *raison d'être,* the *odnodvortsy* were no longer subject to the state's concern and protection. As they occupied lands that lay directly athwart the path of the nobility's agricultural expansion into the fertile black-soil steppe, they were hard-pressed by landowners from the central provinces who by hook or by crook were acquiring land and settling their serfs on it.[41]

Impoverished as they were, the *odnodvortsy* were defenseless against the encroachments of nobles who had connections in the capitals and the means to bribe officials. The poorest among them lost their land and sank to the level of hired laborers and sometimes even became serfs.[42] At the same time, they continued to claim privileged status, their right, as servicemen and freemen, to own serfs themselves. Because of their own economic weakness they resisted and mistrusted everything that

[40] T. Esper, "The Odnodvortsy and the Russian Nobility," *Slavonic and East European Review* 45, no. 104 (January, 1967):124–34.

[41] For a contemporary description see A. T. Bolotov, *Zapiski Andreia Timofeevicha Bolotova, 1773–1795* (St. Petersburg, 1873), vol. 3, pt. 16, chap. 141.

[42] See Semevskii, *Krest'iane v tsarstvovanie Ekateriny II,* 2:721 ff., for a most comprehensive study of their economic situation.

tended to modernize the economy and to change the traditional pattern of self-sufficiency into production for a market. Their loss of economic and social status paralleled somewhat the fate of the small imperial knights in Germany at the time of the Reformation. As the knights had done in the fifteenth and sixteenth centuries, the *odnodvortsy* reacted to their sense of loss and alienation from the new trends by pinning their hopes on the providential leader or ruler who would bring them salvation by restoring them to their former function and status. It is from their ranks that several of the pretenders arose; and Pugachev, who claimed to be Peter III the czar-savior and restorer, found ready support among the *odnodvortsy* of Voronezh *guberniia*.[43]

If the *odnodvortsy* represented a native social group that had lost its traditional military, political, and economic functions, the foreign colonists who had been settled on the Volga in the reign of Elizabeth were a new and alien element.[44] The foreigners were not too numerous, about 23,000 souls, but they occupied lands on the lower middle course of the Volga, neighboring on the Kalmyk and Don Cossack territories, where the last act of the Pugachev rebellion was to take place. Although one might expect their situation to have been better than that of the Russian peasantry, it was not. In the first place, not all foreign colonists had the same legal status or were treated alike. Indeed, about half of them had been brought there by individual recruiters and were obliged to turn over to the latter one-tenth of all their produce, as well as to submit to their authority in all administrative and police matters. The recruiters' power, however, was more arbitrary and direct than that of the regular provincial administration. Many of the colonists had been recruited hastily, only to satisfy the greed of the recruiters, and they were not prepared for agricultural work—at any rate, not under Russian conditions. The yield of their labor was therefore quite small, for they suffered profoundly from crop failures and famine.[45] In addition, they were much exposed to raids and

[43] F. I. Lappo, "Nakazy odnodvortsev kak istoricheskii istochnik," *Istoricheskie Zapiski* 35 (1950):232–64; Sivkov, "Samozvanstvo v Rossii"; Mavrodin, *Krest'ianskaia voina*, 1:464–69.

[44] V. V. Mavrodin, "Ob uchastii kolonistov Povolzh'ia v vosstanii Pugacheva," in *Krest'ianstvo i klassovaia bor'ba v feodal'noi Rossii*, pp. 400–413.

[45] See *Pugachevshchina*, 2:71–73, for a description of the crop failure of 1773.

incursions by their nomadic neighbors, which added physical insecurity to their hardships.[46] In 1764 new regulations improved their status by placing them under the special supervision of regular state organs. But this compromise did not satisfy the settlers, because they wanted to be state peasants and completely free of control by their recruiters or special officials.[47]

Northeast European Russia traditionally had been a region of large Church landholdings. Between the Volga and the northern massif of the Urals there were several large monasteries with huge amounts of land and numerous peasant serfs attached to them. It was to be expected that the confusion which resulted from the fitful attempts at secularization—Catherine's retreat from Peter III's legislation and then her own compromise settlement—would excite the peasants, whose hopes for freedom had been raised high only to be belied by subsequent events. The remoteness of the area from the capital and the nearest episcopal sees (Kazan and Nizhni Novgorod) prevented the local authorities from adequately coping with peasant discontent; by the 1760s thousands of peasants belonging to monasteries were in open rebellion.[48]

The longest and most dramatic revolt was at the Dalmatovo Monastery in the Urals, the so-called *dubinshchina* in 1762–64. General A. Bibikov (future commander of the forces against Pugachev) and Prince A. Viazemskii (future procurator-general of the Senate) were dispatched to investigate the causes of the revolt, put it down, and suggest reforms to prevent its repetition.[49] Obviously, these high officials succeeded in coping with only the outward manifestations of discontent, for we find the peasants of the Dalmatovo Monastery at the center of the Pugachev rebellion in the Urals in 1773–74.

Besides the regular monasteries there were also numerous

[46] *Pugachevshchina*, 3:203–6.

[47] G. G. Pisarevskii, V*nutrennii rasporiadok v koloniiakh Povolzh'ia pri Ekaterine II* (Warsaw, 1914), pp. 1–2, 9–10.

[48] See Mavrodin, *Krest'ianskaia voina*, 1:393–420, for a general discussion of discontent among monastery peasants. The classical account of their economic situation is in Semevskii, *Krest'iane v tsarstvovanie Ekateriny II*, vol. 2.

[49] G. Plotnikov, "Dalmatovskii monastyr' v 1773–1774 g. ili v Pugachevskii bunt," *Chteniia obshchestva istorii i drevnostei rossiskikh pri Moskovskom Universitete* 28 (January-March, 1859), bk. 1, sec. 5, pp. 18 ff.; A. A. Kondrashenkov, *Ocherki istorii krest'ianskikh vosstanii v Zaural'e v XVIII v* (Kurgan, 1962), pp. 74–90.

small monasteries and hermitages (*skity*) of Old Believers in the region east of the Volga. They constituted another element that was receptive to Pugachev's appeals. As a matter of fact, the network of Old Believer *startsy* ("holy men") and hermitages served to propagandize the appearance of Peter III—Pugachev— and his successes, and they also helped him recruit his first followers from among the Old Believer Cossack of the Iaik.[50]

In the middle of the eighteenth century the Urals were Russia's major mining and industrial region. The area had developed at a rapid pace since Peter the Great had allowed factory and mine owners to attach and ascribe (*pripisat'*) serfs to their enterprises. Serfs so ascribed were compelled to work in the mines and factories at those times when they were not needed in the fields. In fact, their obligations were particularly burdensome and intolerable because the time spent in traveling to and from the factory or mine (sometimes as far away as several hundred miles) was lost. Naturally, the serfs' aspiration was to return to their villages for good and be freed from the horrible work in the factories and mines. In the course of the century it had become evident that such compulsory labor was quite unsatisfactory. A decree of Peter III,[51] which prohibited the further ascription of villages and peasants to factories until such time as a new code of laws would settle their status definitely, had raised the expectation among ascribed peasants that their freedom was near and that they would be allowed to return to their homes. The appearance of Pugachev (whom they also believed to be Peter III) was naturally interpreted by them as a signal to rise, leave the factories and mines, and return to their native villages.[52]

In the 1770s, however, the mainstay of the Ural labor force was the workers who belonged to the factories—industrial serfs, we might call them (*possessionnye krest'iane*).[53] As everywhere

[50] Dubrovin, *Pugachev i ego soobshchniki*, vol. 1, and Shchebal'skii, *Nachalo i kharakter, passim.*

[51] *PSZ*, no. 12,067, 27 February 1762.

[52] Mavrodin, *Krest'ianskaia voina*, 1:420–21. See Semevskii, *Krest'iane v tsarstvovanie Ekateriny II*, vol. 2, for economic conditions; documentation is given in *Pugachevshchina*, 2:315, on relations among various groups of workers in the Urals and the Pugachev movement.

[53] Portal, *L'Oural au XVIIIe siècle*, chap. 5, esp. pp. 231–58; A. A. Savich, *Ocherki istorii krest'ianskikh volnenii na Urale v XVIII–XX vv.* (Moscow, 1931), pp. 14, 16.

in Europe at the time, such labor was the lowest of the low, at the bottom rung of society and the economy. Needless to say, the working conditions, with heavy reliance on child and female labor, were appalling by any standards. In addition, the workers had to carry a heavy burden of taxation and various dues. Their quitrent payments rose from one ruble to one ruble seventy kopecks in the middle of the eighteenth century, but their wages did not increase. By the middle of the eighteenth century many of the factory hands and miners were children of the original factory serfs and frequently held the status of hired laborers, who were paid wages. But the pay scale was very low, and working conditions were not good in their case either.[54] Because they no longer tilled the soil they were particularly hard hit by the rise in prices on such vital commodities as salt and grain.

The situation of many workers worsened when in the reign of Elizabeth a number of state-owned factories were turned over to private owners (in fact given away to such favorites as the Shuvalov brothers). The new owners, interested only in obtaining high benefits rapidly, intensified the exploitation of their labor force (and plant facilities) without regard for the future. At the same time, like landowners with respect to the serfs, they stood as a solid barrier between their workers and the government, precluding appeals to, and intervention by, the state for improvement of conditions. With the loss of Russia's competitive advantage on the world market (due mainly to high transportation costs and technological rigidity) the production of the Ural mines and iron-smelting factories declined, hitting hardest the workers who had no other place to go or no other skill to market.[55] Quite clearly, then, there was enough material to support rebellion against the system. By and large the factories supported Pugachev, some voluntarily continuing to produce artillery and ammunition for the rebels (a significant factor in Pugachev's success).[56]

[54] Portal, *L'Oural au XVIIIᵉ siècle*, pp. 245–50; Savich, *Ocherki istorii krest'ianskikh volnenii*, p. 16.

[55] Portal, *L'Oural au XVIIIᵉ siècle*, chap. 6. The owners did not seem to be much interested in technological innovation, because they relied mainly on cheap labor. The situation is reminiscent of what we find in a "plantation" economy; see E. Genovese, *The Political Economy of Slavery* (New York: Pantheon Books, 1965).

[56] The ascribed serfs tended to "vote" with their feet by taking advantage of Pugachev's approach in order to return to their villages. It was the *possessionnye* who had to make the decision of whether to join Pugachev or not; they had nowhere to go.

The workers' support of Pugachev frequently had another motive as well: their need of protection against Bashkir raids on factories in the southern Urals. (In the north, where this danger was minimal, the factories were more divided in their loyalties.) The Bashkirs had been pushed from their traditional winter camps and summer grazing lands as dams were built, flooding encampments and pastures, and forests were cut down to meet the needs of the expanding mining and industrial enterprises. The Bashkirs had to yield their lands, grazing grounds, and fishing places under duress and at derisive prices, much like the American Indians selling Manhattan Island. Not surprisingly, they hated the factories and took their revenge whenever possible by raiding them or attacking their workers.[57] That is why some factories appealed to Pugachev, whom the Bashkirs supported, for protective charters (*okhrannye gramoty*) and in return worked for him.[58]

The conflict between the factory population and the Bashkirs highlighted the fact that the region affected by the Pugachev revolt comprised many non-Russian, non-Christian native peoples. Such a heterogeneous population created special problems for the government, and it provided opportunities for those opposing the state and seeking support among the discontented, as yet unassimilated natives. Instead of considering separately each one of the many non-Russian peoples caught up in the revolt, let us look at three major "problem areas," as contemporary jargon has it, that were the sources of discontent and opposition to the central Russian government and its agents.[59]

In those areas which had been under Russian control for a long time and whose native population was primarily sedentary,

[57] *Pugachevshchina*, 2:268–70. For a picturesque account see the historical novel by Stepan Zlobin, *Salavat Iulaev* (Moscow, 1941).

[58] For example, *Pugachevshchina*, 1:202–4 (no. 250). See also *ibid.*, 2:316–17; A. I. Dmitriev-Mamonov, *Pugachevskii bunt v Zaural'e i Sibiri: Istoricheskii ocherk po ofitsial'nym dokumentam* (St. Petersburg, 1907), p. 65.

[59] The numerous Soviet histories of the relevant constituent republics and autonomous regions provide many interesting facts and documents, whatever their interpretation. Of particular interest to us are: *Ocherki istorii Mordovskoi ASSR*, vol. 1 (Saransk, 1955); *Ocherki po istorii Bashkirskoi ASSR*, vol. 1 (Ufa, 1956), pt. 1; V. D. Dimitriev, *Istoriia Chuvashii XVIII veka: Do krest'ianskoi voiny 1773–1775 godov* (Cheboksary, 1959); the collection of documents *Materialy po istorii Bashkirskoi ASSR*, ed. N. V. Ustiugov, 4 vols. (Moscow, 1956), esp. vol. 4, pt. 2; and *Kazakhsko-russkie otnosheniia v XVIII–XIX vekakh: Sbornik dokumentov i materialov* (Alma-Ata, 1964).

the major problem was conversion to Orthodox Christianity. This was the case in the upper valley of the Volga and its north-eastern tributaries, a territory dependent upon the archdiocese of Kazan, the native population of which consisted of Tatar Muslims and primitive groups of hunters, fishermen, and tillers such as the Cheremys, Mordvinians, and Chuvash. Initiated by Empress Anne and continued under Elizabeth, an active program of conversion had been promoted under the aggressive aegis of the archbishops of Kazan.[60] With respect to the Tatar Muslims the results had been disappointing, and the conversion campaign only resulted in the destruction of many mosques, the digging up of cemeteries, and various economic and social hardships determined by the whims of local officials and land-owners. In any event, it seems that the Tatar Muslims did not play an active part in the Pugachev uprising, even though large numbers of them lived in and around Kazan.[61]

But the peoples and tribes which practiced various forms of paganism, shamanism, and animism offered much less resistance to conversion. Allured by promises of tax advantages (e.g., exemption from capitation for three years) and quick to bow to the pressure of local authorities, they converted—at least formally—in large numbers in the eighteenth century. But the act of conversion itself became the source of further exactions and a shameless abuse of their trust. With the full support and active participation of provincial officials, local clergies collected "gifts" and the tribute in kind (*iasak*) under various pretexts; noticing (or deliberately planning) evidence of inadequate fulfillment of ritual and dietary prescriptions on the part of the newly converted, they would impose heavy fines or exact bribes. Confused and impoverished by such illegal collections and exactions, the natives became restless. They tried to bring their plight to the attention of the central government; elections of deputies and the meetings of the Codification Commission of 1767 afforded them the long-sought opportunity to voice their

---

[60] See the comprehensive memorandum of Colonel A. I. Svechin in *Pugachevshchina*, 2:3–40; see also Dimitriev, *Istoriia Chuvashii XVIII veka*, chap. 10.

[61] They also seem to have been kept under particularly close surveillance because they were suspected of having contacts with the Turks. Perhaps, too, the revolt had negative effects on trade, which was one of the main occupations of the Kazan Tatars.

grievances.[62] But their last hopes were shattered when their petitions were turned back, their access to the sovereign being impeded by local officials. They were ready to join a movement of discontent or rebellion.

While conversion was not a major issue for the natives farther east—Muslim and Buddhist nomads in the open steppes beyond the Volga—the advance of agricultural settlement brought in its wake serious and far-reaching conflicts. Throughout the eighteenth century the imperial government consistently pursued a policy which aimed at changing the nomads' way of life by transforming the cattle raisers into sedentary tillers of the soil (which in the long run would bring about their cultural and social Russification as well). The successful outcome of such a policy would make it possible for greater numbers of Russians to move onto new arable lands without fear of raids from neighboring nomads.[63] Thus the grazing lands of the Bashkirs and Kirghiz were relentlessly whittled away. The Kirghiz were hard pressed on the lower Volga and the Irgiz, while the Bashkirs were gradually dispossessed of their summer grazing spots on the southern slopes of the Urals. At the same time, the nomads were pressured into abandoning their traditional ways and taking up sedentary agricultural pursuits.

The Bashkirs were the main target of this conversion effort: their elders and tribal chiefs were promised rewards of rank, money, gifts, and medals if they would lead their people into social and economic change.[64] The effort was not fruitless, for some chieftains and their clans began to settle down and till the land. Not surprisingly, however, this development caused considerable tension within Bashkir society, and the breakup of traditional links and solidarities resulted in friction and unrest.[65] In addition, the turn to agriculture frequently required

---

[62] See *Sbornik imperatorskogo russkogo istoricheskogo obshchestva*, 148 vols. (St. Petersburg: Russian Imperial Historical Society, 1867–1916), vol. 115, where the *cahiers* of delegates of the natives are reprinted.

[63] See, for example, *Materialy po istorii Bashkirskoi ASSR*, vol. 4, pt. 2, nos. 497 and 498; see also B. Nolde, *La Formation de l'Empire russe: Études, Notes et Documents*, 2 vols., Collection historique de l'Institut d'Études slaves, no. 15 (Paris, 1952–53) vol. 1, esp. pt. 2.

[64] *Materialy po istorii Bashkirskoi ASSR*, vol. 4, pt. 2, *passim*.

[65] The claim of Soviet historians that the rich chieftains, becoming involved in agriculture, played the government's game while the poor strata rose in revolt against both the chiefs and the government does not seem substantiated. The leaders of the Bashkir revolt, Salavat Iulaev, his father, and Kinzia Arslanov came from the ranks of the richest and most respected clan chiefs.

the settlement of a new, alien element—non-Russians of various origin, known as *tepteri,* who provided a landless agricultural labor force for the richer, settled Bashkirs. Friction was great between these exploited and scorned *tepteri* and the Bashkirs among whom they lived, so that when the latter rose in revolt the *tepteri* remained loyal to the Russian government, in whom they saw a protector. The Russian state was also using fiscal policy to tighten its control over the Bashkirs and to push them onto a new path of social and economic development. Indeed, the basis of taxation was changed from the tribute in kind, normally levied on all non-Christian peoples of the east, to compulsory purchases of salt in state-owned stores at fixed prices. Eventually the Bashkirs were put on the *obrok,* albeit at a low rate. All these measures tended to introduce the elements of a market and money economy by government fiat, and they were bound to upset the traditional equilibrium.[66]

There was, of course, also the usual conflict between nomadic peoples and their settled neighbors, a conflict heightened by national, religious, as well as political, rivalries. The Cossacks on the Don clashed with Kalmyk and Kirghiz nomads, and the foreign colonists were frequently the object of ruinous raids by Kirghiz tribes. We have commented on the conflict that pitted Bashkirs against factory workers; in addition, there were clashes between Bashkirs and Russian agricultural settlers branching out from the regional center, Orenburg. Finally, old rivalries between nomadic peoples (Kalmyks versus Kirghiz, Kirghiz versus Bashkirs) were cleverly exploited by the Russians (especially by I. I. Nepliuev, the governor-general of Orenburg from 1742 to 1758). All of these developments kept the region seething with discontent, and pretexts for defection from the central government were never lacking.[67]

The third and final aspect of what in modern parlance would be called the nationality question involved the relationship between the natives and the central government. This relationship was no longer a live issue along the banks of the Volga, because the central government was well in command there and the administrative setup followed the usual Russian pattern. Where

[66] Nolde, *La Formation de l'Empira russe;* for a convenient summary see R. Portal, "Les Bashkirs et le gouvernement russe au XVIIIᵉ s.," *Revue des Études slaves* 22, nos. 1–4 (1946):82–104.

[67] National rivalries were taken advantage of by both the government and Pugachev.

central control was a more recent development, however, the areas of friction were numerous. The establishment of Orenburg had been viewed by the Bashkirs as a symbol of the physical presence and control of the Russians, and this view was confirmed by the colonization drive and the protection given to Russian settlers by the governors of Orenburg. (Pugachev's promise to abolish the *guberniia* of Orenburg was designed to arouse the Bashkirs, who indeed would join him enthusiastically in besieging the hated city.[68]) But the Russians had not only built the fortress of Orenburg and settled and administered its territory, they had also imposed service obligations (frontier guards, auxiliary troops against the Turks) on the Bashkirs and had levied large numbers of horses for their own military needs. These policies provoked bitter and long-lasting revolts (1735–41, 1755–57) that required a great military effort before they were quelled; but each repression was followed by heavy levies of horses, fines, and more stringent service obligations.[69] Undaunted, in 1773 the Bashkirs were once more ready to shake off the most burdensome aspects of Russian rule, and they listened with favor to Pugachev's promise to restore to them the right to "be [free] like steppe animals."[70] Their antagonism toward the government explains why they joined the revolt, in spite of their own quarrels with the Iaik Cossacks and their profound aversion to everything Russian. They would provide Pugachev with some of his best and most loyal lieutenants.[71]

[68] *Pugachevshchina*, 2:415–16. Failure to take Orenburg in a way predetermined the Bashkirs' eventual loss of confidence and interest in Pugachev's movement. They did not follow him outside their territory in the second phase of the revolt.

[69] For a superficial account of these revolts, their causes and immediate consequences, see Alton S. Donnelly, *The Russian Conquest of Bashkiria, 1552–1740: A Case Study in Imperialism* (New Haven, Conn.: Yale University Press, 1968).

[70] *Pugachevshchina*, 1:27–28. For a comprehensive discussion of the aspirations and "ideology" of the various groups involved in the Pugachev rebellion (especially good on the natives), see D. Peters, "Politische und gesellschaftliche Vorstellungen in der Aufstandsbewegung unter Führung Pugačevs, 1773–1775" (Inaugural diss., Freie Universität, Berlin, 1968).

[71] Iu. A. Limonov, V. V. Mavrodin, and V. M. Paneiakh, *Pugachev i ego spodvizhniki* (Moscow-Leningrad, 1965); A. N. Usmanov, "Kinzia Arslanov: Vydaiushchiisia spodvizhnik Pugacheva," *Istoricheskie Zapiski* 71 (1962):113–33. There is no place here for a discussion of the situation and role of other nomadic nationalities, especially the Kirghiz (Kazakhs) and Kalmyks. For an introduction see "The Kazakhs and Pugachev's revolt," *Central Asian Review* (London), 8, no. 3 (1960):256–63; A. Chuloshnikov, "Kazakh-kirgizskie ordy i vosstanie Pugacheva, 1773–1774 g.," *Novyi Vostok* 25 (1929): 201–15; and the literature cited in note 59.

Several times in the preceding pages passing reference was made to the Cossacks. It is time now to turn our attention to them, because they triggered the revolt and provided the mainstay of Pugachev's military power to the very end of the uprising. Since the middle of the seventeenth century (when the Zaporog and Don Cossacks came under Moscow's sovereignty), Cossack societies had been undergoing a dual process of transformation.[72] Their social organization, political autonomy, and military function steadily yielded to pressures from the central government in Moscow and St. Petersburg, and by the middle of the eighteenth century the latter was asserting complete and direct control.[73] The Cossacks' right to elect their chiefs (*ataman* and *starshina*) and to follow their "democratic" traditions was steadily eroded and restricted. In the case of the Don Cossacks, from whose midst Pugachev had come, *Ataman* S. Efremov tried in the 1760s to stem the tide and obtain a loosening of controls by St. Petersburg. His attempt failed (1772), and the way was opened for the complete incorporation of the Don Cossack Host into the regular framework of the military organization of the empire, which was completed in 1775 by G. Potemkin.[74] Other aspects of St. Petersburg's growing control were the increases in the number of Cossacks obliged to serve on the border and the formation of new Cossack regiments to be held in constant readiness. In this way the Volga Cossack Host was formed in 1732. In 1770 a special regiment, *Mozdovskii Polk,* was detached from this Host and sent to the Kuban frontier for permanent military duty.[75] In short, the fear was ever present that the loose and traditional Cossack organization would be changed to the rigid regimentation of the regular army (*reguliarstvo*). It was a constant cause of agitation that easily turned into open rebellion.

[72] G. Stökl, *Die Enstehung des Kosakentums* (Munich, 1953); S. G. Svatikov, *Rossiia i Don, 1549–1917* (Belgrade, 1924); V. A. Golobutskii, *Zaporozhskoe kazachestvo* (Kiev, 1957).

[73] Mazeppa's turning against Peter the Great forced part of the Dnieper Cossacks to go into exile in Turkey. The episode further split the Cossacks and cast an additional shadow of suspicion on them from the government's point of view. We shall leave the Ukrainian (Dnieper, Zaporog) Cossacks centered on the *Sich* (headquarters of the Dnieper Cossack Host) out of this account.

[74] Svatikov, *Rossiia i Don,* pp. 210–16, 223; M. Raeff, "Russia's Imperial Policy and Prince G. A. Potemkin," in *Statesmen and Statecraft of the Modern West,* ed. G. Grob (Barre, Mass.: Barre Publishers, 1967), pp. 8–10.

[75] Dubrovin, *Pugachev i ego soobshchniki,* 1:105–6.

But the traditional Cossack pattern was also eroded from within. Indeed, a process of economic and social differentiation was taking place: the *starshina* (elders, i.e., "officer" group) was becoming more prosperous, more influential, and it increasingly identified with the way of life, ideals, and aspirations of the regular Russian elite.[76] The Cossack elders were accumulating land, estates on which they settled serfs (or used their poorer fellow Cossacks like virtual bond labor). They petitioned for and received ranks from the central government which gave them the status of regular noblemen and at times secured for them political advantages as well. Obviously, such developments in the midst of what at one time had been a "military democracy" brought friction and discontent in their wake. The ever-present antagonism between the government-oriented *starshina* and the rank and file erupted into open conflict at the slightest provocation.[77] Only shortly before the appearance of Pugachev, the Dnieper Cossacks had been shaken by a rebellion of the lower and foot-loose elements, the *koliivshchina*.[78]

Of the several Cossack hosts in existence in the eighteenth century, that of the Iaik was most directly and completely involved in the Pugachev revolt.[79] This particular Cossack society was an offshoot of the Don Host: most of its members were Old Believers who had settled along the Iaik (now Ural) River, from its estuary at Gurev to the upper course, where the main center, *Iaitskii gorodok*, was located. They guarded the empire's borders primarily against the Kirghiz nomads that roamed the steppes beyond the Iaik; on occasion they were also called to participate in other temporary operations, particularly against the Turks. Their main occupation and source of revenue was fishing in the plentiful Iaik River. In the reign of Peter the Great the fishing rights had been farmed out to the Cossacks, the Host having to pay a fixed annual sum. The collection of this payment was the responsibility of the *ataman*.

[76] Golobutskii, *Zaporozhskoe kazachestvo;* V. A. Miakotin, *Ocherki sotsial'noi istorii Ukrainy v XVII–XVIII vv.* (Prague, 1926).

[77] Contrary to what Soviet historians are wont to claim, the loyalty of the *starshina* to the imperial government should not be taken for granted.

[78] V. A. Golobutskii, "Gaidamatskoe dvizhenie na Zaporozh'e vo vremia 'Koliivshchiny' i krest'ianskoi voiny pod rukovodstvom E. I. Pugacheva," *Istoricheskie Zapiski* 55 (1956): 310–43. Soviet historiography sees this rebellion as a prologue to the Pugachev movement.

[79] Pugachev himself was a Don Cossack; as a matter of fact he came from the same *stanitsa* (Cossack settlement) as Stenka Razin a century before him.

In the person of M. Borodin the *ataman* in fact came to control the life of the Cossacks—hiding and falsifying the figures of the payments due and of collections made. He assessed individual Cossacks on the basis of their actual catch rather than by merely prorating the fixed amount set by the government, and thus he pocketed the appreciable difference. He had become very wealthy and was in a position virtually to buy the acquiescence of the officers as well as to keep the rank and file in line. But his conflict with one of the *starshina*, Loginov, who wanted to be cut in on the large profits reaped by Borodin, precipitated the Cossacks' open rebellion against the *ataman's* authority. We need not dwell on the details of this long-drawn-out affair.[80] At first, the commission of investigation sent by the government sided with Borodin; a second team decided in favor of the rank and file. The Host was split into two factions—those loyal to the government, led by the *starshina*, and the discontented rank and file. The petitions of the latter were usually disregarded by the central government, especially as long as Count Z. Chernyshev remained at the head of the College of War.

The Iaik Cossacks had still other causes for discontent. To increase the revenues the government received from the Iaik Host, the fishermen were ordered to purchase state-owned salt at set prices. Salt was essential to preserve the catch, and forced purchase at high prices heavily burdened the Cossacks. As the war against Turkey dragged on, causing heavy losses in manpower, the College of War suggested the formation of an auxiliary "Moscow Legion" from the ranks of the smaller Cossack Hosts, each of which would furnish a set number of recruits for the legion (1769). The proposal was greeted with deep suspicion because it aroused the fear that through this indirect method the government would try to assimilate the Cossacks to the regular army, to impose *reguliarstvo*. It was a clear threat to the Cossacks' autonomous and traditional organization; the implied subjection to drilling, the use of unfamiliar weapons,

---

[80] For the fullest traditional account see Dubrovin, *Pugachev i ego soob-shchniki*, vol. 1; see also "Volnenie na Iaike pered Pugachevskim buntom: Zapiski kap. S. Mavrina, sostavlennaia na osnovanii doprosov kazakov v 1774," in *Pamiatniki Novoi Russkoi Istorii*, ed. V. Kashpirev, 3 vols. (St. Petersburg, n.d.), 2:250–94; I. G. Rozner, *Iaik pered burei* (Moscow, 1966).

the wearing of regular uniforms, and the shaving of beards and cutting of hair were anathema to a Cossack Host, whose members were mostly Old Believers. Finally, the government planned to control the Host's membership, to prevent escaped serfs from hiding in its ranks, and to keep accurate accounts for purposes of taxation and military service. To this end the Cossacks had to be registered, and the accession of new members became almost impossible.[81] The role of the Cossack assembly (*krug*) also was drastically reduced, to the benefit of the *ataman* and appointed officers.

In short, as the Petrine state threatened to eradicate most of their old privileges and traditions, the Cossacks' temper rose to the boiling point. With their petitions and requests disregarded in St. Petersburg (and even in Orenburg) and with the official commissions of investigation apparently siding with the *ataman* and the *starshina,* the Iaik Cossacks revolted. In 1772, provoked by the way General von Traubenberg was carrying out his investigation, they rioted.[82] They murdered Borodin, von Traubenberg, and several subaltern officers. The revolt was put down by a military detachment from Orenburg, but the tension remained.

The Iaik Host was prepared to follow any leader promising the return of the good old times, especially if he claimed to be the "legitimate" sovereign, Peter III. In due course such a pretender did appear—he was the Cossack Bogomolov. But Bogomolov did not have a chance to make much of a stir; he was seized and deported to Siberia (and died en route). Naturally, when Pugachev "revealed" himself as the true Peter III he immediately found support among the Iaik Cossacks. They not only were his first followers, but they also staffed his headquarters and provided him with his most loyal combat force and personal guard.[83]

While the deep involvement of the Iaik Cossacks with Pugachev may have been due in large part to the accident of their

---

[81] Dubrovin, *Pugachev i ego soobshchniki,* 1:106.

[82] Note the foreign name of von Traubenberg, and of quite a few officers and officials linked with the revolt. But there is no clear evidence of generalized xenophobia on the part of the rebels.

[83] Some historians go as far as to claim that the Iaik Cossacks kept close surveillance on Pugachev, who in fact was their prisoner throughout the revolt. This seems a bit excessive in my opinion.

geographical location and to the particular troubles that immediately preceded Pugachev's appearance, there is no doubt
that in general the Cossacks were a major factor in the revolt.
The Don Cossacks, it is true, did not support Pugachev in the
last phase of his revolt, when he was seeking their help after
his flight from Kazan.[84] (They may have been reluctant to join
someone whose success was then very much in doubt, but more
important, their combativeness had been pretty much broken
after *ataman* Efremov's attempt a few years earlier, and they
were under close government surveillance.) But Pugachev himself had stemmed from their ranks, and in the earlier period of
his career as a rebel (*buntovshchik*) he did find some support
among them. The Iaik (Ural) and Volga Cossacks, of course,
did follow him. What is even more interesting is the fact that
all the Cossacks idealized his memory and his rebellion, weav-
ing much of their folklore around it.[85] They exemplified the discontent and rebelliousness of a traditional group in the face of
transformations wrought (or threatened) by a centralized absolute monarchy. Like the feudal revolts and rebellions in the name
of regional particularism and traditional privileges in Western
Europe, the Cossacks opposed the tide of rational modernization
and the institutionalization of political authority. They regarded
their relationship to the ruler as a special and personal one
based on their voluntary service obligations; in return they
expected the czar's protection of their religion, traditional social
organization, and administrative autonomy. They followed the
promises of a pretender and raised the standard of revolt in the
hope of recapturing their previous special relationship and of
securing the government's respect for their social and religious
traditions.

As our brief survey of the difficulties experienced by the government with respect to the Cossacks, Bashkirs, and monastery
peasants must have indicated, local administration left much to
be desired in the eastern frontier regions. Inadequate local government was characteristic of the empire as a whole, but the

[84] A. P. Pronshtein, *Don i Nizhnee Povolzh'e v period krest ianskoi voiny,
1773–1775: Sbornik dokumentov* (Rostov-on-Don, 1961), esp. the editor's
introduction.

[85] I. I. Zheleznov, "Predaniia o Pugacheve," *Ural'tsy—Ocherki byta
Ural'skikh kazakov*, 3d ed., vol. 3 (St. Petersburg, 1910), pp. 135–222;
A. I. Lozanova, *Pesni i skazaniia o Razine i Pugacheve* (Leningrad, 1935).

deficiency was greater and fraught with more dangerous consequences in the east, where the population was sparse and
diversified ethnically, the distances great, and the territory still
open to incursions from the outside. We read with astonishment
and almost disbelief that the Kazan *guberniia,* with six provinces and a population of about 2.5 million, was administered
by only eighty regular officials.[86] The towns were sadly under-
populated, in most cases little more than walled-in villages,
and their officials were ill-prepared to meet any serious challenge. They panicked and fled rather than take decisive measures, as seen in the numerous cases of *voevody* and other func-
tionaries who deserted their posts at the first rumor of
Pugachev's approach.[87] We might add that prior to and during
the revolt the governors of Orenburg and Kazan (D. Volkov,
I. Reinsdorp, and von Brandt) were of low caliber. Given these
circumstances, the weak and inefficient response of the authorities to the first signs of the rebellion becomes understandable
and its rapid spread comprehensible.

It is only fair to point out that the few and inadequately
prepared officials had little military power they could rely on.
The garrisons of provincial fortresses (with the exception of
such centers as Orenburg and Tsaritsyn) were ridiculous both
in number and in quality.[88] There is no need to insist; we have
only to read the description of a small provincial garrison in the
east as accurately and vividly drawn by Pushkin in *The Captain's Daughter.* In the east only a few landowners actually
resided on their estates; the majority of the peasant serfs were
supervised by unreliable and corrupt managers and a few government officials.

[86] Alexander, "The Russian Government and Pugachev's Revolt," p. 20.
[87] Ia. K. Grot, ed., "P. S. Potemkin vo vremia pugachevshchiny," *Russkaia
Starina,* July-December, 1870, p. 496.
[88] Dmitriev-Mamonov (*Pugachevskii bunt v Zaural'e i Sibiri,* pp. 44–45)
gives the following list of military personnel in Chelyabinsk: 1 poruchik
(lieutenant), 4 corporals, 1 drummer-barber, 30 privates, 206 recruits,
6 retired officers, 7 retired non-commissioned officers, and 97 "retired recruits." The figures adduced by Dubasov ("Chuma i Pugachevshchina,"
p. 120) are no more impressive: in Shatsk there were 12 non-commissioned officers, 42 privates, 17 officers—and only 50 rifles! Incidentally,
most of the soldiers were invalids. See also the memorandum from the
College of War concerning garrisons in the eastern and southeastern regions in Dubrovin, *Pugachev i ego soobshchniki,* 1:377–86 (app. 3). The
over-all total of military personnel for this vast and unprotected region
was 27,779 men; the College proposed a reorganization which, among
other things, involved the raising of that figure to 32,761 men.

To summarize, the eastern borderlands shared the general features we have noted for the empire as a whole, with a double dynamic pattern which differed somewhat from the one encountered in Western Europe in the preceding century. On the one hand, we have a shrinking of the "frontier," the extension of direct state control over regions and social groups that heretofore had lived in a traditional and autonomous framework (Cossacks, natives). On the other hand, this same "rationalizing" and centralizing state was removing itself from the exercise of direct control over the common people by allowing the "interposition" of serf- and landowning nobles. In so doing the state gave inadequate protection and security to those forces which might have made for economic and social modernization. In view of this basic ambiguity and disarray, it was natural for the people to seek a sense of security and order by escaping from the present and, with the help of a "true ruler," to try to restore their direct personal connection with the source of political authority. The first goal, therefore, was the elimination of what M. Cherniavsky has called the new "priesthood" of the secular state. In Russia this priesthood was not so much the bureaucracy of the king's men (as in Western Europe) as it was the serf-owning state servitors, who lacked authority in the government but had complete and arbitrary control over their peasant serfs. In short, the main enemy was the serf-owning noble, who exercised evil power without bearing its moral burden as did the czar, the saintly, suffering prince.

Without going into an account of the revolt itself, which would throw little light on its causes and background, we may, however, note a few of its characteristic features in an effort to understand better its dynamics and impact. The history of the revolt may be divided into three phases whose specific traits should be noted briefly.[89] The first period, the fall and winter of 1773–74, was characterized by the revolt of the Iaik Cossacks, who, with the assistance of the Bashkirs, attacked Orenburg, the seat of government authority in the region. The siege, which

[89] A. Kizevetter, "K istorii krest'ianskikh dvizhenii v Rossii," *Krest'ianskaia Rossia* 8–9 (Prague, 1924):3–26; see also R. Portal, "Pougatchev: Une révolution manquée," *Études d'Histoire moderne et contemporaine* 1 (1947):68–98.

lasted several months, ended in failure; Pugachev could not take the city and was forced to withdraw into the Ural Mountains and the Bashkir region. There he remained until late spring, 1774, when the second phase of the revolt began. Having replenished his arsenal in the Ural factories, and expecting support from the peasants attached to factories and monasteries, Pugachev sallied forth westward from the Urals in the late spring or early summer of 1774. Most Bashkirs refused to follow him, and at first his support was limited to the Cossacks and some factory workers and peasants. But as he emerged from the Urals and turned toward the Volga he was well received by small towns, as well as by state and monastery peasants. He managed to capture Kazan but failed to hold it. Forced to retreat, he first went north, then crossed to the right bank of the Volga and turned southward down the river toward the region of the Don Cossack Host. At this point, after Pugachev had crossed to the western shore of the great river, the serfs rose *en masse* in the adjoining regions. The uprising became general: landowning nobles were killed or put to flight, and their estates were burned; bands of serfs roamed the countryside almost to the gate of Nizhni Novgorod, striking fear and panic into the hearts of landowners in and around Moscow. This phase of the revolt had a flavor strongly reminiscent of the *Grande Peur* in France fifteen years later, except that in Russia the rising was sparked not by fear of bandits but by the actual forays of peasant gangs invoking the authority of the true Czar Peter III, Pugachev.

It has been argued that, had Pugachev properly understood the dynamics of the peasant uprising he helped to provoke, he would not have turned south but would instead have marched west; with the help of the widespread and spontaneous serf uprising he would have been able to conquer the center of Russia and even Moscow.[90] But like his Cossack forerunner in

---

[90] Well known is the memoir account by Bolotov, *Zapiski*, vol. 3, chaps. 177–78; see also "Perepiska Ekateriny II s Moskovskim glavnokomanduiushchim kn. M. N. Volkonskim," *Osmnadtsatyi Vek* (Moscow), 1 (1869):79–183. The question remains open as to what Pugachev could have done even had he managed to enter Moscow. It is unlikely that the regime would have toppled (there was nothing to replace it with); at best there might have been a palace *coup* in favor of Grand Duke Paul, but this would not have changed the fate of either Pugachev or the Russian people.

the seventeenth century, Stenka Razin, Pugachev was not interested in the fate of the peasants and preferred to recoup his forces by arousing the Don Cossacks (or perhaps merely to take refuge there). But he failed to capture Tsaritsyn; and in the manner typical of primitive rebellions his own Cossack lieutenants turned him over to the imperial troops who were pursuing him.[91]

We should note that, in the first place, Pugachev failed to hold any major urban center; his movement was confined to the open countryside, especially in the territory of Cossacks and natives. In the second place, we ought to keep in mind that the real serf and peasant revolt started only after Pugachev's defeat at Kazan; it was an anticlimax, even though it turned out to be the bloodiest phase of the rebellion as well as the greatest threat to the social status quo. The Cossacks thus were the permanent, solid core of the movement; the other groups and regions were involved only through the accidents and fortunes of Pugachev's struggle with the imperial army.

These facts raise the question about the nature of the revolt that has much agitated Russian and Soviet historiographers: Was it a "conscious" effort to change the social and political systems, or was it merely a spontaneous, violent outbreak of anger and discontent? The Soviets believe that it was a regular peasant war;[92] but this interpretation hardly seems justified in the light of what we have seen of the background and causes. At best it is a simplification which applies only to the last phase of the rebellion. The movement, it seems to me, was primarily a "frontier" and Cossack affair, and its leadership never understood the possibilities offered by the serf uprising and a direct move against Moscow. This fact may also help to explain why the Pugachev rebellion was the last large-scale peasant rebellion not limited to a locality.[93]

As pretender, Pugachev endeavored to project himself in the image of the ideal ruler. The folkloristic tradition has empha-

---

[91] E. J. Hobsbawm, *Primitive Rebels: Studies in Archaic Forms of Social Movement in the 19th and 20th Centuries* (New York: Frederick A. Praeger, 1959).

[92] Some interesting and valid comments on the differences between the *Pugachevshchina* and the German Peasant War of the sixteenth century are made by Peters, "Politische und gesellschaftliche Vorstellungen."

[93] Firsov, *Pugachevshchina*, p. 109; Mavrodin, *Krest'ianskaia voina*, 2: 22–25.

sized this image by providing the typical medieval validation:
he was the real czar as long as he was successful; his very failure destroyed his claim and opened the way for a new pretender
(there were several of them after 1774).[94] He could not be defeated in open combat, but, once his success had been ques-
tioned, his own closest followers turned against him, rejected
him, and delivered him to those authorities whose success had
proved their legitimacy.[95]

According to folk memory and contemporary legends (confirmed both by Pugachev and his followers at their interroga-
tion), Pugachev appeared as the pretender-liberator. He was
Christlike and saintly because he had meekly accepted his dethronement by his evil wife and her courtiers. He had not
resisted his overthrow, but had left sadly to wander about the
world. He had come to help the revolt, but he did not initiate it;
the Cossacks and the people did that. The image, therefore, is
that of a passive leader, strongly reminiscent, of course, of the
image of the saintly meekness of the Kievan and medieval Russian ideals of kingship.[96] The pretender's wanderings, in truly
holy fashion, took him to Jerusalem and Constantinople first;
he then returned to Russia which he crisscrossed as a pilgrim.[97]
Wandering about the Russian land he learned of its condition
and needs; he helped his people through his counsel and
prayers before he accepted again the leadership to restore rightful authority. But how did one know that he was the rightful
czar? He had the imperial magic signs, like stigmata, on the
chest and on the head. Pugachev uncovered them to prove his
identity to the doubters. With a ceremonial that reminds one of
the Muscovite and Byzantine tradition, he made himself awesome and difficult of access. As head of the movement, he acted
primarily as ultimate judge, punishing and pardoning at will.
The very arbitrariness of his actions was a sign of his regal

---

[94] Sivkov, "Samozvanstvo v Rossii"; see also K. Bosl, *Frühformen der
Gesellschaft im mittelalterlichen Europa* (Munich, 1964).
[95] Hobsbawm, *Primitive Rebels*. Note the Christlike parallel of betrayal.
[96] Cherniavsky, *Tsar and People;* G. Fedotov, *The Russian Religious
Mind: Kievan Christianity* (Cambridge, Mass.: Harvard University Press,
1946), chap. 4.
[97] *Pugachevshchina*, 2:188. In *Pronshtein Don i Nizhnee Povolzh'e*,
p. 83, mention is also made of Egypt. The legend is reminiscent of F.
Tiutchev's famous stanza on Christ's wandering and blessing the Russian
land ("Eti bednye selen'ia," 1855).

sovereignty and nature.[98] He intervened only when called on to make a final decision or render a verdict of justice. Under the circumstances one may wonder how the people accounted for his failure. Interestingly enough, they did it in terms of God's law: Pugachev failed because he appeared before his time; he allowed himself to be tempted by human considerations (of pity and mercy) rather than abide by the will of God, Who had ordained that twenty years elapse between his dethronement and his return. In addition, he sinned by marrying a Cossack girl while his own lawful wife (whatever her crimes) was still alive; these acts of hubris predetermined his ultimate failure.[99]

Yet the image projected by Pugachev was not entirely medieval or traditional, as the legends and folklore might lead us to believe. There were also clearly elements of the modern Petrine notions of political authority. Like Peter the Great, the pretender had gone abroad to learn; like the first emperor, he was of foreign birth (here both positive and negative elements of the popular image of Peter I merge in a curious fashion). Pugachev tried to appear, in M. Cherniavsky's felicitous phrase, as "Sovereign Emperor."[100] The medals struck for him show him in neoclassical profile, in armor. Some presumed portraits make him look very much like Peter the Great, with the cat-like mustache and wild eyes. Finally, in some of his proclamations he had his name written in Latin (he was illiterate, of course); he was also alleged to have said that after he regained his throne he would make *Iaitskii gorodok* his "Petersburg."[101]

More significant than these externals were Pugachev's attempts at reproducing the St. Petersburg bureaucracy, the Petrine state. He established his own College of War (*Voennaia Kollegiia*) with quite extensive powers and functions. He created his own Count Chernyshev; he appointed to the rank of

---

[98] We are reminded of C. Schmitt's definition of sovereignty; see his "Soziologie des Souveränitätsbegriffs und politische Theologie," in *Erinnerungsgabe für Max Weber*, ed. M. Palyi, 2 vols. (Munich-Leipzig, 1923), 2:1–35.

[99] *Pugachevshchina*, 2:109–10, 114; V. Sokolova, "Pesni i predaniia o krest'ianskikh vosstaniiakh Razina i Pugacheva," *Trudy Instituta Etnografi Akademii Nauk SSSR*, n.s., 20 (1953):17–56.

[100] Cherniavsky, *Tsar and People*, pp. 97–99.

[101] *Pugachevshchina*, 2:111–12; R. V. Ovchinnikov, "Obzor pechatei na dokumentakh E. I. Pugacheva, ego voennoi kollegii i atamanov," in *Voprosy sotsial'no-ekonomicheskoi istorii i istochnikovedeniia perioda feodalizma v Rossii* (Moscow, 1961), pp. 328–35.

general, conferred titles, granted estates in the Baltic regions, and even gave away serfs.[102] He accepted and approved petitions for retirement from government service. Yet he also ap-appointed a *dumnyi diak* (secretary of the czar's council in the seventeenth century) to act as his main secretary—an interesting amalgam of old and new titles similar to what was practiced even by the immediate successors of Peter the Great.[103] Particularly striking for someone who is alleged to have risen against the burdens of the state, Pugachev in his proclamations did not promise complete freedom from taxation and recruitment. He granted only temporary relief, similar to the gracious "mercies" dispensed by a new ruler upon his accession.[104]

We have here perhaps the main clue to Pugachev's and his followers' concept of the state. They believed that the basis of political organization of society was service to the state (sovereign) by commoner and noble alike. It was the notion which Peter Struve has aptly termed "liturgic state."[105] Thus all soldiers were changed into Cossacks—i.e., free, permanent military servicemen, and so were all other military personnel, even the nobles and officers who joined Pugachev's ranks (voluntarily or under duress). Symbolically, in pardoning a noble or officer who had been taken prisoner, Pugachev's first act was to order that the prisoner's hair be cut in Cossack fashion (paralleling the "shaving of the forehead" which signified conscription into the emperor's regular army). All peasants also should be servants of the state: they were to become state peasants (instead of serfs of private owners or of monasteries) and serve as Cossacks, i.e., militia. (Note, they were not to be given personal freedom.) The nobles in turn were no longer to be

---

[102] *Pugachevshchina*, 2:113. Volume 1 of this collection reproduces all the decrees and orders that were issued by Pugachev's College of War; see also *ibid.*, 3:7, and Mavrodin, *Krest'ianskaia voina*, 2:12.

[103] *Pugachevshchina*, 2:107 and 1:136.

[104] *Ibid.*, 3:110. Only at the very end of the revolt, on the last day of July, 1774, did Pugachev issue a proclamation virtually inviting the peasants to take the law into their own hands, to do whatever they wanted; see Ia. K. Grot, "Materialy dlia istorii Pugachevskogo bunta: Bumagi otnosiashchiesia k poslednemu periodu miatezha i poimke Pugacheva," *Zapiski imperatorskoi Akademii Nauk* 25 (1875), app. 4, p. 53.

[105] *The Cambridge Economic History of Europe from the Decline of the Roman Empire*, vol. 1 (Cambridge, 1941), p. 419; for a discussion of this notion with respect to the "feudal" period of Russian history, see M. Szeftel's article in *Feudalism in History*, ed. R. Coulborn (Princeton: Princeton University Press, 1956).

pomeshchiki, i.e., estate and serf owners, but were to revert to their previous status as the czar's servicemen on salary.[106]

Was there no concept of freedom in this movement? There was: freedom from the nobility, which implied the natural freedom to be what God had made one to be—a tiller of the soil, who was free to work and possess the land he had made productive, or cattle-raising nomads, who were free "like steppe animals."[107] Naturally, too, old religious practices were to be tolerated, for Pugachev "granted beards and the cross," i.e., the freedom to be an Old Believer. He talked about the nobles as traitors to himself and to the people, and of his intention to restore the natural direct bonds between himself and the people —there need not be any intermediaries, any "secular priesthood" of nobles. Pugachev's statements here are reminiscent, *mutatis mutandis,* of Ivan IV's missive from Aleksandrovskaia *sloboda* in which the awesome czar demanded the right to eliminate the boyars, who had interposed themselves between him and his loyal people, betraying both.

The ideal of Pugachev's followers was essentially a static, simple society where a just ruler guaranteed the welfare of all within the framework of a universal obligation to the sovereign. The ruler ought to be a father to his people, his children; and power should be personal and direct, not institutionalized and mediated by land- or serf owner.[108] Such a frame of mind may also account for the strong urge to take revenge on the nobles and officials, on their modern and evil way of life. This urge manifested itself with particular force, of course, in the last phase of the revolt: the serfs destroyed the estates of the nobility especially their most modern features (e.g., glass panes, windows, and mantlepieces), for these were symbols of the new, alien, secular civilization; there were also some instances of "Luddite" actions on the part of factory workers in the Urals.

Taking these features of the movement's ideology and symbol-

---

[106] *Pugachevshchina,* 2:135, 194.

[107] Firsov, *op. cit.,* p. 127; *Pugachevshchina,* 1:28. Note also the traditional threats of dire punishment if they do not accept his "merciful grant" (R. V. Ovchinnikov and L. N. Slobodskikh, "Novye dokumenty o krest'ianskoi voine 1773–1775 g. v Rossii," *Istoricheskii Arkhiv,* 1956, no. 4, p. 131). The dissertation of Peters, "Politische und gesellschaftliche Vorstellungen," gives a detailed summary of the notions of state and power held by those who participated in the Pugachev movement.

[108] *Pugachevshchina,* 1:74–75.

ism as indications of its participants' basic attitudes and aspirations, it is quite clear that they felt disarray stemming from a sense of crisis of the old and traditional order.[109] Somehow they were aware that there could be no going back to the old forms, but neither could they accept the dynamic implications of the new. They were particularly frightened by apparent economic and social changes, and they rejected the individualistic dynamics implicit in them; they wished to recapture the old ideals of service and community in a hierarchy ordained by God. Most significantly, it seems to me, they were not able to come to terms with the functional organization and impersonal institutionalization of authority. In this inability they were not alone, nor the last, as the Decembrist movement and the history of the intelligentsia have shown. Pugachev and his followers needed a palpable sense of direct relationship with the source of sovereign power and ultimate justice on this earth. The Cossacks were, of course, most keenly aware of the loss of their special status and direct contact with the czar and his government; but so were the serfs and, in an inchoate way, some of the non-Russian natives as well. The movement was thus "reactionary" in the etymological sense, with its predominance of negative-passive ideological elements; at time it seemed a childlike desire to return to the quiet and security of the protective family.

Not surprisingly, in view of this childlike urge to return to the protective family, we detect on the part of the rebels a naïve desire to be loved by their elders, i.e., the true czar and his good boyars. Was this not the mirror image of the ambivalence the upper class felt, vis à vis the common people, which

---

[109] The same point was put somewhat differently in the seminar discussion of the present essay: The serfs, the Cossacks, and the *odnodvortsy* revolted ultimately in defense of their traditional closed system of social patterns and values. In their view the mortal threat to this system came from the "modern" (Petrine) state's going beyond its traditional (negative) function of dispensing security and justice by interfering with the form and content of men's traditional actions and appearance. They felt, in short, that the new state was attempting to change man's very being for the sake of a secular (evil) purpose. The noblemen (*pomeshchiki*) in their role as serf owners, also were threatening to break up the traditional patterns of peasant action and belief by interfering in their ways of tilling the soil, disrupting their family structure, by promoting a new, western and non-Russian, way of life. Religion having retained its traditional binding character for the Weltanschauung of the peasants, the revolt against innovation and modernization was most forcefully expressed by the Old Believers, who constituted a sizable minority of the peasants and an overwhelming majority of the Cossacks.

became noticeable at about the same time? Both the peasants and upper class dimly perceived that they had become alien to each other, that they had ceased to be members of the same God-ordained, harmonious order. This realization may go a long way in explaining the excessive panic and fear that the last phase of the rebellion aroused in the nobility of Moscow and St. Petersburg. Little wonder that the educated nobles reacted by trying to create a new image of the peasant which would emphasize those very qualities that could put their fears to rest. Instead of the view of the serf as an uncouth half-beast who could be kept down only by force, we observe the emergence of the notion of the peasant as a child, a child who has to be protected against himself and carefully guided into the new "civilization."[110] While this reaction was clearly defensive, it also bespoke a subconscious and correct understanding of the psychic mechanism that had driven the people to rebellion. The dim awareness that for the peasant—as with children—feelings of justice and the need for personified authority outweighed the possible advantages of rationalized and institutionalized power not only started a new trend in Russian literature but also helped to shape the basic attitudes of the elite: a feeling of ambivalence toward, and alienation from, the people, coupled with an almost overpowering sense of social responsibility and moral guilt. These were to be the driving forces in creating modern Russian culture with its double aspect of guilt and distance with respect to both the state and the people.

Pushkin was perhaps the first to become fully aware of this ambiguity in modern Russia's elite and its culture. He also was the first to give artistic expression to this new—post-Pugachev—relationship between the upper classes and the people, a relationship he depicted with great psychological and historical insight and artistic felicity in *The Captain's Daughter*.[111] For our

---

[110] J.-L. Van Regemorter, "Deux images idéales de la paysannerie russe à la fin du XVIIIe siècle," *Cahiers du Monde russe et soviétique* 9, no. 1 (1968):5–19. One cannot help being struck by the parallel development in the United States after Nat Turner's rebellion.

[111] Pushkin was also the first historian of the Pugachev rebellion. His *Istoriia Pugachevskogo Bunta* is valuable as a symptom and for the documentation included and appended therein; by today's standards and tastes it is pretty boring, being only what L. Febvre's school derides as *histoire évenementielle*.

generation it is of course tempting to interpret his famous depiction—in Grinev's dream—of the ambiguous relationship between the elite and the people in Freudian terms, as a restatement of the Oedipal conflict. In such an interpretation the dream would express the feelings of young Grinev (representing the westernized nobility) toward his castrating father (i.e., Pugachev, his love-hate of the father who possesses the mother (i.e., the people).[112]

But may not another great Russian poet, Marina Tsvetaeva, have seen deeper into Pushkin's meaning?[113] Instead of fastening on Grinev, who is the concern of modern Freudians, she focusses on Pugachev. She notices his craving for Grinev's full, unquestioning love—as father or perhaps an older brother would want to be loved. Tsvetaeva's reading of the dream brings out the sense of loss of the elite's affection that Pugachev— symbolizing the people—may have felt. Is Pugachev's love not the love of someone enchantingly closer to nature, someone completely possessed by genuine feeling? Pushkin speaks of Pugachev's magic (*char*), to which Grinev succumbs against his better judgment. Is this primitive, magical love not the saving force? Twice it saves Grinev from the evils of nature and/or men. The ultimate tragedy of Pugachev (the people) may have been that Grinev (elite as well as the people's child) could not accept this free gift of love.[114] Was not the almost magical intervention of the natural brother's gift of love an attempt to save the last representative of the old intelligentsia, Iurii Zhivago?

The rebellion of Pugachev was in truth the prologue to the history of modern Russian culture, and as such, it marked also the very beginning of the great Russian revolution of the twentieth century.

[112] A. Besançon, "Psychoanalysis: Auxiliary Science or Historical Method," *Journal of Contemporary History* 3, no. 2 (April, 1968):153–54; *idem, Le tsarévitch immolé: La symbolique de la loi dans la culture russe* (Paris, 1967), pp. 164–69.

[113] M. Tsvetaeva, "Pushkin i Pugachev," in *Moi Pushkin* (Moscow, 1967), pp. 105–60 (article was written in 1937).

[114] James Baldwin echoes this same sentiment in *The Fire Next Time* when he points out that the only gift the downtrodden and the slave can bestow is the gift of love; and on our ability to accept love depends the creation of a meaningful relationship between the polar extremes of society, and of a livable civilization.

Bibliographical Note

The literature on the Pugachev rebellion is enormous. I make no pretense of having covered it fully. The most comprehensive bibliography that has come to my attention appears in the dissertation of D. Peters referred to earlier; it contains over five hundred items. The most up-to-date general history is a proposed three-volume work, of which the first two volumes have appeared, V. Mavrodin, *Krest'ianskaia voina v Rossii v 1773–1775 godakh: Vosstanie Pugacheva* (Leningrad, 1961–66). The first volume is a valuable (in spite of its bias) and detailed historiographical and bibliographical survey. A recent, brief account of the revolt itself is I. G. Rozner's *Kazachestvo v krest'ianskoi voine 1773–1775 gg.* (Lvov, 1966). A summary account of the revolt is contained in the recently published study of the government's reaction to the *Pugachevshchina*, John T. Alexander's *Autocratic Politics in a National Crisis: The Imperial Russian Government and Pugachev's Revolt, 1773–1775*, Russian and East European Series, vol. 38 (Bloomington: Indiana University Press, 1969).

Notes on Contributors

J. H. ELLIOTT has been Professor of History at King's College, University of London, since 1968. He studied history at Cambridge University and subsequently was a lecturer there until taking up his present appointment. His specialty is sixteenth- and seventeenth-century history, with special reference to Spain and Spanish America. His published works include *The Revolt of the Catalans* (1963), *Imperial Spain* (1963), and *Europe Divided, 1559–98* (1968). A study of the impact of America on Europe will be published in 1970 under the title of *The Old World and the New, 1492–1650*.

ROBERT FORSTER has been Professor of History at The Johns Hopkins University since 1966. Educated at Swarthmore College, Harvard University, and The Johns Hopkins University, he taught at the University of Nebraska and Dartmouth College before coming to Johns Hopkins in 1965. His specialty is the social history of France in the eighteenth century. His principal published work is *The Nobility of Toulouse in the Eighteenth Century* (1960). Another book, entitled *The House of Saulx-Tavanes: Versailles and Burgundy, 1700–1830*, will be published in 1971.

JACK P. GREENE has been Professor of History at The Johns Hopkins University since 1966. He received his university education at the University of North Carolina at Chapel Hill, Indiana University, the University of Nebraska, Bristol University, and Duke University, and has taught previously at Michigan State University, Western Reserve University, the College of William and Mary, and the University of Michigan. A specialist in seventeenth- and eighteenth-century Anglo-American history, he has published a number of books and articles, among them *The Quest for Power: The Lower Houses of Assembly in the Southern Royal Colonies, 1689–1776* (1963).

203

ROLAND MOUSNIER has been Professeur d'Histoire moderne en Sorbonne since 1955 and Directeur du Centre Recherches sur la Civilisation de l'Europe modern since 1958. He studied in the Faculté des Lettres de Paris and at the École pratique hautes Études, and earlier taught at various *lycées*—Corneille in Rouen, Janson-de-Sailly, and Louis-le-Grand in Paris—as well as at l'Institut d'Études politiques de Paris and the l'Institut d'Études politiques de Strasbourg. His main interest has been in early modern France. Among his many books are *La Vénalité des Offices sous Henri IV et Louis XIII* (1945); *État et Commissaire: Recherches sur la Création des Intendants des Provinces (1634–1648)* (1958); *L'Assassinat d'Henri IV* (1964); and *Fureurs Paysannes* (1968).

MARC RAEFF has been Professor of Russian History at Columbia University since 1965. He was educated in France and at Harvard University and taught at the University of Washington and Clark University before coming to Columbia in 1961. He is primarily interested in eighteenth- and nineteenth-century Russia, and his published works include *M. M. Speransky: Statesman of Imperial Russia* (1957); *Siberia and the Reforms of 1822* (1956); and *Origins of the Russian Intelligentsia* (1966).

J. W. SMIT has been Queen Wilhelmina Professor at Columbia University since 1968. He studied and taught at the University of Utrecht before coming to Columbia in 1965. He is interested in sixteenth-century European history, with special reference to the history and culture of the Netherlands. Among his principal publications is *Fruin and the Political Parties at the Time of the Republic* (1958).

LAWRENCE STONE is Dodge Professor of History at Princeton University and Director of the Shelby Cullom Davis Center for Historical Studies. He studied at Oxford University, where he was subsequently a Fellow of Wadham College before assuming his present position in 1963. Primarily interested in early modern British History, he has published *Sculpture in Britain: The Middle Ages* (1955), *An Elizabethan: Sir Horatio Palavicino* (1956), and *The Crisis of the Aristocracy, 1558–1641* (1965), as well as numerous articles on the social, economic, educational, and architectural history of modern England.

Index

Abbott, George, archbishop of Canterbury, 81
Administration. *See* Bureaucracy
"Administrative revolution," in England, 70–71
Agenais, 144
Agriculture: in England, 74, 96; in France, 135–37, 155; in Russia, 164–65
Aides, 133
Aides et gabelles, in France, 155
Aksakov, S., 174
Alburquerque, duke of, 117
Alcald, duke of, 117
Alsace, 131
Alum, 68, 69
Alva, duke of, 48, 49, 50
Amsterdam, government of, 29, 30, 39, 42
Andalusia, 109
Angers, in France, 151–54
Anglo-Scottish War, 85, 103
Anjou, estates of, 149
Anne, queen of England, 108, 182
Annese, Gennaro, 126
Anomie, Merton's study of, 24
Anti-colonial feelings, in the Catalan revolt, 58
Antwerp, economy of, 39, 43
Apothecaries, 152
Apprentices, in England, 62, 102
Aragon, 113
Aristocracy, in England, 61, 72, 82–83, 84, 99, 100, 104. See also *Gentilshommes*; Gentry; *Grands*; Nobles
Arminianism, 100
Army, British: 69–70, 103–4; lack of employment opportunities in, 94
Arrêt d'Union, 146
Artisans: in England, 62, 88, 93, 101; in France, 152, 157; in the Netherlands, 30, 37–40, 41

Assignats, Russian, 164
Ataman, Cossack, 186, 187, 188, 189
Attainders, in England, 72
Attorneys, French, 141, 144, 152, 153

Bacon, Francis, 92, 111
Bailliage courts, 142
Bande d'ordonnance, 31, 47
Banditry: in Catalonia, 117, 127; in Naples and Sicily, 125
Ban et arrière ban, at Angers, 151, 153
Barcelona, 116, 119, 128
Barshchina, 166. See also *Corvée*
Bashkirs, in Russia, 9–10, 181, 183–84, 185, 192, 193
Bastwick, 101
Bates case, 90
Bazadais, 134
Béarn, provincial estates of, 149
Bedford, duke of, 105
Berry, estates of, 149
Bibikov, General A., 178
Bigorre, estates of, 150
Billeting, in Catalonia, 122, 128
Bill of Rights, 108
Bishops, English, social origins of, 79
Bogomolov, 189
Book of Rates, 69
Bordeaux: *généralité* of, 133–34; Parlement of, 142, 156
Borodin, murder of, 188, 189
Bouillon, duke of, 138
"Bourgeois Revolution": and England, 55; and the Netherlands, 20, 23–24, 37, 52. *See also* Classes; Marx
Bourgeoisie: in England, 63; in the Netherlands, 32, 53
Bourgogne, provincial estates of, 150
Boyars, in Russia, 198

Brabant, 28, 30, 32, 38, 39, 40, 50
Braganza, duke of, 115, 122
Braudel, Fernand, 52
Bread, price of in France, 110, 134
Bread riots, in France, 136
Bristol, earl of, 94
Brittany, provincial estates of, 149
Brotherhood of Saint Nicholas at Angers, 151
Buckingham, George Villiers, duke of, 83, 85, 90, 93, 101
Bureaucracy: as a cause of revolt, 6–8, 14; in England, 66, 69, 70–71, 84–85, 96, 103–4; in France, 132, 138–49; in the Netherlands, 33–34, 36; in Russia, 9–10, 190–91, 196–98; in the Spanish Monarchy, 117–19, 121–22, 124, 129. *See also* Constitution
Burton, 101

Calvinism, in the Netherlands, 46
Campoix, 135–36
Canterbury, archbishop of, 105
Capet, Hughes, 138
Capitalism. *See* Economy
Castile, 113; dominant position of in the Spanish Monarchy, 118; economy of, 117; lack of revolt in, 109
Castilianization, 6, 118–19
Catherine II, empress of Russia, 164, 169, 170; attempts at codification of law by, 172*n*; peasants' attitude toward, 170
Catholicism, abolition of in Holland and Zeeland, 50
Catholics, in England, 72, 80, 95, 97
Cavaliers, in England, 101, 105
Cavendish case, 69
Cecil, William, 85
Cecil faction, at the English court, 84
Censitaires, of *gentilshommes*, in France, 137, 155, 156
Censorship, under the Tudors, 73
Census, in Russia, 168
Centralization. *See* Bureaucracy
Cerdanya, 111
Chalais, conspiracy of, 137
Chambre des Requêtes, in the Parlement of Provence, 144
Chambres des Comptes, 142
Champagne, province of, 135
Champs-de-Mars, general assembly of Franks in, 147
Chancellor, office of in France, 139, 156
Chancery (England), interference

with, 88
Char (personal magic), of Pugachev, 201
Charlemagne, 147
Charles I, king of England, 77, 84, 101, 102, 103, 106; conservative politics of, 98; economic policies of, 99; foreign policy of, 97; ideology of, 177; influence of Catholics over, 97; unpopularity of, 86
Charles V, emperor, 27, 31, 38, 43, 50, 138; political methods of, 32–33; religious policy of, 45
Châteaux, demolition of, in France, 134
Cheremys, attempted conversion of, 182
Church: in England, 68, 71–72, 75, 85, 97; landholdings in Russia, 178; Russian government's policy toward, 169–70
Church-and-King men, 63
Church, Catholic, of the Netherlands, 4; attacked by mobs, 48
Church of England, 78–81, 93, 95, 96, 102; hierarchy of, 104; lack of employment opportunities in, 94; parish clergy of, 79–80; patronage in, 72, 81; property of, 78; public opinion of, 78–80
Chuvash, attempted conversion of, 182
Cing-Mars, marquis de, 138
Clarendon, Edward Hyde, earl of, 55
"Classes," 13; in France, 157; in the Netherlands, 23, 31, 37, 39–40, 49. *See also* Marx
Clergy: in Catalonia, 114–16; in England, 78–82, 93, 148; in France, 153
Clientele of nobility, in the Netherlands, 31. See also *Créatures*
Cloth manufacturing, in England, 74, 89, 99, 102
"Club-men," 62
Coal, 68
Coal mining, in England, 74
Codification Commission of 1767, in Russia, 167, 182–83
Coke, Sir Edward, 59, 81, 88, 101
"Collective behavior," theories of, applied to the Netherlands, 46–47
College of Economy, in Russia, 170
College of War, of Russia, 188; created by Pugachev, 196
Colonies, British, in North America, written constitutions of, 138

Colonists, in Russia, 177–78
Commerce, closed to *gentilshommes*, 155
Commission on Fees, 100
Common lands, 62
Common law, in England, 59, 66, 67, 68, 84, 89–91
Commonwealth, ideal of, 104, 107
Concini, Concino, 139
Condé, prince of, 138, 157
Condomois, 135
Conscription, in Russia, 162
Conseiller d'état, 142
Conseillers du roi, 142
Constable, 139
Constitution, 16; of England, 4, 61, 91, 95, 101, 104, 106; of France, 7–8, 133, 138–40, 142–43, 147–49, 154; of the Netherlands, 31–36, 44, 52; of the Spanish Monarchy, 113–15, 119, 122–23. See also *Patria*
Conti, prince of, 138, 157
Contract. See Constitution
Copyholders, in England, 62, 75
Corporate bodies: in France, 142–49, 152; in the Netherlands, 27–29; in the Spanish Monarchy, 115. See also Magistrates; Municipalities; Officials
Cortes, in the Spanish monarchy, 115. See also Constitution
Corvée, in Russia, 10, 166, 167, 173–74
Cossack elders (*starshina*), 175–76; estates of, 175
Cossacks, 17, 179, 185, 186, 187–89, 192, 193, 194, 199; government's attempt to register, 189; revolt of, compared to feudal revolts in Western Europe, 190
Council of State: in France, composition of, 139–40; in the Netherlands, 47
"Country," English, 4, 87, 96, 104; versus court, 95; ideology of, 91–92
County, English, as focus of loyalty, 71
Coup d'état, 2, 8, 89, 122; of William of Orange, 50
Cours des Aides, 142
Cours des Monnaies, 142
Court of Admiralty (England), 70
Court of Exchequer (England), 70
Court of High Commission (England), interference with, 88
Court of Wards (England), 70
Courts, common law, 70, 88, 91
Créatures: of central government in the Netherlands, 33; in France, 139–40, 156, 157; nature of in France, 141
"Credibility gap," in the English Church, 78
Croij, clan of, in the Netherlands, 31
Crue de gernisons, 142
"Cultural Revolution," as preached in 1641, 61
Curia Regis, 147, 148
Currency: of Castile, 120; of Catalonia, 120
Customs. See Taxes
Czar, links of peasant community with, 163

d'Alais, Count, 156
d'Alesi, Guiseppe, 126
Dauphiné, provincial estates of, 150
"Days of Dupes," 137
Decembrists, 199
Demagogues, roles of in popular revolts, 111
d'Epernon, duc, 156, 157
Devereux faction, at the English court, 84
Diputació, 115, 122, 123
Diputats, of Catalonia, 17, 122, 129
Divine Right of Kings, 61, 93, 95
Dnieper Cossacks, 187
Don Cossack Host, 175, 193
Don Cossacks, 177, 184, 186; role of in Pugachev's rebellion, 190, 194. See also Cossacks
d'Orléans, Gaston, 137, 138, 150
Downs, battle of 1639, 121
Dubinshchina (rebellion of peasants belonging to monasteries), 178
Dudley faction, at the English court, 84
Dumnyi diak, 197
"Dysfunctions," 3, 9, 17; in England, 67, 74–96

East India Company, 99
Economic conditions, in the Spanish Monarchy, 117, 120–21, 129
Economic ideas, in eighteenth-century Russia, 166
Economy: of England, 74, 85–86, 96, 99, 101–2; of France, 132–34, 135–36; of the Netherlands, 20, 37, 40, 41–43, 51–53; of Russia, 167. See also Agriculture
Education: attitudes toward, and societal change, 24; in England, 73, 88
Edward I, king of England, 59
Edward II, king of England, 58
Edward VI, king of England, 72

Efremov, S., *ataman* of Don Cossacks, 186, 190
Élection, creation of new, in
Agenais, 144; of Angers, 151
Eliot, Sir John, 94, 101
Elites: alienation and fragmentation of, 3, 6, 13, 17; in Catalonia,
112, 113; in England, 64, 65, 67,
76–86, 100, 107; in France, 137,
142–47; in Naples, 14, 112, 127;
in the Netherlands, 31–32, 41–
42, 47–48; in Portugal, 112, 123,
127; in Russia, 163, 165–66, 187.
See also Cossacks; Gentry;
Grands; Magistrates; Nobles
Elizabeth I, queen of England, 73,
77, 79, 81, 85, 86; persecution of
the Puritans under, 97; policy of
procrastination of, 95–96; reign
of, 59, 66
Elizabeth Petrovna, empress of Russia, 162; industrial development
under, 162–80; policy of, regarding Church peasants, 169;
religious policy of, 182
Elus, corporate body of, 142, 143,
144, 150
Enlightenment, 55
Epidemics, 134; in Russia, 169. *See
also* Plagues
Episcopal Church, destruction of
during the English Revolution,
107
Episcopate, in England, 4
Established Church, destruction of
during the English Revolution,
58, 61
Establishment, English, 78–85
Estates-General: of France, 139,
198; of the Netherlands, 5, 17,
27–28, 35, 47, 48
Estates, provincial, 6; in France,
149–50; in the Netherlands, 3, 17,
31–35, 50; in the Spanish Monarchy, 115, 123
Evora (Portugal), 1637 riots at, 119
Executive, limitations of in England, 108. *See also* Constitution

Family, attitudes toward and
societal change, 24
Fermiers, 155
Feudal dues, revival of in England,
99
Fidélités, 7, 141
Fiscal policies. *See* Monopolies;
Taxation
Five Knights case, 90
Flanders, 40, 50; economic situa-
tion of, 39; religion of, 45; town

government in, 28, 30; urban
revolts in, 38
Forest laws, 99
Francs-fiefs, at Angers, 151, 154
Franks, 147
Free Economic Society, propaganda
of, 166, 167
Freeholders: and Charles I, 98;
economic position of, 75
French Revolution, 65, 82
Friesland, 27
"Frontier conditions," in Russia,
10–11

Gabelle, 153; at Angers, 151
Gages, 143, 144, 145, 146
Garonne valley, economic condi-
tions in, 134
Gelderland, 28
Gent, 29, 32, 40
Gentilshommes, in France, 137,
154–57
Gentry, in England, 56, 59, 60,
63–64, 71–72, 75, 84–88, 90–106,
107. *See also* Landownership
Germany, 31, 74
Gold, 68
Gondomar, Count of, 86
"Good Catholics," 132
Gouda, 40
Grain prices, in Russia, 165. *See
also* Agriculture
Grammar school. *See* Education
Grande Peur, Pugachev's rebellion
compared to, 193
Grand Privilege (the Netherlands),
28
Grands, in France, 6, 137–39, 156–
57
Great Council of 1640, 98
"Great Rebellion," 55, 57
Greniers à Sel, 142; at Angers, 151
Grisons, Swiss, 131
Groningen, 28
Gros fermiers, 136
"Guild democracy," in the Nether-
lands, 50
Guilds: at Angers, 152; in Cata-
lonia, 128; in England, 99; in the
Netherlands, 29, 30, 50
Guise, duke of, 138
Gustavus, Adolphus, king of
Sweden, 78
Guyenne: economic conditions of,
134–36; land survey of, 135

Habsburgs: Austrian, 131, 132; and
France, 131; Spanish, and the
Netherlands, 33. *See also* Philip II
Hainaut, nobility of, 41

Hampden, John, 101
Harrington, James, 56
Harvests, of 1630s, in England, 102. *See also* Agriculture; *Mortalités*
Héjar, duke of, 109
Henry IV, king of France, 137, 139
Henry VIII, king of England, 59, 66, 67, 77, 86; religious policy of, 71–72
Historiography: of the English Revolution, 55–56, 61, 102; of the Netherlands Revolution, 19–24; Soviet, of Pugachev's rebellion, 163, 194
Hobbes, Thomas, 58
Holland: economy of, 39–40; Estates of, 44; role of in the Netherlands Revolution, 49–50; towns of, 29
Hondschoote, economic situation of, 39–40
Hoogstraten, count of, 41
House of Commons: increasing self-confidence of, 71, 84, 88; Puritan lobby in, 90, 95; under the reign of Elizabeth I, 86–87
House of Lords: destruction of in the English Revolution, 58, 107; hostility toward, 99
Huissiers, of the parlements, 144, 156
Humanitists, of the Netherlands, 45
Hunger, in Sicily, 110. *See also* Plagues

Iaitskii gorodak (center of Old Believers), 187, 196
Iasak (tribute in kind), 182
Ideology, 15–16; and the English Revolution, 89–93, 107–8; and the *Fronde*, 8–9, 147–49; and the Netherlands Revolution, 16, 34–35, 43–46, 48–49, 52; and the Pugachev rebellion, 199–201; and the revolts in the Spanish Monarchy, 114–17. *See also* Constitution; *Patria*; Puritanism
Ile de France, 135
Income, English national, 75
Independents, 57
Indirect taxes. *See* Taxes
Industry, in Russia, 162
Inflation, in eighteenth-century Russia, 164
Inns of Court, 88, 90, 94
Intellectuals, alienation of in England, 94. *See also* Ideology
Intelligentsia. *See* Ideology
Intendants, 133, 140, 143, 145, 156
Internal duties. *See* Taxes

Internal war, concept of, 21–23, 25, 26–46, 51, 55
Ireland, 77–78; earl of Strafford in, 98
Irish land settlement, 99
Irish Rebellion, 105–6
Italy, and Thirty Years' War, 131
Ivan IV, 198

"J curve," in England, 102
Jacqueries, 2, 5–6, 12, 13, 15. *See also* Popular revolts; Urban revolts
James I, king of England, 78, 79, 86, 89; lack of popularity of, 86; pro-Spanish policy of, 84; religious policy of, 81; selling of offices under, 69; succession of, 77
James II, king of England, 103
Jerusalem, 95
Justices of the Peace, in Elizabethan England, 87–88, 95

Kazan, in Russia, 178, 182, 191, 193, 194
Kent, gentry of, 63
King: in France, 138–39; in Russia, 189
"King in Parliament," 66, 71
Kingship: absentee, in the Spanish Monarchy, 113–14, 123, 129; ideals of in Russia, 195; Renaissance, 73; reputation of in England, 86
Kirghiz, 183
Koliivshchina, 187

Laborers: in England, 62, 75; in France, 149; in Russia, 180
Landownership: in England, 75, 82, 88, 102; in France, 135–36; in the Netherlands, 41; in Russia, 168, 178
La Pilosa, Antonio, 126
La Rochelle, siege of, 150
Laud, archbishop, 59, 97, 100–103, 105
Law of inheritance, in Russia, 174
Lawyers: common-law, 88–89, 94, 96; in England, 59, 75, 90–91, 93, 94, 100, 104; in France, 141; in Naples and Sicily, 126; in the Netherlands, 32
Leiden, 40
Lemousin, 135, 149
Lerma, duke of, 117
Lettre de jussion, 143
Levellers, 57, 59, 65, 107
Lex Salica. See Constitution

"Liberties." *See* Constitution; Corporate bodies
Ligueurs, 132
Lisbon, 116, 119
Lit de justice, 148
"Liturgic state," 197
Local Government. *See* Bureaucracy
Locke, John, 108
Loginov, *starshin*, 188
Long Parliament, 60–61, 91, 99, 104–7
Longue robe, 41
Lord Treasurer (England), 70
Lorraine, 131, 135, 137
Louis XIII, regency for, 132, 137, 138–39, 149
Louis XIV, 9, 78, 138–39
Louvain, 40
"Luddite" activity, in Russia, 198
Luynes, duc de, 139

Magistrates: in France, 140–41, 142, 143–47, 153; in the Netherlands, 30, 33, 41, 47, 48. *See also* Corporate bodies; Officials
Magna Carta, 91, 96, 104
Magnates. *See* Aristocracy
Maîtrises des Eaux et Forêts, 142
Maréchaussée, 151
Marian exiles. *See* Puritans
Marie de Medicis, 132, 137, 150
Marillac, Keeper of the Seals (France), 132, 137
Marprelate Tracts, in England, 79
Marx: and the English Revolution, 61; and the Netherlands Revolution, 20, 23–24, 37–38, 43; and revolution, 13
Mary, Queen of Scots, execution of, 77
Masaniello, rebel leader of Naples, 111, 126
Mazarin, cardinal, 132, 139, 153
Mazarins, 153, 157
Medina Sedonia, duke of, 109
Mercenaries, in England, 69
Merchants: in England, 62, 75, 84, 93, 100, 104; in France, 152–57; in the Netherlands, 30, 37–40, 41, 50, 53
Messina, against Palermo, 123
Migration, in the Netherlands, 40
Militia: in England, 70; in France, 133–34; in the Netherlands, 30, 47
Millenarianism, in the Spanish Monarchy, 111
Millenial Petition, in England, 81

Mineral monopolies, in England, 68, 69
Mining, in Russia, 11, 179–81
Mobility, social, 3; in England, 62, 94, 98; in the Netherlands, 40
Monarchy, in England, 58, 86, 107. *See also* Kingship
Monasteries: in Russia, 178; seizure of in England, 68
Monopolies: in England, 68, 85–86, 95, 99; in Russia, 162
Monsieur, duc d'Orléans, 138
Montmorency, Henri de, 138, 150
"Moral communities." *See* Municipalities (in the Netherlands)
Mordvinians (Russian tribe), 182
Mortalités, in France, 134–36. *See also* Plague
Mozdovskii Polk (Cossack regiment), 186
Münsterism, in Netherlands, 46
Municipalities: in Flanders, 28, 30; in France, 150–54, 157; in the Netherlands, 28–30, 42, 51

Nationalism: in Catalonia and Portugal, 114–17, 128; in England, 71, 86; in the Netherlands, 20, 36, 44, 49, 51–52; in Russia, 181–86. See also *Patria*
Natural law. *See* Ideology
Navy, English, 85
Neapolitan revolt. *See* Sicilian and Neapolitan revolts
Nepliuev, J. J., governor-general of Orenburg, 184
Newcastle, 74
New learning, in England, 5
Nizhni-Novgorod, episcopal see of, 178, 193
Nobility. *See* Aristocracy; *Gentilshommes*; Gentry; *Grands*; Nobles
Nobles: of Catalonia, 14, 117; of England, 98; of France, 136–37, 144, 148, 154–57; of Naples and Sicily, 123–25; of the Netherlands, 23, 31–32, 41–42, 47–49, 51; of Russia, 10–11, 162–66, 172, 175, 192, 199–200. *See also* Aristocracy; *Gentilshommes*; Gentry; *Grands*
Nomads, in Russia, 11, 183, 184, 187
"No Popery," 101
Nordlingin, battle of, 132
Norfolk, peasant unrest in, 76
Normandy: parlement of, 144; provincial estates of, 149–50
Northumberland, earl of, 68

Notables ("ruling classes"), of Catalonia and Portugal, 14, 120, 123. *See also* Nobles
Notaries, at Angers, 152
Nouvelle Conquête, 28

Obrok, 166, 174, 184
Octroi, in Russia, 162, 164
Odnodvortsy (homesteaders of the Volga), 168, 176–77
Offices, sale of, 69, 124
Officials, in France, 141, 143–47, 153, 157. *See also* Magistrates
Okhrannye gramoty (protective charters), 181
Old Believers, 10, 170–71, 179, 187, 189, 198
Olivares, duke of, 6, 117–19, 122
Orange, prince of, 31
Orenburg, fortress of, 184, 185, 191
Ornano, conspiracy of, 137
Osuna, duke of, 117
Otkhod, 166
Ottoman Turks, 176

Paganism, in Russia, 10
Palermo, popular revolt in, 126
Pamphlets, use of in the English Revolution, 58
Papacy, and England, 68, 97
Parlamentum, in French law, 148–49. *See also* Constitution
Parlement: of Bordeaux, 157; of Normandy, 144; of Paris, 146–49; of Provence, 144–45, 156
Parlements, French, 17, 138, 142–44, 146, 148–49, 156
Parliament: English, 4, 62, 64, 67, 73, 84–87, 90, 101, 104, 106, 108; in Sicily and Naples, 123. *See also* Cortes
Participatory democracy, 60
Partisans (tax farmers), 133, 140, 143, 144, 145, 146
Patria, idea of: in Catalonia, 7, 16, 114–16; in Naples, 123; in Portugal, 114–16; in Sicily, 123
Paulette, 145–47, 154
Peasants: in Catalonia, 122, 128; in England, 76; in France, 136–37, 156–57; in Russia, 162–65, 169, 170–74, 178, 193–94, 197, 199–200
Penza, province of, 173
Pereira, Solorzano (jurist), 113
Peter III, emperor of Russia, 169–71, 178–79
Peter the Great, emperor of Russia, 10, 161–64, 169, 172, 176, 179, 187, 196, 197

Petite robe, 141
Philip II, king of Spain, 26, 35, 38, 43, 47
Philip III, king of Spain, 117
Philip IV, king of Spain, 117
Physicians, at Angers, 152
Physiocracy, 166
Pirenne, Heni, 20, 28, 37, 39–40, 44
Plagues: and deserted villages, 135; in France, 134–35, 138, 150. See also *Mortalités*
Podushnaia podat' (head tax), 164
Political thought. *See* Ideology
Pomeshchiki (estate-owning nobles), 175
Pomestie (estate using serf labor), 176
Poor, in England, 62, 76
Popular revolts: in England, 58; in France, 137; in the Netherlands, 48; in the Spanish Monarchy, 111, 126–28
Population: in England, 74, 96; in the Netherlands, 38–39; in the Spanish Monarchy, 110
Portugal, 6–8, 58, 109, 110–12, 114–23, 127, 133
Possessionnye krest'iane (industrial serfs), 179–80
Potemkin, Gregory, 186
Precipitants: of the English Revolution, 97–103; of the Netherlands Revolution, 25; of revolutions, 2
Prerogative, in France, 139
Prerogative courts, 61, 70, 88, 91, 105
Prerogative powers, 73, 89, 91, 95, 98
Presbyterians, 57, 81, 103
Présidiaux (royal courts), 142, 144; at Angers, 151
Pretender ("true czar"), in Russia, 171, 177, 189, 194–96
Prévôts (French magistrates), 155
Prices: in France, 134–35; in the Netherlands, 38–39; in the Spanish Monarchy, 126
Primitive Christian Church, 59
Prince, as target for the Netherlands Revolution, 29. *See also* King; Kingship
Princes of the Blood, in France, 6, 137, 138, 139, 148, 156
Pripisat' (ascription of serfs to mines and factories), 179
Privileges. *See* Constitution; Corporate bodies
Privy Chamber (England), 98
Privy Council, 70, 98

Proctors, at Angers, 152
Procureur du roi, 144
Professions, at Angers, 152
Providence Island Company, 90, 101
Provinces: of France, 149–50, 156, 157; of the Netherlands, 28, 50–51; of the Spanish Monarchy, 113. *See also* Constitution; Estates; Parlements
Provincialism, in the Netherlands, 27–28, 35, 48–49, 52
Prynne, William, 101
Pugachev, Emilian, 161, 171, 179, 190, 201
Puritanism, in England, 4, 55, 58–59, 72–73, 84, 88–90, 94–97, 100, 105
Pushkin, Alexander, 191, 200–201
Pym, John, 101
Pyrenees, Peace of the, 132

Quartering of troops, in France, 151
Quarter sessions, in England, 71
Quitrents, in Russia, 166–67, 170, 173, 180

Reformation: and England, 71; and the Netherlands, 40, 45–46
Regalia, in Russia, 164
Regencies, in France, 138–39
Reguliarstvo, 186, 188–89
Religion: in England, 78–81, 93, 107; in France, 140; and the Netherlands revolt, 20, 43–46, 52; new concepts of in Russia, 182; Pugachev's policy toward, 198. *See also* Puritanism
Remonstrance, right of, 142–43
Renaissance monarchies, as model for Tudors, 66
Rentes, in the Netherlands, 43
Rents, in England, 102
Requests, Court of, 70
Richard III, king of England, 58
Richelieu, cardinal, 132, 134, 139, 143, 144, 153
"Rising expectations," in England, 102
Robe nobility, in the Netherlands, 41
Royal commissioners, in France, 133, 140, 143. See also *Intendants*
Royal Council, in France, 132, 146, 154
Royal court, of England, 4, 83–86, 93, 102
Royal demesne, in Naples, 124
Royal edicts, in France, 138–39
Royalists, in England, 57, 62, 64, 107

Royal magistrates, at Angers, 151–53
Royal salt monopoly, in France, 142
Rural society: in Catalonia, 127; in England, 62. *See also* Peasants
"Russification," 10
Russo-Turkish War (1768), 161, 164, 188

Sale of crown lands, in England, 99
Sale of offices, in France, 144–45, 154
Sale of titles, in England, 82, 98
Salisbury, earl of, 104
Salt, state monopoly of: in England, 69; in Russia, 164, 184, 188. See also *Grenier à Sel*
Samozvantsy (pretenders), in Russia, 171
Sandys, archbishop of York, 79
Say and Sele, viscount, 101
Scotland, union of with England, 78
Scottish Church, 103
Scottish Wars, 98
Scutage, in England, 99
Secretaries of state, in France, 140, 156
Seigneurial system, in France, 137. *See also* Landownership
Selden, John, 79
Selivanov, Kondiatii, 171
Sénéchaussée courts, in France, 142, 151, 153
Separatism. *See* Nationalism
Serfs, in Russia, 10–11, 163, 167, 170–76, 178–81, 194
Sexuality, attitudes toward, and societal change, 24
Sharecroppers, in France, 137
Ship money, in England, 69, 90, 99
Shuvalov, 162, 180
Sicilian and Neapolitan revolts, 14–15, 109–12, 123–27
Silver, American, 120–21
Simony, in England, 78
Skepticism, in England, 92–93. *See also* Ideology
Skity (small monasteries and hermitages of the Old Believers), 179
Skoptsy sect (Old Believers), 171
Smelser, Neil, theories of, applied to the Netherlands Revolution, 46–47
Soissons, count of, 138
Soldiers, in France, 133, 136
Sovereign. *See* Constitution; Kingship
Sovereign courts, in France, 142–43, 146, 154. *See also* Parlements

Spanish America, and France, 134; and Portugal, 120

Squires. *See* Gentry

Stände revolt: characteristics of, 34–35; the Netherlands Revolution as, 20

Stapleton, Sir Robert, 78–79

Star Chamber, Court of, 70

Starshina (Cossack chiefs), 175–76, 186, 187, 188–89

Startsy (holy men), in Russia, 179

State. *See* Constitution; Bureaucracy; Taxes

"Status crystallization," in England, 94

"Status inconsistencies," 6, 13; in England, 62, 94

Statute of Monopolies, in England, 86

Stenka Razin, 194

Strafford, earl of, 98, 101, 102, 106

Stuarts, financial policy of, 69

Superintendent of Finances (France), 140

Surgeons, French, 152

Tabouret, 144

Taille, 133, 142, 156; at Angers, 151–53; exemptions from, 143, 155; in Languedoc, 150

Tatar Muslims, 182

Taxes, 7, 14; in England, 68–69; 98; in France, 133–34, 135–36, 150–51, 154; in the Netherlands, 34, 43; in Russia, 162, 164, 169, 184; in the Spanish Monarchy, 110, 124, 129

Tepteri, 184

Terror of 1793, 140

Textile industry, in the Netherlands, 37, 39

Thirty Years' War, 78, 121, 132; and France, 131–32; French allies in, 133; and the Netherlands, 131

Thorough, policy of, 99–100, 103

Tiers état, 148, 154

Titles. *See* Sale of titles

Tocqueville, Alexis de, 82

Toleration, demands for in the Netherlands, 5, 48

Toleration Act, 108

Toulouse, 150; parlement of, 150

Touraine: estates of, 149; merchants of, 152

Toussaert, J., 44–45

Town magistrates, in the Netherlands, 33–34

Town militias, in the Netherlands, 30

Town oligarchies, in the Netherlands, 30

Towns. *See* Municipalities

Towns, Dutch: economic position of townsmen in, 42, 43; internal politics in, 29–31; political and social conflicts in, 32

Trade, English, 74

Tradesmen, English, education of, 88

Traitants. *See Partisans*

Transportation, cost of in Russia, 165

Trésoriers généraux de France, 142, 143, 144, 150

"Triggers," of the English Revolution, 103–7

Tsaritsyn, 191, 194

Tsvetaeva, Marina, 201

"Tudor despotism," 66–67

Tudor state: central administration in, 70–71; financial problems of, 68–69; instability of policy in, 66–74; religious policy of, 71–72

Tyrannicide, duty of, in France, 140–41

Ukraine, 165

Unemployment, in the Netherlands, 40

United Provinces, 75

Universities: English, 73, 88, 94; French, 153

Urals, 172, 178; Church lands near, 178; factories in, 193

Urbanization, in Italy, 125

Urban revolts: in Catalonia, 122, 127–28; in Naples and Sicily, 110–11, 126–27; in the Netherlands, 30, 50. *See also* Popular revolts

Ustensile (quartering of troops), in France, 133

Utrecht, 27, 40

Vagrants: in France, 135; in the Netherlands, 24, 40

Van der Wee, H., 39, 40, 42

Venality of Office, 154. *See also* Sale of offices

Verlinden, Charles, 38–39

Viazemskii, prince, in Russia, 178

Viceroys, in the Spanish Monarchy, 113

Villari, Rosario, 124

Vodka, taxes on, 164

Voennaia Kollegiia. *See* College of War

Voting rights, of English yeomen and artisans, 101. *See also* Constitution

Wage-earners, urban: in England, 62; in the Netherlands, 20, 30, 37–40. *See also* Urban revolts
Wages, in the Netherlands, 38
Wardship, in England, 69
Warwick, earl of, 101
Wentworth, Sir Thomas, 101. *See also* Strafford, earl of
Westphalia, Peace of, 132

William III, king of England, 77, 108
William of Orange, in the Netherlands, 27, 31, 44, 46, 48–51
Williams, bishop, in England, 100

Yeomen, in England, 62, 75, 88, 93, 101
Younger sons, in England, 94–95

Zaporog Cossacks, 186
Zeeland, role of in the Netherlands Revolution, 49–50